WHERE WHALES SING

14 YEARS SAILING THE SOUTH PACIFIC

By Daniel H. Van Ginhoven

Vero Beach, Florida

2015

BOOK 1 of 2

Copyright © 2015 by Daniel H. Van Ginhoven

All rights reserved. This book or any portion thereof may not be reproduced or used in any manner whatsoever without the express written permission of the author except for the use of brief quotations in a book review.

Printed in the United States of America

First Printing, 2016

www.WhereWhalesSing.com

This book is dedicated to Peggy...

You clasped my hand
As we have stood on mountains.

You clasped my hand
As we have sailed on stormy seas.

You clasped my hand
As we have walked life's pathways.

You clasped my hand
And together, we shall ever be.

Dan speaks these words to Peggy, which are a derivation from the song *You Raise Me Up* the music of which was written by Rolf Lovlander and lyrics by Brendan Graham © Peermusic (UK) Ltd; Universal Music Publications, AB.

Peggy Ann Woodall clasped the hand of Daniel H. Van Ginhoven when she was twenty years of age and he was twenty-one.

They remain happily married.

Acknowledgments

Overhearing my father's discussion regarding international monetary rates of exchange which in my very early youth had a ten to one advantage to the US in purchases from China, caused my consideration of what China may have that I might buy. Chinese sailing junks were the first entrants into my mind; and my sailing interest was born.

Emmett Early, a friend of early sailing days, flew me to Oxford, Maryland from Arlington, Virginia where the 41 foot sailing sloop *Osprey* was found and "who" soon welcomed my wife Peggy and me into her water world of the huge Chesapeake Bay.

Good Ed Cutts, owner of Cutts and Case Boatyard, is a naval architect who designed a full keel for this center-boarder, and transformed the *Osprey* into the proud and powerful ocean sailing yacht upon whose magic carpet we spent a 14 years sailing voyage, which included crossing the South Pacific from Panama to Australia via most of the tropic islands from East to West, and from Fiji in the North to New Zealand in the South.

Our wonderfully good friend Buddy Hart is recipient of our accolade for longest sustained duration of assistance to us for the length of time during our entire voyaging. Buddy maintained a perpetual watch over our financial matters, and enabled our peace of mind that our funds be available via our system of access at the far flung and often quite remote locations of our ventures. Buddy, we salute you, and we thank you!

And my very good wife Peggy, whose accompanying presence during this voyage brought beauty and elegance everywhere we went; is herewith presented with the epitome of all highest acknowledgement from this simple sailor and husband, that though not a sailor herself, I could not have done it without her.

Acknowledgements for the great professional assistance in preparing the book for publication was the work of the editors, Justine Goldberg of Write by Night, Austin, Texas; and formatting the book and designing both the interior of the book and its artistic cover; my grateful thanks and praise are warmly extended to Cynthia Noonan, renowned owner of Advanced Graphic FX, Inc. of Vero Beach, Florida, USA.

While these acknowledgements have voiced praise worthiness, there is one portion of the author's participation in which he hopes for your recognition that he is a sailor, not an aspiring photographer. Yet the photos in the book, though not of artistic quality, still speak with a worthy voice regarding these events that will enhance your voyage with us.

Introduction

I intend to have you feel the wind at sea, to taste the salt on your lips, to hear the wave as he rushes toward you, to smell the sweet scent of land yet beyond the horizon. I want to put your hand on the smooth varnished spokes of the teak wheel so that you feel the living motion of this sailing yacht, and have you brace your feet against the roll of the ship as you reef the mainsail at sea.

But there is so much more than this. There is the beauty of quiet anchorages, in waters of such startling clarity that illusions of unreality are experienced. When looking from the shore, you can see not only the yacht above her waterline, but also see her full keel and the anchor chain arching downward from her bow. She can seem to be suspended in air, because the lagoon is invisibly so clear.

It is my intent, not just to have you hear my voice as you read this book, but if you wish, you can be part of this voyage.

It gives me pleasure, indeed honor, to welcome you aboard.

Table of Contents

Chapter 1: The Osprey 1

Chapter 2: The Osprey Reborn 13

Chapter 3: The Osprey Takes Flight 23

Chapter 4: The Bahama Islands 39

Chapter 5: Haiti 49

Chapter 6: Panama 63

Chapter 7: The Galapagos Islands 91

Chapter 8: The Vast Pacific Ocean 103

Chapter 9: The Marquises Islands 111

Chapter 10: Tahiti 123

Chapter 11: The Day Fish Rained From The Sky 145

Chapter 12: Samoa* 157

Chapter 13: Tonga 173

Chapter 14: Fiji 187

Chapter 15: A South Pacific Storm 219

Chapter 16: Fiji Again 253

Appendix A: A Detailed Look at the Boat Handling Arrangement 263

Appendix B: Peggy's Log I: The Galapagos 271

Appendix C: Peggy's Log II: Tahiti 275

* At time of publication, Western Samoa had changed its name to:
The Independent State of Samoa

CHAPTER 1

 The Osprey

The fangs drooled wet foam from its jaws. We could see the claws curling downward. The beast was up about 50 feet when it crashed down on us. The monster is the biggest thing on the earth. It is the sea. And that wave curled over the entire yacht and pushed us way down under itself. Deep blue was the color of the water outside each of the ports until she came up for air, to snarl back at the sea.

The name of the yacht is *Osprey*, which is the name of a bird accustomed to flying above the water, diving to shallow depths to grab fish with its talons. This 41 foot sloop will do battle in the grip of that far away sea.

Will she be out of her depth? Will we? These few pages will speak to those two questions. And perhaps paint a few glimpses of events that will span fourteen years of our lives.

This is the voyage of a few planks of wood that became a boat upon whose magic carpet we will be cast way beyond the horizon. This is a true tale of two people, who cast a look turned backward in time, to when a man walked alone with his woman.

Here, there are no cities filled with the hubbub of people jostling each other. Here, there is no other sound than the sound of the sea. Here, no other person lives within a thousand miles.

As the cave man strode his way, always mindful of the beasts of the land, he could nonetheless sit down on that moss-cushioned log and smile at the day. Even so do Peggy and I, for our "dragons" wait another day.

* * *

It was really Emmet's fault. He is a good friend whose family used to go camping with ours. I had just read an advertisement of a sailboat for sale in Oxford, Maryland which had caused that all too familiar instant flow of my saliva glands. So I called Emmet, "If you're taking a flying lesson today, you've got to fly somewhere, so how about flying me to Oxford, Maryland? My schedule is too packed for me to drive."

I got on the backbench seat of this aircraft, which impressed me mostly as being terribly small. I asked the instructor if I could move to the left or right on this seat, needing to know if I would upset the balance while flying. With a knowing smile, I was assured that I could safely do so. Then I silently asked myself, "Am I nervous?"

The engine roared! I gasped a full breath of air, not previously realizing how much I cherished the taste of it, and we were off the ground. Wow, what a sight! What a rush of marvel. To this day, the concept of hurling one's self into the air still spins my mind. Yes, I too know the function of lift resulting from the greater length of travel of the air over the top of the wings than the travel of the air under them. The exact same thing is true of the sails on a boat. But the concept of flight still moves me.

Soon we were over the Chesapeake Bay, eastward from home not much more perhaps than a hundred miles as this creature flies. As we approached the eastern shore I could see countless waterfowl covering a huge part of the bay. And then suddenly, the world changed.

As though these multiplied thousands of waterfowl were one living creature, they rose in an instantaneous breath-taking choir of vision, as seen from the vantage point of being above them. A marvel of life whose symphony I can recall without the loss of even one of its woodwinds, without the loss of one of its roll of the drums.

The reality of the advertisement for the boat was better than its words. Her name was Vega and she was a star. Amazingly, instead of grim and oily water, she had dust in the bilge. She was built in South Africa. And the sea had now conspired to have romance claim her people. For after sailing to our shores a child had been born and priorities had changed. The boat was for sale.

But alas, though I could have bought the boat on my own, I had just bought a small apartment building and could not jeopardize that venture by consuming this additional cash. I needed Emmet to buy the boat with me. He too liked the boat, but the problem was that she had only three bunks. It would have been fine for us, but he had five in his family.

So I bought the plane with Emmet instead. It was an old tail dragger with almost no electronics, so it was astoundingly inexpensive. He had two others who were buying it with him and I offered to make it one more.

I took lessons. My flying career was neither glorious nor long. For on a solo flight I turned the plane into wreckage. Pride bruises easily, but no other damage was done, except to my family's wallet. I could not, of course, have my partners suffer at my hand.

Emmet, however, was not finished with his diabolical influence. He bought a boat. She was a Brixham Trawler, gaff rigged and a thing of beauty. She had a fifteen-foot traveling bowsprit that could be withdrawn in areas of close dockage, and her mizzen boom went 5 feet aft of the transom. She spread sail 75 feet fore and aft and worked her sails aloft without winches, using multiple-fall blocks and a strong grasp of the halyards. This was my world, and Emmet gave me the pleasure of "showing him the ropes" as he had introduced me to airplanes.

My saliva glands knew neither bounds nor etiquette.

One afternoon, two fellows asked themselves aboard. These guys were yacht brokers who were doing what I was, they were looking for a boat for themselves. As we compared mutual disappointments, they told me about a boat which they recently had seen in Oxford, Maryland. Right away, I thought they were going to tell me about the Vega. But no, this boat was named *Osprey*. They loved everything about the boat in every respect, but the price was too much for them. They tried to get a listing for the sale of it, but the boatyard owner would have nothing to do with them. Overcoming my apprehension of the price, the information was enough to launch me to that charming little town that I came to love.

When I had first seen her, she was entirely under winter cover. Ed Cutts, the boatyard owner and great architect of gracious and able sailing yachts, held up a corner of the canvas as I crawled under and then through the hatchway into a barely lit world by which I was instantly possessed.

Peggy decided that for this boat she would unleash the beast, which for so many years had paced about within the soul of her husband. We made an offer of purchase in an amount which we could afford. It was very different from the listed price, but this lovely and beautiful vessel welcomed us into her family.

My destiny was cast. Her name was *Osprey*. Forty-one feet never seemed so complete. She was strip planked of African mahogany about two inches thick on laminated oak frames. Her deck was of teak, approximately two inches thick, also strip planked, which for decking is very unusual and very strong. Below decks she was all non-glare varnish, the softness of which has always been so welcoming when entering below from the brilliance of the sun.

She of course presented all the required necessities of "gracious" living, including a stainless steel coal stove. A large circular cover plate on deck opened into a coal shoot, which in turn delivered the coal to an enclosed bin upon which the stove was mounted. With the smoke passing through her chimney, and a "Charley Noble" spinning at the top to add draft, the result was a wondrously comfortable dry heat on wintery sailing days.

With a couple of apples baking in the oven, the boat was filled not only with comfort, but the air was enhanced with aromas of delight as well. And if the sailing time was to be longer, a roast in its oven would far out do any restaurant ashore. Oh how she enriched our lives.

Chesapeake Bay opens to countless charms, up myriad twistings of her shoreline, with rivers and deep water creeks to explore. It is an area graced not only with wilderness, but also abounding in the loveliness of huge estates whose manicured lawns caress the water's edge. It is lovelines interrupted only by magnificence. So the question is, "Why would anyone wish to go anywhere else?"

That question is difficult to answer sanely. Yet there it was, that horizon thingy. Has all mankind been bullied by the need to know? There it was, that fermenting, unspoken, unsettling, silent unidentified gnawing – some-where, is that where the soul is? I can only ask. But I knew that one day I would answer that question. And I probably knew that to do so, would make all the difference.

It was a glorious time. I would drive from Arlington, Virginia to Oxford, sometimes a couple of times a week, busily thinking about small changes to the boat or to small changes in her sail trim.

The voice of that horizon problem never spoke in words. It talked in a much more primitive manner and directly to my innermost spirit. I don't think of that as an entity of any kind, but some say that emotion is the rudder by which the ships of our lives are steered. Though I knew it was still there, the aura of the boat's possession and its sailing had muffled my senses. Yet I knew this thing wasn't gone. Might the solution be to just glimpse the horizon by sailing to — how about Bermuda?

There were 3 of us; my wife Peggy, our son David, and me. I kept checking the radio weather forecasts while underway. We were motoring most of the time in either complete calm or almost breathless breeze since we left our home port of Oxford, Maryland, on our way to the southern reaches of the

Chesapeake Bay. We still needed to go through the process of checking for faulty readings from our radio direction finder due to possible electro-magnetic interferences aboard the boat.

This is a special radio which has a rotatable antenna attached to it. By tuning to a station whose broadcasting antenna's location is marked on a chart, the boat can be run on courses around the compass to see if the direction of the receiver aboard differs from where the station is known to be. One can then record the course at which the error occurs and the quantity of that error, so that when on such a course elsewhere, you can know that the broadcasting station's antenna is not where your radio antenna says it is, and you can plot a line from that antenna ashore, knowing that your position is approximately somewhere on this corrected line. This adds to your navigation accuracy accordingly. A radio direction finder is a very inexpensive tool, so why not have it aboard.

We were running such course directions, each for about 10 minutes or so in duration. It takes time to set the course, record it, go below to realign the RDF antenna, record all the data, etc., before changing to another course, when we heard whistle signals from a ship at least a mile east of us. There was no other vessel between them and us. Whistle signals on ships are in fact not given by whistles, they are given by the ship's horns; an almost earth shattering blast of sound.

Our course would have crossed theirs with no close encounter of any kind and I would have rejected the request to pass port to port had the vessel been any other than a United States Coast Guard Cutter who has the right to demand. So I altered my course to pass him accordingly. My only thought was that they must be wanting to give some verbal word to us in passing, so we proceeded. As we drew nearer, we saw the entire crew including the cook, lined up along their port deck where we would be passing. This is never done unless great formality is occurring.

Well, I realized that our first ocean trials with the *Osprey* was about to commence, however, this does not call for anything at all, much less anything like this formality. I certainly had a sufficient enough grasp of reality to know that the CG does not go around bestowing such formality upon yachtsmen such as we. So in total befuddlement I looked back again to see who might have been coming up from way behind us. And there it was; a submarine with only her sail out of the water.

I've always thought it an interesting homage to the past to refer to the conning tower as a sail even on a submarine. But back to the show:

It was in perfect unison that the three of us passed each other. The CG with all its crew on deck was going westward. The submarine was going eastward, and the *Osprey* also going eastward was right between both of them at the instant of passage.

The poor CG Ensign who may have been savoring the entry in the ship's log about how, under his command, this vessel of The United States had so gloriously maintained the best of seamanly tradition, with modest record of his command during this distinguished ceremony. As it all turned out, it was with such an uncontrolled fuming frustration that his young voice cracked as his shout to us, "I WASN'T SIGNALING YOU!"

But alas, in his excitement that's exactly what he had done. He must have assumed that a wee yachtsman wouldn't know what such whistle signals mean, but even so, he might have called us on channel 16 for us to disregard his signal. I nodded my head slightly to convey regret with not the slightest smile upon my blank expression. Once clear, we went back to the work at hand, with maybe just the very slightest possible smile at enthusiasm.

I may poke a little fun at this young man in the CG, because I now wear one of their uniforms with a silver oak leaf. As a volunteering civilian, presently I'm doing coastal surveillance flying as observer; from Vero Beach Florida to the Dry Tortugas south of Key West, done for Homeland Security, via the Coast Guard Auxiliary.

***

Chapter 1   The Osprey

It was hot! Norfolk, Virginia, our point of departure for Bermuda, was stifling. We were waiting for some favorable wind by which to sail. And with no air conditioning available aboard, I decided to take us all to a theater to watch a movie where air conditioning was certain to be enjoyed. The name of the movie was, "The Poseidon Adventure," which at that time had no meaning to us at all. This was to be Peggy's first time at sea. And to have her launched by the watching of a disaster happening on an ocean liner was perhaps not the very best of all possible choices; a fact not entirely unmentioned by her. The air conditioning, however, was a joy! We went to two other theaters that same day and basked in the comfortable irrelevance of what was happening on the screen.

The next afternoon the wind was up. I phoned the airport weatherman and received a detailed report, which included NE wind forecast at 20 knots. I told the fellow that, "She likes a bit of breeze" and was told that he wished that he were going with us; presumably, but not necessarily, spoken out of courtesy. We slept well and after a hardy breakfast we were off.

This was a "shakedown" cruise. Although we had enjoyed the boat's behavior in the bay for more than a year, this trip held a particular excitement for us, as she was to show us her sea legs.

All adventures quicken the spirit and enlarge the smiles. What a gorgeous day to be aboard this boat and making toward Bermuda! Life is good!

Our son Dave was 18, a great and enthusiastic sailor and enjoying every moment of the spectacle of the sea. The two of us had fallen into a long discussion about "Flying Fish" and we finally agreed that they were swimming out of the water with great tail motion which firstly hurled them out of the water, after which they glided beautifully on their giant "wings" [pectoral fins] as they churned the lower edge of their tails on each subsequent wave's crest.

Though Flying Fish have been found on the decks of ships, their "flight" is never more than quite close to the sea surface. With amazing agility they dodge about when trying to escape perusing predators. Perhaps when they are just at the right spot aside the bow of a fast moving ship when they launch themselves into the air to escape this perceived danger, they could be caught on this air wave and be sailed all the way up to the deck.

I may have to omit this paragraph from your book if it embarrasses Peggy, who was not seeing the Flying Fish any of the times that Dave or I would call out, "There's another one!" I had failed to notice that she was always looking up into the sky to find it, which simply shows again that no one is born really knowing anything; a group among whom I am most accustomed to be found.

I wanted to swim in that magnificently clear water. We were in the Gulf Stream going NE with the current, so tethered to the boat by a rope, over I went. Oh it was great. Even the temperature was perfect for a good swim, but the speed of the boat, though slow, was much beyond my non-Olympic abilities. Besides, what was that moving way down there in the shadow?

A day or so later, as I was on deck moving toward the mast, one of those truly magic moments occurred, and I was fortunate enough to be just at the right place at the right time to see it.

I don't know what caused me to look up. But at that instant the wind had blown a film of water off the face of a wave and passed that film of water over the boat above the spreader and entirely enveloped us within a bubble. I found myself looking at a bright blue sky through a lens of water that a tear could hope only dimly to emulate. How unspeakably moving and joyous is that memory amidst those conditions. It was a spectacle!

Chapter 1 								The Osprey

It also indicates that the waves were increasing their size. The Gulf Stream flows NE ward. The wind, blowing from the NE against the Gulf Stream, was slowing the upper part of the wave while the under part kept going NE. The result is a very high steep wave lacking any pleasantness of any kind. On deck, we now disappeared when in the trough of the waves and only her mast could see the horizon.

The weather had continued to worsen. The blue had now been scrubbed from the sky by black brushes that rushed toward us. The western horizon was a wall through which nothing could be seen. When the wall was upon us however, we must have startled Neptune by his suddenly seeing us there, because what had looked so menacing was in fact a very small mouse with no teeth at all.

Neptune was not in the menacing blackness of the cloud. But it was Poseidon who shortly rode up from the depths of the sea in a chariot whose wheels sparked blinding lightning! The hooves of his sea horses shook the entire world with thunder! His trident had killed the monster who had slept in the blackness of that cloud and now only strangeness filled the earth.

It was then that we saw his face. The cavern of his foul mouth gapped open as he hurled a blast of wind that threw the *Osprey* over on her side as though she were a toy daring to occupy space in his personal bathtub. He needed a bath. But I would have preferred a less revealing event in my wife's presence.

This Poseidon fellow had not even had the courtesy to make a reservation with the weatherman! And with this fellow stirring everything up like this and with no indication as to when all of this public bathing and splashing around was going to stop messing up our bathtub space, after a day or so of this inconsideration, I indignantly changed course.

If one were escaping from some land of danger or threat to life, the course toward our destination could have been held. Our cruise was of lesser need. And our shakedown exercise had regretfully displayed a serious fault with the good ship *Osprey*. We made toward the Chesapeake Bay and to Oxford and to Ed Cutts.

"Ed, the boat is not up to the job. Firstly, she is too tender. And secondly, the centerboard sounded as though it would bash the trunk to pieces. I had to bring it up to one quarters draft to ease it, resulting in an insufficient hold to her coarse. Either we can solve this or I need a different boat."

I really liked the boat. She was sloop rigged; had a great sail inventory; a Ford tractor diesel engine which has great parts supply; a wheel with Edson worm gear stout as a horse; large cockpit seats to stretch out in or on which to sleep; back rests and coaming angled to my personal comfort; strip planked toe rails with a base of about three inches wide tapering gently upward to about two inches with a cap that extended not only outboard but also inboard. The height of the rail is about five inches plus the cap.

The big deal about all of this is the fact that while sailing to windward, when she occasionally puts her deck partly under water, I could walk in the water on the inside of her toe rail with excellent footage and the cap's inboard extension held my foot from slipping overboard. Usually one walks on the upper side, but there is work at the mast on the lee side occasionally, including for sail handling, which on very many occasions afforded praise to Ralph Wiley her architect and builder, for this practicality.

Ralph Wiley happens to have been the prior owner of the yard now named Cutts and Case Boat Yard. And he was the builder of many fine yachts during his able tenure, the *Osprey* among them.

If form, meeting efficient function, is the logical goal of design without "gilding the lily," then the below decks of the *Osprey* would be a welcome sight to you too. Everything was done by unhurried craftsmen, directed to the strength of each item's intended use, rather than just to its decorativeness. Yet in contrast, men had sat around carving 2-inch piano like legs to form the fiddle rails on the cabinet tops to prevent things placed there from being dislodged when heeling. Not one of these is perfectly the same as the others, though almost. And having to look closely for the differences, plus the mental picture of the crew sitting on kegs doing the carving, adds to the charm of the atmosphere of her birth. The inside of one of the cabinets in the main saloon (living room) was given tailor-made racks for the crystal glasses still aboard, with the original owner's family crest on each. In all of our sailing, not once was any crystal broken.

Ed said, "Let's fix it." And the metamorphosis began.

CHAPTER 2

THE OSPREY REBORN

I started with shotgun lead. Bags and bags of lead shot, which I dragged aboard and carefully put into the bilge. Days went by and I continued to load lead into the bilge until I thought my profile was forever formed as a question mark. Ed would come out, look at the waterline and pronounce the words, "More lead."

Finally, we sailed her in the Chopptank River under Ed's very careful and watchful eye. More lead was required to satisfy Ed's eye as well as to my lesser-tuned feel of her handling, but wow what a difference! I lived with her like this for a while, sailing as often as I could in all types of wind and was delighted! In the meantime, Ed was designing a keel extension. The lower end would be of lead in the quantity as presently in the bilge.

He bought 30-inch wide Loblolly Pine planks; 6 inches thick and about 12 feet long, which were to form laminations to acquire the needed downward reach of the keel. The only sculpture ever attempted by my artless appendages, finally took the form of actual art. This accomplishment was due entirely to the step by step instructions of the very patient skillful boat building architect, His Eminence (titled by my hand), the right honorable Mr. Ed Cutts, Naval Architect.

Next came the lead to be shaped and attached. Ed bought a chunk of lead. And it became my task to cut it to shape. I was surprised at Ed's instruction of tools to use. I used a handsaw, and finally an adz, finishing with a carpenter's plane.

By this time, Ed seemed entirely captivated by our anticipated voyage and the way to marry the keel to the boat. He bought an old crane to lift the boat out of the water and lower her onto the keel, propping the boat in this position for attachment.

There were dangers. The crane must be close enough to the water's edge to reach the boat, but not close enough to have the crane crumble the edge of the shore and have the crane topple over onto the boat. It was not a very large crane. The boom didn't reach a great distance, so this was a real problem. There was deep water to the edge, so the boat could get close, but how solid was the shore?

Contrary to popular belief, boat people are not risk-takers. Now that may seem contradictory, but at least if we are slightly risk tolerant, we think of ourselves as being cautiously so.

The day was here. We had strengthened the shore with a system to disburse the weight of the crane, and it is a total exaggeration that witnesses reported my complexion actually turned a deep purple before taking my next breath. She was out safely.

I don't remember the next couple of hours too clearly. The boat was set up. She rested on big athwart ship timbers fore and aft of the new keel position, and securely braced to hold her up for when the crane could be released. I did no other work that day. For me, the night began while the late afternoon still hung around. How soundly rests the head of him whose well-being is secure.

One of the many disappointments in my life was finding no magic wand to wave about for the union of this keel to the boat. Work, however, was not invisible to the task. Long bolts were to pass through the bed log, and the present keel, and the new keel — including through the lead. These bolts were to pass through holes, of course. And as Ed turned away having finished explaining to me how I was to go about making these holes, I could have sworn I caught a wry grin of his face. Surely he didn't take pleasure from seeing simple folks suffer!

The keel was raised to the boat with jacks and propped securely. The drill bit would need to be about five feet long plus about three feet to reach up from my foot level to my hands. That's 8 feet of space required inside the boat before even attaching the heavy-duty drill to the bit. There isn't that much space on the boat! And can you imagine the mid section of such a bit when drill pressure at one end meets resistance to turning at the other? It would be bowing outward as it spun around causing all manner of problem, not the least of which was keeping hold of the drill. The bit was never thought of as being that long. Obviously, extensions would be welded as depth continued. Even so, bowing was a perpetual problem.

Had bolts been able to be passed at 90 degrees to the floor, downward through the center, the keel could have been brought up fully snug by tightening the bolt nuts. But bolts left and right of the trunk inside the boat, if passed vertically down, would have missed the keel extension entirely due to its taper, wherefore they needed to be angled. And here lay the problem. The bolts most assuredly held the tonnage of the keel securely to the boat. But they were never able to bring it up tightly enough to be watertight due to their apposing angles. Water was always in the centerboard trunk thereafter. And the damp aft end of the trunk always looked accusingly in my direction.

But oh my! The *Osprey*, whose potential was previously hidden — now as though with a dignified flourish of her fan she stood forth with all the poise and grace of a Duchess. Her entire being was regal. I smiled.

There were a few other things that had given me pause however. As always there are pluses and minuses on the scorecard of wishes, wants and needs. To wit; I loved the size of the ports. They were big, 18 x 6 inches, with 3 on each side of the cabin. Two were on each side of the main saloon, one in the galley and, on the other side, one in the head. They let in a wonderful airflow for summer comfort.

They needed greater strength, however, and though we found them adequate for the moderate conditions that we encountered on the ocean shakedown trip for keeping the sea at bay, the overhead was thick with a layer of salt from the air entry. And where salt air can go, can the sea be far behind?

My favorite solutions have always been those of simplicity. I fitted a thick Plexiglas to the outside of each port which overlapped the opening by 2 inches, removable by two bolts each, whereby the benefit of harbor pleasure was easily returned.

One of the early small additions done by the boatyard was to build an anchor sprit at the bow to carry two 45 pound CQR anchors for easy access. These were the primary anchors. For unusual anchorage conditions I had bought a 60 pound Danforth and a wonderful storm anchor designed by L. Frances Herishoff. This was a *fisherman* style anchor, such as what an artist would depict if asked to draw an anchor.

It was a 75 pounder that separated into three parts by extracting two stout pins. The boat's pull on the anchor put pressure of the parts against each other, not against the pins. The flukes and arm and shank were kept lashed in the bilge and carried separately to the fore deck, making it easily handled. In the fullness of time, these anchors all found their call to duty well answered.

Annapolis, Maryland is on the western shore of the Chesapeake Bay and has always been an enjoyable car stop for me. It is the present seat of the US Naval Academy, whose lovely grounds and stately buildings are at the center of town. The patina of early times graces the old buildings and stately courthouse. Were it not for the horde of its car traffic, living there could hold very great appeal.

This is where Emmett's fine Brixham trawler, the *Zephyr,* was docked in the close quarters of the city marina, and where I met G. D. Dunlap.

Good Mr. Dunlap, with Captain H. H. Shufeldt, is responsible for the text of the Twelfth Edition of *Dutton's Navigation and Piloting*, which was the Naval Academy's textbook for its young officers to be. I first met Mr. Dunlap at Weems and Plath, where he was president. I had come to buy a *C. Plath* micrometer sextant made in Hamburg, Germany.

There are basically two schools of thought about sextants. Some like them light and plastic and cheap, and some like the feel of the steadiness of a heavier and admittedly more expensive instrument whose devotees would argue are also more accurate due to a lesser tendency to transmit one's hand shaking into the measurement of the angle of horizon to star to sextant. The plastic ones are also said to warp. But having no experience with the type, I cannot say if this is true or false.

When I came to Weems and Plath, a shop specializing in nautical publications and sextants, good Mr. Dunlap was just placing some brief notices on the counter regarding a celestial navigation class that was shortly to commence. At that point I was totally unaware of the prestigious authority of the instructor and the reason for the course.

Mr. Dunlap had written a book which I have, and which I hold in highest recommendation to you. If you can find, *Successful Celestial Navigation with H.*

O. 229, by G. D. Dunlap, buy it. He wanted to teach the subject to an average group of yachtsmen to judge whether he needed to tweak the manuscript. I don't find that he changed a thing. And having sailed well over 20,000 miles of blue water by now, with no other navigation than a sextant and a clock, I praise the book, its author, and those ancient wizards upon whose shoulders we navigators stand.

Today we have the annual Nautical Almanac by which we can know for every second in time where the sun, moon, planets, and navigation stars are directly overhead on our planet. And using HO.229 for the sight reduction tables, one need only learn to lift the appropriate three figures from their pages, and using simple addition and subtraction and a plotting sheet, know within a couple of miles on a trackless sea, the position of your location. To solve the spherical triangle by hand is to me as a non-mathematician, immensely cumbersome and vastly time consuming.

I became more acquainted with good Mr. Dunlap, upon finding that he also owned the *Antique Scientific Instruments* shop on Fourth Street & Seventh Avenue in Annapolis. It is here that I found that lovely super heavy bronze encased compass which has its compass card viewable only from underneath. It took residence over the pillow of my boat bunk. It yielded a ready reference during the night as to any wind direction change, which the windvane steering is slaved to follow.

Two other great finds there, were the flare gun and anchor light. Today's flare guns are plastic. This one was made for the old British Infantry, and is of solid heavy bronze with a flared muzzle. It takes modern flares perfectly. The anchor light is about 15 inches high, has a proper *Fresnel* lens and a small kerosene lamp with its own oil reservoir and its own glass chimney inside it.

The entire lamp lifts out to trim and adjust the wick for burning oil for ten hours of illumination. And the flame, being encased by its traditional glass chimney, was never once threatened by the winds. I hasten to confess, however, that the usual anchor light used, was atop the mast using battery power.

The taffrail log was also found at Dunlap's hand. This very heavy bronze devise is mounted aft, as the name indicates; and shows by a full face sweeping finger, one hundred miles; a small indicator on the face turns for ten miles; and another small indicator turns for one thousand miles of travel.

The device that causes the turns is a 12 inch long, light metal *fish*, having three blades attached to its body's length at such an angle that, when attached to the taffrail log by a length of long braided line which is turned by the fish, the gears speak with clear accuracy to the dials and made for wonderfully accurate distance of water having passed under one's keel. Thus, with distance known and direction sailed, *dead reckoning* navigation is accomplished. Such were the *gifts* that I bought — for the boat.

*　*　*

However, this present I bought for Peggy. I bought her a boat.

She knows that I like to row. Were I ever to have the opportunity of satisfying a fondness for such perfection in a pulling boat, I would most likely choose a sixteen foot *Whitehall*. The beauty of those lines is enough to moisten the eye of the most hardened of true sailors.

In one of the places to which we subsequently sailed on the voyage of which I have written in this book, I was in a movie as an extra while in New Zealand. It was a pirate movie by Paramount Pictures.

A girl of about twelve, dressed in her finery, was rowing a Whitehall across the small harbor with her little dog sitting in the stern sheet, [back of the boat]. How perfectly lovely it was. Two huge square-rigged sailing vessels formed the background. If truth be known, I may likely never own a Whitehall. But if such is the greatest type of life's regrets, I might possibly have cause to smile.

One always wishes the best for one's wife, which is why I bought her a boat for her birthday. No, not the *Osprey*. [Was that for me?] I bought her a dinghy. It was a sailing dinghy, nine feet in length. A sixteen footer could never fit aboard the *Osprey*. It became the first and third dinghy of the *Osprey*. The second one was also bought before we left on the trip, and was the result of my addiction to the beauty of wooden boat designs by the likes of L. Frances Herreshoff, who heads my list of great architects. And when Ed Cutts, who was one of Herreshoff's protégées, told me about the dinghy which Herreshoff had designed for the Bermuda race when the rules changed to require dinghies to be carried, my antenna was activated. Ed found one, and at a very reasonable cost. It was covered in many very old layers of unattended varnish inside and out. So I took it to an antique furniture restorer who soaked it in a vat of paint stripper, from which she arose in all her glorious nakedness. Not one corner of varnish remained. And all that was called for was to stroke her gently with sand paper before dressing her in a few layers of white paint inboard and out, except for her upper most strake [plank] which I varnished. Oh my, how she smiled at me! And the well of my inner eye was caused to moisten.

She rowed best with one person aboard. But such as she, should surely not be subjected to nit-picking, should she? Afloat or aboard, she was a joy to see, and not until much later would she be judged wanting.

Time was stopped there on the Chesapeake Bay. Though approaching, it was not yet time for either of our retirements from Marriott Corporation. And though the call of distant worlds became ever-louder, the press of daily responsibilities built ever-greater dams within my mind to reduce my hearing, while within my mind a conspiracy was always seeking to hide and divert my attention from those quiet murmurings.

The dam burst open when my retirement date arrived and Peggy's was to follow the next year. Upward I swam with lungs burning for air! I could almost see the surface. And when, after a millennia, I broke the boundary and caught my breath when seeing the length of the list needing to be accomplished by the time Peggy would be ready to leave, I set myself to the task.

I had thought perhaps to sail singlehanded to Greenland during the year that Peggy still had to work. I have always been interested in sailing into some of those fjords but alas, I was pleasurably enslaved by the needs of the preparation list for departure.

There was that matter of selling the apartment building. This is what was to sustain us during a voyage around the world. And about the time that my wife's retirement arrived, I had a buyer for the building, and to the benefit of all, I agreed to take a second mortgage for a considerable amount. The quarterly payment of that note is what maintained us during our sojourn. I smiled.

Shelves were installed in the forecastle. We had learned that the Church of Latter-Day Saints had developed special food cans designed for longevity. After sampling them and their contents we bought a two years supply of food. I was in no hurry to finish this trip. And if we were to come upon an island with good water and great beauty, we would not refuse to consider lingering for as long as pleasure may reside. The fact of weight being a factor spoke loudly for this choice as well. The food was dehydrated.

A place was selected in the boatyard. Saw horses were assembled, planks placed, cans lined up, wrappers removed and placed under the appropriate cans, rust-inhibiting paint was poured into pails, and the cans were dunked, three quarters of the way first for one end and then, after it dried, the other end was dunked. Permanent marker in black stated the contents. The absence of fancy advertising as was on the labels seemed not at all to affect the delights to the pallet in future years to come. The shelves that were built in both sides of the forecastle were designed for these food cans and were kept there perfectly in place.

This, of course, was only the beginning of the stores brought aboard, of which each item was awarded absolute critical consideration of yea or nay. Peggy had a box of filing cards that listed everything that came aboard, food or otherwise. She could retrieve a card listing the item's name, and know where it was and how much was left. And the inventory was kept that way for all of the years of our voyage. Wow, she's good!

For instance, the history of the consumption rate of a roll of toilet paper necessity was recorded over time for each of us, so that stocking requirements would be judiciously rather than haphazardly determined because stores will become fewer as time progresses. Everything from soap to rope, carrots to cloths was recorded. Our departure was getting close.

Winter raised his head over the horizon with no expression of pleasantness on his face. Were we going to be bitten by the frosty breath of this guy, or could we get away? Peggy's retirement party from her company was scheduled for today. That long awaited event had not been overshadowed by the unfortunate fact that those in charge of investing the corporate profit-sharing funds had gambled wrongly. Both of our portions of those funds, which were heralded as being of such wonderfully grand amounts, became only about what we ourselves had put into it. But, as they say, that's why belts come with all of those holes. We knew that we would need to inwardly adjust ours.

I stood in the background of the crowd at the party and inadvertently overheard two ladies talking. After all, they were standing right in front of me just three feet away. The word was out. Peggy had mentioned to someone that her husband was going to take her on a trip around the world. So Miss A said to Miss B, "These rich people! Nothing to do but go around the world." I said, " No – I know them -- they're not rich! They're sailing their own boat!" And immediately realized how that sounded. However, I knew what the reality was. I knew what kind of extreme budget was going to control our lives. And if you were to pull back the curtain of time, to see some far-off places, perhaps even the cupboard may be found wanting.

CHAPTER 3

 The Osprey Takes Flight

Tomorrow we are leaving. No, we aren't ready. It can't be because I haven't had enough time, yet here we are leaving tomorrow and I still don't feel ready to go. But we either leave now or we are stuck here. The ice of winter is almost here. Let's run!

David and his wife Sherri, are shoehorned into the forecastle. I don't know where all their stuff has been put. Dave has tons of tools aboard. The boat is way down on her water line. Morning is here and we're still stowing stuff. But there is a smile on everybody's face. We had a makeshift breakfast.

Everybody was scurrying around in all directions. Noon came and went. We needed to get going. I could see that Ed had company at the house. I needed to have a bath before we got underway but didn't want to reduce the quantity of the water aboard, so I was sitting on the dock somewhat in front of Ed Cutt's house, scrubbing myself generously with an abundant display of soap suds when Ed came walking down the dock.

Well I wasn't naked! I had on a bathing suit and I was bathing.

Okay, I knew that it wasn't perhaps the picture setting that Ed might have chosen to show off the boatyard, but that wasn't the message of complaint that he brought. These very lovely people were here to *send us off* and had been oh so politely waiting without a word for hours. In a flash I hosed off – except, as I recall, the inside of my bathing suit – put on some acceptable clothing, and with a hardy wave to those of this gathering, we started motoring past the group. We were just at the edge of the boatyard when a chill ran down my back. All the hairs on the back of my neck jumped to attention as I fought back genuine tears. Good Mr. Ed Cutts had pulled the cord on the Herreshoff cannon and a resounding boom literally shivered the timbers of my sailor's soul, for such is the salute which eons of history has heard given to those noble men who have gone down to the sea in ships. Oh Ed, thank you for thinking so kindly of people such as we, though I am clearly "the very least of these my brethren."

A wee chill was in the air and shortly a mist of rain moistened the half-mile of visibility that was available to us as we sailed through the night. Before dawn the mist had formed itself into a softness equal to powdery snow, while below our coal stove wrapped everyone with its arms of complete comfort. We were on our way.

The second night, our entire world was engulfed in very dense fog, which gave our presents a perception of, if not otherworldly, an easy excuse to play at being from another time. We rang the ship's bell at the required intervals called for by the rules of vessels underway in fog. As we left the bay; almost ghostlike as though we were back in 1775, was our passage up this tiny river whose banks were invisible to us.

I had a chart. And I could tell where its turns should be. There were estates that lined these banks from which we were invisible. So just for fun I went to the foredeck and threw the lead line forward with a slight splash. As the slack came taut, and with my best voice of bygone times, I hauntingly called, " Byyy the mark fooourrr," as the old sailing ships measured the water depth with a lead line when approaching an unfamiliar shore.

It was a lovely quiet night, made snuggly comfortable by the warmth of the coal stove. Sleep was sound. And then the sun brought with it a world entirely changed. Our calendar had leaped forward suddenly by 200 years. It was 1977 again, and back on the bay again the sails added their patina to the seascape. The snow continued to cloak the world within its mantle and by now had covered us entirely with 1-1/2 inches of white, ghostly apparition, which had frightened away the gods of wind. Will this be as "cold as the night the *Crissie Wright* came ashore?"

The old-timers of the city of Beaufort, North Carolina, still use that expression. In January of 1886 a fine three-masted schooner came to grief in freezing conditions while those ashore were helpless to assist. The tragedy is still mourned in the stories told to their children.

We were motoring again when a sound of extreme horror shattered all other sound with a banshee's screech from below. And the motion of my hand toward the engine cutoff was simultaneously matched by Dave's yell, "Turn it off!" The engine ground to a stop with even my unskilled ear in recognition of a major problem.

In order to set sail, we needed to rid the boat of her cover of snow. We bailed bay water by the bucketful thrown over the house and deck. We needed secure footing. We needed sails up, while keeping all hands aboard! We were not in close quarters, so urgency was not master of the day. We were ruled by very light winds. Any sailor would choose a blow if the choice were to be offered, but very light remained the wind. As expected, night followed day. The world turned.

The scene changed again. The race was intense. We had sailed day and night for three days straight and then the race started. Never has every fiber of my being been so concentrated on winning. This was a sailing race. My race opponent was painted red. It seemed like hours passed while we were inches ahead and then inches behind our adversary's position. The tidal current was fast. Our opponent was a stationary buoy marking the beginning of a channel. Yes, I was racing against the current with a buoy, trying to make it into the channel. The wind remained light. An anchorage beckoned from within.

Once beyond the entrance, we were out of the narrows that had squeezed the current to that fast speed and though the wind had nearly given up for the day, we managed to get to an acceptable place out of the shipping lanes to anchor for the night. This was our second anchorage nights sleep in five consecutive days. We, of course, had alternated watches throughout those days and nights, so there was nothing herculean about this.

The next day, upon gaining a marina's dock, we could take some serious look at the engine problems. I clearly recognized David's mechanical skills and the fact of his tools with which to work. But we were less than a hundred miles from Don Wilson, the man who was the mechanic of Cutts and Case boatyard.

One of the people who kept a sailboat in the yard had called one day with engine problems having just gotten through Hell's Gate at New York City; and the next morning, Ed had flown his plane with Don Wilson and me to come to the rescue. Ed as flying chauffeur, Don to cure the engine, and me [though it wasn't mentioned to me until we got there] to crew for the owner to get the boat back to Oxford. I wasn't being hijacked though. Had the owner been able to get another crewman, I would have just had the diversion of a flight up and back. My schedule was not cluttered at the time.

There was one fun event of that trip which otherwise was uneventful. The canal that joins the bays of Delaware and Chesapeake has a very pleasant restaurant directly on its edge which has an excellent dock to receive yachtsmen who can thereby enjoy their tables. And one of my favorite events is beautifully done by this restaurant.

When a ship is transiting the canal at night, the lights of the restaurant are dimmed to the extreme as the ship passes your windows, and a voice comes over the audio system saying, "Ladies and gentlemen, this ship is the [we'll say *Indian Pride*], a ship of 50 thousand tons, carrying … " and the voice will proceed to list a typical cargo manifest for this vessel, further saying, "her ports of call include …" and list numerous countries of her voyages.

Even in my early youth I was drawn to the romance of the sea; and now the sight of these ships moving from darkness into the lighted area supplied for us diners, was always a pure delight to see. And following them into darkness and beyond was at least one mind in pleasant yet unanswered wonderings.

The point of specific interest, however, is the fact that a very strong current can occur in this canal. The flow was westward, toward the Chesapeake Bay, therefore behind us, and was strong indeed. Other yachts were lined up, each with its bow to the stern of its neighbor in front of it at the long dock. There was enough space between two of them for us to fit. It was time to eat! The exercise was to turn the boat around in the space of the canal with that much current. This was not a major problem for us, but the distance that we were swept down current in the process seemed alarming to my friend. The fun was from talking the owner into the vacant space on the dock. I showed him how we could be perfectly motionless in all of that current by the use of exactly the right amount of engine power, and then how, by just the slightest amount of rudder change, to be able to move the boat parallel with the dock to the left and right, still maintaining canal position fore and aft, while moving closer to the dock space or farther from it by a slightly opposing rudder change. So I readied a spring line of proper length and a bow line of proper length both belayed to the boat and a bowline knot tied in the shore end of each.

The boat went oh so gently sideways into the space. I stepped onto the dock, dropped the bowlines over their designated pilings, [spring line first], and after securing the other lines appropriately, the RPMs of the engine were slowly reduced, the lines came taut, and the engine was turned off. There was a sheen on the brow of my friend, but I tried to not be found having seen a gigantic smile of satisfaction coming over his face in having so nicely done a truly seamanlike maneuver. My having put that smile in place, carried over to my enjoyment of the very delightful hors d'oeuvres. It was more personally rewarding than having done it myself. I smiled.

But for our present problem, to call Don Wilson or not was the question, quickly answered by the enthusiasm of Dave's intent to show his stuff in our present need. It's fun to be proud of one's son. And with the aid of a length of wood dowel as a stethoscope for initial diagnoses, the complete disassembly of the engine commenced and quickly displayed the correctness of the first conclusion. The crankshaft was broken in half. Clearly, this was not the fault of the Cutts and Case mechanic to have sent us on our way with any discernible problem. This was a fault in the crankshaft construction and could have occurred in a much more remote place on the planet than here. David, of course, was great. He took the block to be bored, installed new rings and new crankshaft, all with virtually no workspace at all. And within the span of a couple of weeks, that lovely purr was back, if a diesel engine can be so described.

I'm reminded of a friend who would visit the boatyard on occasions. He was not to be described as avant-garde. No conversation ever occurred in which he failed to scoff at engines in sailing craft. On one such occasion my response was, "I agree! Down with engines – down with sails! Oars never fail!" It was a joke, taken in good spirit, showing neither of us convinced by the other. And so I still remain ready to use that iron mainsail most gladly as conditions warrant. Thanks Dave, for all that work.

* * *

As Norfolk was left behind, we had entered the smaller waters of The Intracoastal Waterway. We slept at anchor every night. And aboard, gentle peace reigned supreme.

As I luxuriated this morning in contented pleasure I let my eye roam the loveliness of the main cabin. I was almost totally content. This is the area into which one descends from the outside cockpit, via the companionway ladder. To left and right were our two single beds, which went outward to the hull. They served as couches or dining room seats during the day. Between the beds was the centerboard trunk with table leaves folding upward for the table. Overhead, the side deck covered half the bunks width and then the cabin sides with their two "windows" supporting the sides of the curved cabin top with no framing under it. The cabin sides likewise had no framing.

I was enthralled by neither of these facts. But the loveliness of it all could not be denied. The imp at my ear was always harping the same tune — "Tear along the dotted line," talking about this magnificent one solid piece of thick African mahogany, in which the "window" openings were cut. This cabin side was of a plank about two feet wide and a length of about ten feet, on edge of course. Each side was so built. My unease arises from the fact that the grain of this beautiful wood also runs its entire length and is broken by the "window" openings: and hence the weakening of its centerline. The cabin top had not been as critical a concern to me by virtue of the strength of its curved shape, until I heard Dave walking on it and saw from my bunk the overhead sagging with each step. All of the above is readily resolved by proper framing. But I was loath to do anything that would destroy the pleasure that I enjoyed from the elegance as it was. However, one does not go seriously to extended ocean voyaging with a vessel of which one has concern. We had escaped being iced in for what was looking like a severe Chesapeake winter, but in doing so we were out of reach of Ed Cutts' guiding hand of design.

Dave and Sherri were able to abide the claustrophobia of the forecastle for another couple of weeks more as we gained our southing. And perhaps he felt that giving his parents this wee nudge to get them out of the nest fulfilled his sonly duty sufficiently by setting them off on their own. I miss their presence.

The boat voyaged on, and in the proverbial fullness of time, there entered another hand of good fortune. He was an artist. He was a cabinetmaker. He was there at a boatyard where we had stopped to haul the boat to repaint the bottom of the keel. A buoy had been drug out of position by a barge driven by a tug having run into it and moved it away from its charted position. And being unaware of this, we took the buoy as marking the turn. We went hard aground. And although I had a worm shoe in place, the anti-fouling paint that protects the wood from sea boring worms was off part of the sides of our prized new keel. The boat had to come out of the water to restore her paint and here was found our wanted craftsman.

We were at the Masonboro Boat Yard at Wilmington where we were surrounded by the most friendly and accommodating folks it was our pleasure to have been fortunate to meet. Not only were the day-to-day encounters of each person a genuine family like experience, but everyone was happy to share what they had, from advice, to a car. Everyone was welcome to use it, so long as they left enough gasoline in the tank and oil in the engine to get the next person to the gas station. The gasoline consumption seemed only slightly less than that of the oil [poetic license liberally taken and only in jest]. It was a lovely accommodation extended to all those who came to their dock.

Our talks were long and intense with Bill. I wanted knees at each end of each window, which would receive frames under the overhead from side to side. Bill was certain that he could do it in such a way that beauty would be enhanced not destroyed. I was not convinced.

He drew it out and I said okay. As he made each piece I sanded it through the many sandpaper choices until perfection took possession of each item. And along with the strong exterior timber joining the edge of the side of the house, and the inboard edge of the deck, I could almost hear the sigh of satisfaction as the *Osprey* took a deep breath of contentment.

She was a mighty and seaworthy ship, pleased as well by the beauty she possessed as seen in the eye by him whose hand was steady on her helm, as well as by her newly gained strength. She was pleasing in every way. I smiled. She would easily have spent her days in sheltered waters with the strength with which she was born, but now she would look the sea fully in the face and not flinch. I was happy.

It was great welcoming Buddy Hart for a jaunt aboard. Buddy is a friend from church who was quickly up to his elbows in soapy dishwater during the after service dinners. No one was ever able to beat him to the sink, and I often was one of those grabbing an assisting dishtowel. Not because I have any born talent to display, but mostly for the fun of listening to the slight South African accent of Buddy's speech and the stories that he willingly shared. Both he and his good wife, Bikie, are gracious kind and caring folks whom it is our distinction and pleasure to call friends. Many indeed are the witnesses to his gifted talents. Buddy is a church architect firstly, but hotels and many other structures have been benefited from his occasionally soapy hand.

We were off shore, north of Florida in one of those super dense fogs. The ocean bottom slopes up gently to the shore in a uniform manner here as the chart displays, and simply sailing along the ten fathom line is an excellent choice, because an electronic depth sounder will reliably show it to you and is perfectly following the shore line at the same distance off and very far from any hazards.

We were the only show in town for the porpoises. They couldn't see the surroundings any better than we could. They came by the hundreds. And as all actors of any show will tell you, it's great to see the smiles of the crowd!

We seem to have been a great success in our performance. The front row was packed. To port and starboard was a perfect line of about twenty five porpoises stretching out shoulder to shoulder in two perfect lines as though seats had been supplied at the aft corners of the boat in both directions. Everyone seemed to strain to not miss the slightest nuance of any movement or expression on our face. No Shakespearian actor could want for a more dedicated audience. And as with all actors, we too were fed by the response of those before us.

Those in the front row were almost touching the boat. Others were all around us, in front of us, beside us, behind us, all packed into the scope of vision within the fog. We had no way of knowing if it may have been a standing-room-only crowd with others waiting outside the theater of our vision. It was grandly wonderful for us to be there.

I wanted to touch one but didn't want to scare them by anything that might appear threatening. But I put my hand and then my arm over the edge of the boat. No one moved. I started very slowly reaching downward toward the water. No one moved. I was by now reaching so far that my upper body was out of the boat. No one moved. The fingers of my hand were inches from the water. No one moved. Then one inch. No one moved.

One finger touched the water, and was greeted by a simultaneous loud slap of the tail to the water surface by one in authority and just as simultaneously they were all well out of reach. And so it should have been. When my finger entered their world I was judged a foreigner and thereby an unknown. The boss had commanded. And instant obedience was universal.

We had religiously been sounding the bell, which was mounted on the aft side of the mast and struck by the pull of the bell rope that reached into the cockpit. As you recall, that's the only "rope" aboard a vessel. All these of similar construction are called either lines or halyards or sheets, which I know sounds silly. But every such device aboard a sailing ship has a further defining identification by name, such as topsail halyard, etc.

The origin of "learning the ropes," though now rather landlubberly in expression, comes from the absolute necessity of a sailor knowing which of many lines to ease or to haul on command, especially aboard a square rigger. And aboard all sailing vessels, homage is paid to such as these things, though dimmed by days gone by, but they linger yet in the sailors' lexicon by honor gladly paid to those iron men in wooden ships who sail the oceans of our mind. At sea, such memory is called tradition.

Peggy and Buddy were below. Both were asleep when I heard it. A faint regular beat of a sound, which I immediately identified as the pulse of a ship's engine. I called for them to come to the deck.

We did not have radar so in fog we are blind. I had a radar reflector in the rigging to brighten our reflection, but someone needs to be looking at the radar equipment to see us. Recognizing that the engine of a commercial fishing trawler at close range may sound somewhat similar to the sound of a large ship a long way off, if a collision were to occur, I none the less wanted everyone on deck, and life jackets at hand.

Nothing ever presented itself. I was interested to note that the "sound" (vibration) was amplified through our hull. Sound is odd stuff.

As we entered the St Johns River of North Florida, we did so with the engine heat exchanger leaking water, but cooling enough to get by for brief intervals, when a rather unique event occurred. I wanted to come to a dock to look into the heat exchanger problem but with the progressing mechanical difficulty, chose to lay out an anchor from which we could swing to the dock by using the current.

We were treated to the unheard of apparition of a 45-pound CQR anchor floating on the surface. It was our anchor being kept up by this swiftly rushing tidal outflow. What a sight.

Of course, it was extremely brief but spectacular.

We found a nice little marina a short distance up the ICW and secured the boat. And with dinner time approaching we followed directions to drive to a buffet restaurant that became a frequent delight. It was an all-you-can-eat place for one price. After having fried chicken, I had fried chicken — a couple of times again.

Can you smell that? Ah yes, I must remember that you can't jump around inside my mind; you need a word or two.

Whenever I think of chicken, instantly I see a deep pot on the coal stove in winter sailing on Chesapeake Bay, while mysterious magic transforms the pot into providing a delight, which delays of dinnertime cannot affect. If we anchor when expected, dinner is ready. If we anchor two hours later, dinner is still ready.

Having only browned the chicken, equal parts of Heinz 57 catsup and Pepsi-Cola are added to cover the chicken as it cooks slowly on the stove. And if dinner is delayed, just pour in some more Pepsi-Cola. For casual dining after sailing with friends, a huge amount of food can be prepared with virtually no fuss at all. And what a delicious result.

This is one of my favorites afloat. I scoffed inwardly when I too was told of such a weird recipe, but for the purpose as used, it was great, and deserving of the name which was given to it. Since those early days it has always been known as "Chesapeake Chicken."

The business at hand for the boat was the heat exchanger problem. It was happily resolved by a bright new replacement. But what about Peggy's shoulder? That seemed to be getting progressively worse.

At Beauford, North Carolina the boat was at the city dock. Dinnertime was approaching, so we were going to find a restaurant. The dock was very high. The tide was very low, but the *Osprey* had ratlines. We were port side to the dock. While standing on the house, a judicious twist and swing of the body while grasping the aft shroud, the right foot can reach the lowest ratline and up you can go.

In this case, however, the farther up one goes, the farther one gets toward the mast rather than toward the dock. Peggy did not think that she could make it. And the only way to enable this would be for me to pull her up as she stepped.

I was on the dock, Peggy on the ratline. The signal was defined. At the instant of "three" which would not be spoken, she would do a jump step and I would pull. Indeed she started at exactly the right moment, as did I.

Unfortunately she hesitated after starting. I didn't. And up she came onto the dock. But too much of that achievement was my doing and I had done damage to her shoulder. This became evident now, as she had begun favoring that shoulder by not moving her arm at all.

The Jacksonville hospital diagnosis was that her shoulder was "frozen." Surgery was required to physically break the bone adhesion due to her rotator cuff damage. A long period of time passed during a season of physical therapy done at the hospital. Poor Peggy! The pain was terrible.

We had gotten to Jacksonville in March and left November of that year. We had been monitoring my father's condition for over a year now as well. I had flown a number of times to see him, more frequently prior to November, a month which he did not survive.

There was a steady rain at the cemetery. I had been helping folks to seats under the tent. It was Buddy Hart who saw that the last seat had been taken and that I was in the rain.

He came out. He gave me his seat. It was on the front row.

Peggy's arm was improving at Saint Augustine, Florida, which is the oldest city in the United States; having been commenced there by the hand of Spain. It's a lovely place, festooned by old houses of commerce and residence. Our first sightseeing was at the old fort.

Not long after our arrival we had met the young couple in the rather small bright yellow sailboat with two big eyes painted on her bow. They were young, as bright-eyed as the boat, and also bound toward the Bahamas.

Peggy wanted some groceries, but the plan was that the three of us were to see some of the sights first. So Buddy Hart, who had returned to the boat a few days before leaving Jacksonville, got into my prized Herreshoff dinghy with Peggy and me, bound for the shore.

None of us was of great personal proportion, but it did not go well. This is the first time the dinghy was asked to carry this much weight. Her pram bow was uncomfortably close to the water, which wanted with some apparent determination to join us. It did. It chose to do so in small quantities at a time as each very small wave spoke ever so gently with each approach.

No disaster threatened, but the pain of opening my eyes to see this fault and then to be forced to admit its truth to myself was a torturous anguish. She was such a beauty! I had shunned the fact of good Herreshoff's design of this dinghy being for the minimum-most space aboard the yachts in the Bermuda race, and yet comply with the new rules requiring the carrying of a dinghy. Alas, I was forced to accept the fact that, as nice as she was, she could not do the job of carrying any quantity of load in any chop at all.

We rented a station wagon, mounted the dink on the roof. We were taking her to Oxford to have Ed sell it for us. So Buddy's voyage this second time was about 30 miles. All this time, Buddy had wanted to be aboard for the short ocean crossing to the Bahamas. Almost a year had gone by and we were still not there. Buddy is as focused as he is determined, and planned to come back with us to try again. The young couple of the two-eyed boat agreed to watch over the *Osprey* who was stoutly anchored and secure.

Chapter 3 — *The Osprey Takes Flight*

I had hung Peggy's birthday Dyer dinghy in the Connecticut overhead of her nephew's two-car garage from which we retrieved it. And after visiting friends in various places and retrieving our good friend Buddy, we were off again to the *Osprey*, whom we found in good stead, thanks to both eyes of the yellow sailboat and its people.

* * *

Just north of the Jupiter inlet from the sea, a drawbridge crosses the Intracoastal Waterway. As we approached, the bridge tender dutifully started raising the bridge. We obviously were coming through, because there was no place else to go. However, to the befuddlement of this good man we swung sharply around and then appeared to be coming back again, so he started to open a second time before completely getting his bridge down. "What are they doing now?" must have been his shout. He closed it again.

Something had happened to our transmission. I got an anchor down but the current was dragging us toward the bridge. I got a second anchor toward the other shore and secured our position. The bridge tender I'm sure by now was totally baffled.

Buddy and I launched the dinghy. With such a current the row was for one person only. High-rise condominium buildings lined the eastern side of the waterway. In hindsight, I hope some folks were able to get some chuckles from our comic drama. More was to come.

There was a private marina for apparent use of the cliff dwellers, and people were on the dock. I wanted to ask where service could be called for and one fellow presented himself as a mechanic and offered to take a look. So I hopefully delivered him to the boat, but the prognosis was of a major problem and recommended the boat be taken to a marina about a mile or so from where we were.

A cute little plastic boat about 25 feet or so in length, made up like a miniature tug, came by regularly and had asked if we needed help. We found out later that an average of 44 boats per month were coming aground on a shifting sand bar inside the inlet and this fellow had found a gold mine for his toy tugboat. But again I told him that I was going to row to the marina to discuss the problem.

The row was of some reasonable effort. And they did not have a tow to offer me but recommended a little red tugboat. It was the one of which we were acquainted. In the meantime, the bridge tender was offered a good view of our comic opera, especially upon my return. Peggy's apprehension had increased over the unknown state of our transmission and my possibly being swept out to sea, wherefore she inadvertently failed to keep hold of the dinghy's painter (a line from the dinghy's bow), which I had handed to her. As I stepped aboard the *Osprey*, the dink took off down current and I, having jumped out of my clothes, was after it in my underwear. Much to the amusement of those in the glass cliff who may have been watching at the moment, an event to likewise have cemented the bridge tender's prior opinion regarding the state of our mental condition. I got the dinghy amidst some serious huffing and puffing, got aboard it and rowed back home again.

I hailed the tiny tugboat. He wanted one hundred dollars for the tow to the marina. Now remember, this was some time ago, and the dollar was worth more then than it is at the date of this publishing. We settled for twenty-five. And again, the *Osprey* was found hosting those intent on restoring her health. Buddy and I rented a car and were off on sundry buying trips for parts and paint. While aboard, Buddy was in happy display of his "eye splicing" skills, which is a seamanlike way of making a permanent loop in the end of a line. He was also somehow able to completely hide his frustration over our eternal lack of headway toward his sea passage. I went blithely from hauling the boat because she had touched bottom again to the next small emergency, enjoying myself completely. Time passed with only Buddy's awareness.

Good Buddy Hart had volunteered to care for a matter of immense importance to us. The apartment building had been sold with a second mortgage requiring quarterly payments upon which our ability to stay financially alive depended. And Buddy had agreed to see to it that if these payments did not arrive, that he would contact the people accordingly. For his faithfulness in this regard, we shall be always indebted. But Buddy finally gave up on our ever putting to sea. He left for the third and last time from Lake Worth. It was fun having him aboard. I wish he could have taken that additional time off from his work to come to sea with us.

The engine-cooling seawater pump finally got replaced and half a dozen other things were now also completed. It was January 12, and the *Osprey* waved her flag to her home country for the last time.

CHAPTER 4

☸ THE BAHAMA ISLANDS ☸

Just south of the inlet of Miami is a small park with a lovely quiet water anchorage where we stayed a day or two until the wind was right for a pleasant little passage to the northwest of the Bahama Islands. We rode the Gulf Stream Express. I chose to make it a night sail so that the morning light would show the island area to best advantage. It was such a short little sail, but it marked the commencement of a voyage so very different from the one we expected.

Three or so years prior to this time, Peggy had said, "Well, how long is this trip going to take?" A question which one does not answer flippantly. I had been "sailing in those waters vicariously" for years of pleasurable research and had found that a circumnavigation can be done in three and a half years. There are storm seasons around the world that should be avoided. And such a schedule would provide for that necessity. As it turned out, after 14 years, we would be only half-way.

The boat, dressed in the fullness of ocean-voyaging capabilities, graced the sea as much as any prima donna who has ever paused before her audience. This sail was just as expected. The name of the new girl in the cast of ocean performers was *Osprey*. And the windvane steering system performance was to the pride of its manufacturers. The boat felt comfortable with this new hand at the wheel. And I, well I sat in cushioned comfort in the cockpit and watched it all happen. I watched the boat, now gentle in this sea way, smoothly caress the waves. I watched the sails set just right for her course. I watched the sea, the sky, the stars; and I smiled.

This was our second visit here. We had been to the Bahamas once before, but then with Emmett's new airplane. We had split the families so that if the plane were to come down at sea, parts of the families would survive to take care of each other.

The weather was perfect. The plane recently had its annual inspection as required by regulation, so we knew that mechanically all was well. Except that midway there, it felt as though a giant baseball bat had bashed us in the nose, shaking the entire plane like some rag doll. Emmett looked to his right where I sat. And I gave him the thumb signal that we should turn around. If we were going down, I'd rather be searched for by our coast guard than someone else's. The plane behaved perfectly all the way back. As well as with a local Florida aviation mechanic who flew with us when we got there.

We flew high above the airport doing maneuvers to cause misbehavior but to no avail, so we loaded up again and were off for the Bahamas with no further incident. After subsequent considerations we decided that although the ground temperature was in the 80s, we had probably picked up rim ice particles off the top of a cloud, which momentarily clogged the carburetor.

This was the time when the sputnik had just been launched. And it was interesting to hear the local folks understandably saying, "Those big countries are always dreaming up a bigger lie than the other one."

Most tourists came to this island for the fishing! I'm not a devoted sport fisherman. But the hotel folks seemed anxious that we take one of their guides to show me the spectacle of Bone Fishing. Although I didn't catch any, I was interested in seeing how the guide got the bait.

He had a stick about eight feet in length. While walking along the shore with his feet in the water to his ankles, he was watching for crabs. He would pin one down with the end of his stick, pick it up and with a short practiced swing, knock off the legs and claws on one side and without missing a beat repeat the process on the other side of the crab. The body was then dropped into his bait bag.

The guide spoke quietly but incessantly in the charming undulating sound of his language, speaking about bonefish in general and about some individuals whose personalities and skills at avoiding the hook hiding in the fisherman's bait are well documented in the minds of all fishing guides. These fish were thought to be friends of the local spirit. He lives in a Cottonwood tree on the island, and has a reputation of disturbing the lives of people who do things that he doesn't like. If this spirit has some favorite fish, it's best that we not catch them. So no one is unhappy if no fish are caught. This spirit has a great fondness for corn. And many folks carry a small bag of corn kernels to drop along the pathways as they walk about.

***

Immediately before this flight to the Bahamas, our two families had been tent camping in the Everglades National Parks. There is a special spot to which we have returned many times to see the clouds of magnificent water-fowl swoop down to the same cluster of trees each day after their food hunting needs were satisfied. What marvels these creatures are?

Before starting off toward the Bahamas on that trip, we had to do something with our dogs. Each of our families had a dog. The two wives had taken the dogs to find an acceptable kennel since transporting nine people plus two dogs would take more than two trips in a four-seat airplane. Probably over 50 miles of crisscross car driving occurred, but finally the dogs were left in their kennel. Only one was there when we got back. Ours enjoyed the camaraderie of his fellow dogs, but their dog Peanuts, had dug her way out and was gone. The mystery is how she found her way, not northward toward home, but southeastward to the tent way up in the Everglades, seems miraculous.

Our first trip had been by plane. What had struck us so memorably about the Bahamas was the crystal clarity of the water. And as we arrived this time, again we were amazed. Although we have since been to many lands and many islands, never have we found a place with more loveliness to its waters. To place the festooned arrays of the colors of tropical fish upon a canvas of coral such as this is a joy that only *"wow"* can express.

Chapter 4 — The Bahama Islands

As we arrived this time, Stirrup Light had welcomed us brightly. And after the due process of effortless paperwork at the appointed office, the nation of the Bahamas also added its welcome to that of Stirrup Light's lesser formality. There are reported to be 700 islands here and we have subsequently anchored within the rustle of many of their coconut palms. But we are not the sort of folks who dash about unduly as our rambling southward along the Eastern Shore of the US has shown. Of course, as I mentioned, part of that time was spent attending the last presence of my good father.

Many of the small islands show no evidence of people in residence and one assumes that there may be no adequate supply of water to comfortably sustain a residency, for if beauty were the only requirement, ah how loudly heard would be the songs of the mystic sirens of old, and children would soon frolic amongst those palms.

In many of the smaller local fishing boats, one can usually see an old wooden bucket with a glass bottom, the favorite "diving mask" for those leaning over the edge of their boat to peer into the water. It's also favored by those wading in the water who choose to not get their face wet. It works well from a dinghy too, when looking over the side for a good place to drop a kedge or a second anchor. I always avoid dropping an anchor in coral.

Cruising the Bahamas is such a satisfying experience. It is without effort that one is inevitably found to be quickly immersed in the "island lifestyle." To wit: All of the necessary services of life are available, including such as indicated by a sign outside one of the leading banks in that area, which read, "Bank hours 1 to 2 –Thursdays." I knew that I had arrived!

When surrounded by the beauty of the palm-graced islands and the under water sea life dressed in all hues of color, and you mix in the occasional sailing yacht whose people enjoy your company as you do theirs, all of life has the taste of home-baked bread still warm from the oven.

The folks aboard *Kismet* had already completed their first circumnavigation. They are from Istanbul, Turkey. Kismet is a lovely double-ender ketch rigged boat about our size and although this had begun their second voyage, they were concluding that they ought perhaps to be returning homeward for the sake of their young daughter.

The *Kismet* was the first Turkish yacht to have sailed around the world and was gloriously honored by the government's issuing a postage stamp of commemoration of that voyage which beautifully shows their yacht.

The next day I put up a group of International Code Flags saying happy birthday to their young daughter, making the *Osprey* very festive in her dress, as such a celebration is worthy to be. We had great times talking together about all manner of things, including the brain-picking to which all those of some experience are exposed. And I took to heart Bodrum's unshakable insistence that I needed a good downwind-running sail system, proven to be true as your further sailing in this book will show.

So here, where off-the-shelf buying was challenging, I spent some quality time deciding what I *could* build where I was. I did not want to go back to the states. I did not like the idea of attachments to the hollow wood mast for forward-reaching booms, so I conceived a different way, perhaps resulting from some nightmare so far as appearance goes, but eloquent in its behavior. The running booms to hold the sails out both sides of the boat were stout indeed, and were not once threatened by being broken even if dipped into the sea. They were elegant in function and beautiful (if only to the eye of Peggy's husband) with inboard topping lifts, outboard topping lifts and down hauls, foreguys and braces, and sheet blocks. The mainsail boom cannot swing forward of the shrouds, whereas the running booms I made can easily be positioned.

Having only one bow stay, I either had to hank both headsails to it and therefore have to raise and lower both sails at the same time which can be a problem for me to do by myself, or take a single block with a becket aloft above the first jib head. The becket brought aloft the second stay and the block brought up the halyard for the second jib. It was a wonderfully efficient system! With two bow stays to hank sails to and two halyards to raise or lower each one separately, I could handle each sail myself in any seaway. The verbal complexity of this arrangement need only be worked out by those who wish to emulate it.

I had made and affixed three belaying cleats to the sides of the inboard end of both running booms to care for all of the lines needed to run this system. It was all there and capable of any job to which it might be called. Along with her new baggy wrinkle the *Osprey* had taken on a genuine salty expression. Even *Kismet* could have been jealous. I smiled.

Peggy's mother and aunt visited us for several days in Nassau. I had taken the *Osprey* into a marina for their convenience. A good time was had by all. At their departure I returned to anchor in the harbor there in Nassau. I found the bottom to be an impenetrable hardpan with no more than a couple of inches of sand covering it. However, the area was somewhat strewn with debris.

So I dropped the CQR anchor into the hole of a sizable chunk of a ship's deck, the weight of which was several times the weight of our boat. We were very secure. The problem raised its green head upon attempting to leave. I dove down to free the anchor with mask fins and snorkel only to be greeted by a very large green Morey eel, who with each breath opened his mouth with such a menacing display of white teeth and an "All the better to eat you with" sort of glint in his eye. This was his home. I dissuaded his proximity by grabbing the anchor chain with both hands and shaking it loudly against the steel, long enough that he slunk back down to hide in some secret place unseen. Subsequently, I have never had problems with Morey eels being aggressive towards me, but that mouth display still makes me somewhat uneasy. Maybe it's all from the first introduction that one's reactions remain firmly imbedded.

The Bahamians are seriously and justly proud of their marching band. They are magnificently dressed as I see them now in the theater of my mind. The leader with his long golden stick moving up and down in perfect rhythm for the music he directs, high enough for the entire band's visual benefit. He was impressive. The man himself appeared huge. His headgear must have approached 20 inches in height and was stovepipe-shaped and covered in a dark fur. The band wore Leopard skin capes over bright red jackets. They are impressive to see and fantastic to hear. But in this one instance, perhaps time had prevented appropriate planning.

I was embarrassed. The entire event simply was not given opportunity to be properly planned. The Pope was coming. But the stop was only for fuel for the airplane with no audience planned. However, being imploringly urged, it was agreed that He would take the time to be seen.

Then the problem was in the fact that there was not a proper chair for him, but finally a semblance of propriety was redeemed from the residence of one of the church members. People were to come to the baseball field where the Pope would be driven past the bleachers in an open jeep rigged with a bar for him to hold on to while standing in the back.

I say again, all of this was last minute planning. Absolutely no criticism is intended on my part to anyone. To further set the scene, you must know that the most famous tune by the band at this time was *Yellow Bird*.

It was night. The Pope appeared standing in the jeep. The jeep was coming out of the darkness into the lighted bleacher area at one end of the ball field at home plate. The jeep drove slowly, at a speed unaltered during the event. The band, at instruction, struck up the refrain of *Yellow Bird* with its fast and swinging melody. The Pope hung on. The jeep passed in front of the crowd. The band kept to the same melody. The Pope hung on. The jeep was traveling along the edge of the field. It passed the home plate bleacher area and started out toward right field. There were no bleachers there. There were no lights there. The band played on. The wind blew his vestments sideways. The Pope hung on. His proximity could be seen because of the headlights of the jeep. The band played on as instructed. The Pope hung on. The jeep maintained its speed and finally re-emerged from the darkness. The Pope still hung on. The wind still blew. The band still played. I was relieved when it was over.

***

Chapter 4   *The Bahama Islands*

Our sailing of the islands continued. One of these is famous for its population of Flamingos. Here hundreds of these beautiful pink birds grazed as one, and flew as one into a sky which had decided to also turn itself pink. The result created a blaze upon the memory such as few experiences possess.

This was followed by a visit to the immense salt fields beside the sea, where giant ships loaded salt to be brought to the processing plants of Morton's Salt, supplier to the world.

Other memorable meetings of fellow sailors were enjoyed. *Triad*, a South African trimaran sailboat, she was built by those who sailed her. We met again in Papeete, Tahiti. Here, they had an Ocelot aboard, who had a disquieting habit of biting at your passing ankles. And the couple in the yacht *Easy Go* with an electric organ keyboard with them, were in a rather smaller boat than ours. Years later, their son would hold mail for our arrival in Guam. Aboard the *Cat's Paw* were Russ, Jody, and their two sons from Florida, USA. We met them again in Papeete as well. They too were its builders. Russ had the interesting profession of studying sea waves, which had kept him to the Bahamas for several years. The Japanese couple, who had bought a US-built modern fiberglass sailboat by Morgan which they named *Love Love* after a movie that had enchanted them, were also met here. It, of course, properly flew their national ensign and was the only Japanese yacht which we had encountered. It was one of our pleasures to have gotten acquainted with them and their son Hero and daughter Tomo. Hero was often assigned the task of fishing for the table and Tomo's habit of eating his fish bait when he wasn't watching was a perpetual annoyance to him. We were introduced to wasabi and many oriental delights aboard their boat and we very much enjoyed each one of them, individually and as a family. So much so that they chose to sail with us as we went onward.

Not everyone who starts out carries on. One of these were aboard a Canadian ketch who were able to salve their itch of long-distance sailing by having come this far south, even though they had planned on a circumnavigation. And to all others for whom it is enough to keep a boat in a slip just knowing that if they really wanted to go they need only step aboard and sail over their horizon, I say that there is nothing other than reason to applaud. There is no wrong way of doing anything connected to owning a boat.

But those few, those fortunate few, whose view of life is not contained by such horizons, these are they who drink deeply of their cup of grog, and to whom I raise my glass that small bit higher.

A US yacht had just come into the Bahamas from Haiti. I wanted to hear what they had to say about my intended port of entry. "Gifts" to customs personnel *seemed* to be presented here by those coming from Haiti. The arriving Haitian "schooners" came with armloads of what had the appearance of bribery, though appearances can, of course, be deceptive.

I said, "I hear that you folks have come in from Haiti. I'm on the way shortly. May I ask you about your experience?"

She said, "Sure, come aboard. Whatever you do, don't go into Mole Saint Nicholas!"

Well, this is exactly where I was going. It's the logical point of entry from the Bahamas. "What happened?"

"A whole boat load of men with hob nail boots came aboard shouting, 'No anchor here! Take anchor there!' (Just a short distance away.) 'Give me cigarette.' I offered him one. 'No! Give me pack!' I was terrified every minute I was there and never so glad to get away!" she said.

CHAPTER 5

 HAITI

We were off toward many lands and officialdoms, and I was certainly not starting off on a circumnavigation in fear of these guys, as were the couple that we had just left. We checked out of the Bahamas for Haiti, and the first port of entry for us was Mole Saint Nicholas.

We went way up into the head of the bay and shortly after anchoring a longboat came from shore in answer to our Q (quarantine) flag. There were six or seven men, all with menacing scowls on their faces. As they came up and cut their engine, I called out, "Bonjour mon ami, entrée entrée la bateau avec moi s'il vous plait" ("Hello, hello my friends. *Please* come on in the boat with me "), spoken in my best high school smiling French, though lacking in refinement. They tied up. All started to stand. I said "No no my friends. Two persons only." Two came aboard. We talked pleasantly in English through his number two man. The boss asked if I had any guns. I told him yes. He wanted to see them – I showed him.

He fondled a stainless steel Smith and Wesson .38 with a two-inch barrel. "I keep this one."

I responded with an uproarious laugh as though I knew that he was making a huge joke saying, "No, no," as I took the revolver from him.

I told the number two fellow that I had something below that I would like to give to the boss. We went down and I showed him a couple dozen suit ties

Chapter 5 — Haiti

and told him to choose one. He wanted to take all of them, but I laughed and said, "No no, one tie." He chose one.

That was about the extent of hostilities. When I showed a welcoming attitude at first contact, along with my failure to notice their posture of threat, you could see the hostility just melting away.

The afternoon had passed pleasantly. What a difference from the atolls of the Bahamas! Huge, truly gigantic, steep mountains overshadowed the landscape beyond this large village. The mountains were not green. They seemed stark without trees, and we wondered about it.

Looking westward over the length of the bay, out toward the Caribbean Sea, the sky must have felt the urge to outdo itself because it grabbed a handful of brushes and threw paint all over the place. And when we could finally tear our eyes from the show, we turned again first to the mountains for a moment, but then to the life of the village. We were close enough that we could hear the quiet talking going on. Not enough to understand specific words, but enough to clearly designate different clusters of conversations.

As dusk approached darkness, tiny little fires could be seen scattered about throughout the village and up toward the mountainside. Darkness descended. To the right a donkey was heard braying every couple of minutes; to the left were several goats with one kid the most persistent of the group. A gentle creaking of a crooked pole which was the mast of a roughly formed old wooden local sailboat, added to the quiet sounds. There goes the donkey again, and as the background in a theater production, there was the muffled sound of the people talking.

We were anchored only a couple of hundred yards from the village beach close enough to make out an occasional voice. A youngster was crying for a little while.

There were young people's voices and adults'. Their speech was Creole so we couldn't follow their meaning, but could distinguish a word here and there.

I felt a fascination, as though engrossed by an opera being performed in a foreign language. We were so close to them, yet somehow we were worlds apart. Is it this almost tangible difference that grips our attention with such a fist? Is there a means, a bridge across such a gap?

I am part of this scene yet detached from it on this floating island called the *Osprey*. Is this intangible sound and dimly seen sight, just romance pushing for intrusion, or does something speak without words to one's inner self which may be beyond reach of phrase and pen? It is getting even quieter now. And that welcomed strangeness called sleep is not far away as I too take a few deep slow breaths as I now feel the comfort of my pillow. The shore shares the mountains' deeper silence. My sleep seemed less so.

Exploring we shall go! The day sparkled with promise. Upon securing the dinghy, by bringing her up the beach a short distance plus putting down her anchor a bit farther up the beach, we noticed a man some distance away ambling toward our direction. He was walking along the edge of the water.

He made an almost incongruous appearance. I could see that he was tall; almost gaunt it seemed from this distance. He was Caucasian, stooped over somewhat as he walked. And what set him entirely out of our expectation was that here, almost at the equator (although not an especially hot day); he was wearing a brilliantly colored wool cap such as a good Scotsman would wear on the golf course — tassel and all. We needed to meet this fellow!

He was very gracious. He knew that we were from the boat. He saw the US flag and said that he was from Pennsylvania and was the local Catholic priest. His invitation to join him at the parish right now was of such abounding sincerity that we were completely comfortable in happily following along.

His name was John. He had been a graduate pharmacist in earlier days and in addition to being the only priest in the area, he also operated the hospital. The morning clinic, also run by John, was not free. He charged everyone 25 cents. If it were free, he explained, it would not be viewed as professional. There were local spirit men, in some places called witch doctors, who used potions and chantings, who also charged a fee. John's fee of 25 cents, once paid, took care of all expenses be they for long hospital stay, the pulling of a tooth, or for surgery done by John with a book in one hand a scalpel in the other – and a prayer on his lip. What a man! I still applaud you John, and doff the cap of my soul.

We had heard the fishermen going out early that morning. They were singing heartily as they rowed their outrigger canoes. We told John how hauntingly lovely they sounded, which gave him the opportunity to tell us what was really going on.

Although this is a Catholic village, the people seem simultaneously also capable of retaining the old spirit beliefs very devoutly. John explained that there are a host of lesser gods that are believed to control the affairs of people. These gods are very petty. They are very easily offended. And if offended, they will punish the guilty person. One of the favorite ways of doing this is to bring harm to one of that person's children. So to protect their children, they will give them away to others of the village, whereby the spirit can't find the child to harm. This same parent will take several other people's children for the same reason.

He went on to say that there is an even darker side to this. The children who are taken in tend to become slaves to the woman of the house. Her only need is to carry a stick to hurry the children along in fetching water and firewood, etc. She is entirely occupied in doing this, wherefore she need not do any work herself.

So what we were struck with as being a happy singing camaraderie of departure for a day of fishing, turned out to be that they were singing to the gods saying, "Oh, you are such nice gods. We are so happy that you are taking care of us and thank you for being so nice." How things may have changed since we were there, we cannot know.

We had John out to the boat for several meals. He didn't often have an opportunity to talk to people from his neck of the woods and seemed to revel in catching up on missed camaraderie, as we reveled in hearing of his life here in the north of Haiti.

We told him that we were going to the market tomorrow. It is big enough that it has a parking lot for people's use who come from outlying areas. It is a parking lot for donkeys. John told us to tell people that we were his friends. Therefore, no one would cheat us because (regardless of how untrue) they would know that if they got sick, John would get even with them for cheating us. Everyone was very nice to us in the market and very solicitous to help find what we needed, which we took as being completely genuine in every way.

He told us about his early days there. He would ask a young mother, "Do you feed your child meat?"

"No, I am a good mother! Everybody knows that the little white strips become worms in children!"

"Do you feed your child fish?"

"No no no! Everybody knows that just like the water comes up and down [she was speaking here of the tides] fish make fever in children!"

"Do you ever feed beans to your child?"

"No! I am a good mother! Everybody knows that beans grow like seeds in his stomach and make his stomach stick out!"

John very early found that none of the children were getting any protein and was delighted at the prospects of changing all of that. He was excited about the wonderful health improvement that this was going to bring about. Everything was going great. He only needed to tell the mothers and without exception they all said, "Yes father" to his instructions. But it wasn't too long before he found that although saying yes, they were in fact changing nothing. It is a disappointment that still saddened him as we spoke.

John didn't seem to need much urging to tell us more. He told us that two prison guards had brought a man one morning. "What's wrong with him," John asked.

They didn't know. Well John found that the flesh had been beaten off his buttocks. It seems that a fisherman from the Bahamas had been blown here by a storm and he had tied his boat up at the peer. A decision had been made to quarantine the area of the dock where this boat was located.

A man, now prisoner, had come onto the dock and looked at this boat, which had not been seen here before, and thereby he had criminally crossed into the quarantine area. The problem here is the fact that there was absolutely nothing indicating that the area was not to be entered. Nothing marked the dock area in any way.

Our Japanese friends on the boat *Love Love* came to Haiti at the same time as we, and joined us often for lunch at Father John's table which was decoratively presented by the Sisters, whose hospitality we relished the enjoyment of reciprocating. The open camaraderie with John rests as an eternally warm memory. It was an honor sir, to have met you. Be well.

* * *

Having taken our leave of Father John, we began our sail toward Port-Au-Prince, and were delighted to again see the *Tropic Bird*, a truly beautiful bird in flight. You can argue that its tail is the result of DNA gone crazy, but to see this white creature in flight against a blue sky as background, with its long narrow tail, is grace personified. If you are unacquainted with this bird, I think it worth your while to research it. Pictures are always included in bird identification books as well as from Google.

Love Love decided to follow the same course as we, which seemed out of the way until they noticed the hazards on the short cut which they had intended to take. We stopped first at the city of Gonaives. Yusuke, the husband and father, is a photographer.

He sent a regularly scheduled series of reports of his adventures to his hometown newspaper in Osaka, Japan. One such picture was taken here in Gonaives. It truly had the look of *Out of Africa*.

Yusuke needed several five-gallon jugs of diesel fuel and also drinking water. Perhaps about ten containers in total, plus other sundry things, all were being carried atop the heads of people in joyous single file through the dirt streets of Gonaives. Everyone was ecstatically happy, because everyone was being paid by an amount which here was a day's wage for just a couple of hours work. There were very broad smiles all about!

We sailed well south before making directly for Port-Au-Prince, which now was to the east. Again, mountains leaped from the sea those many centuries ago. Now land has stretched from them to the present water's edge and holds in its hand a tide of teeming people all busily hunting for today's needs.

I watched as a crude two-story ladder, propped against a new building was instantly covered from bottom to top by scrambling men at the sound of a whistle. The man at the top had a man beneath him whose head came up to his buttocks, followed in like manner to the ground. A large bucket filled with wet cement was brought to the right hand of the lowest man, who swung it up to the next man above him.

The bucket did not pause nor slow. It flew up two stories high where it was received by the pouring crew and emptied. Many buckets were used. And the fast swing of the bottom man's arm to the next man kept an almost blur of motion.

There may be men lying about under a palm tree, but they would jump at a chance to be "on the ladder." There have been a few misguided folks who, having assigned their opinion loosely regarding folks under palm trees, have been exposed to my pointed speech on the subject.

Subsistence island living can be done if your menu is content with fish and coconuts. And those who stay in their village, as seen by my unlearned eye, are wealthy compared to so many who have flocked to the capital city seeking their fortune. Yet, who has the right to think that these self-possessed persons should not act upon *their* dreams?

It is through nothing other than the accident of being born in favorable surroundings that we ocean voyagers splash about. It is humbling in the extreme to have reality at least partially defog a small corner of one's eyeglasses by being here.

***

We intended securing the boat at a small marina, though not our usual habit to do so. And waiting on the dock was a small cluster of volunteers offering to take our lines as well as to act as tour guides. We wanted exactly this service of guide and chose one of the young fellows. We were absolutely delighted with his help.

The Iron Market was a surprise to us. We have not seen anything so progressive before or since as this roofed-over area for local farming produce, meat and fish—no charge for the flies. But everything from pots to baskets to clothes was everywhere as well.

If I were a local who was selling something, I would be grateful for such a place. The sides were open and it was a little dark in places, but a roof is a wonderful thing.

Willy took us touring throughout the city and then another full day getting some pipe and some welding done, to finish up the running poles. I'm so glad that Rome was not built in a day. I relied on that joyous fact of justification for years to come. Ah, such are the wondrous benefits derived from the depths of historical study.

Departing Port-Au-Prince, the shore continues westward and on our port side where many coves opened invitingly, each seeming to say, "Come in here for a quiet night's anchorage." This one was no exception.

Both boats anchored and both were visited throughout the day by young and old, some to talk via fast Creole spoken by them and haltingly by us; all wrapped warmly in smiles. But alas, Hero's swim fins and some of their clothes, which were drying on deck, were too much temptation for someone. Yusuki was furious.

He went to the police with one of his fins in one hand (to show what was missing) and a bag of candy in the other. He found that the policeman was also the school teacher there, and in his obviously fluent Japanese, aided by repeated gestures of bringing the fin to Hero's chest and presenting the bag of candy to the teacher, not only did he get the message across, but got the fins back the next day.

The following day we anchored in a lovely cove, which opened with high bluffs on each side. A small valley was at the headland, which was its domain.

When any boat enters anywhere, Haiti requires that the event is handled as though newly entering the country. Documents, passports, number of people, country of origin, everything each time again. And here suddenly arrived not one but two yachts!

The poor gendarme fellow, appeared to be somewhat uncertain as to what he should do and what might be reported about him. His mind may have said, "These must be special people."

Of course, I don't know what was really in his thoughts, but he clearly wanted not to be distinguished by any problem. He represented the Country of Haiti and thereby Monsieur Duvalier himself, which seems to have been the bigger deal.

When he got to the water's edge, he had enough people with him that they were able to pick him up and carry him over the water a few feet, and with great and unpracticed effort, got him into the canoe so that his staunchly pressed trousers not be wrinkled by rolling them up; whereby disgracing himself perhaps to reprimand or even discharge.

Chapter 5   Haiti

I turned away quickly enough. I surely did not want the fellow exposed to embarrassment by being seen taking this extreme precaution. I made every cordial effort to justify his effort by praising his professionalism.

Love Love had entered with us, so four Japanese and two Americans landed ashore in their dinghies and were immediately referred to the people on the hill.

The path up the hill was pointed to and the village seemed to be certain that this is what we wanted to do, so we did.

The path was narrow, dirt of course, and very steep where we found Patrick and Mika Devertevil living in a modern house. They were Haitians who had spent a career in Canada and had returned home to retire. They had a friend searching for a place for them to retire to, where they could have some land and where they would not be in the very midst of extreme poverty.

These 25 acres were found and four years ago they had arrived. Their house looks out over the water from its elevation, surrounded by a manicured jungle. It's lovely. The house isn't entirely finished yet, but Mika's school is buzzing with 90 students!

The school is close to the top of the pathway from the village. It has a tin roof, the back was closed in, there were 9 desks, and the others used benches for seats and board tables. School operation was from 8:15 till 1:15. Lunch was eaten at 11 o'clock.

They had improved the attention span of the children by 3 or 4 times by ruling that no food could be taken home. The children had been only eating a few mouthfuls for themselves and saving the rest for the sake of their families. But these retirees could not take care of the villagers too.

The amount of food sent from overseas was determined by the number of students that were in the school. And when the children actually ate the entire meals, their learning and attention span changed dramatically.

Dried milk, beans, wheat, and corn meal is received from an organization like CARE, and to that is added oil and salt and all of this is boiled in a 50 gallon drum which is cut in half.

We came to school the next day, but not at 8:15. We found the students all reading out loud at the same time. Study time was in progress. But entertainment time had now arrived on the schedule, and we were it.

I told them a story about our country. Hero, the 11 year-old son, did a marshal arts show and Tomo, the 4 year-old daughter, was dressed in old-style costume.

It was reported to us that they really enjoyed the martial arts, and everyone now knew that Japan was a very poor country, because Tomo had worn shoes that were made of a wooden platform with wooden cleats, wherefore the country could not afford leather shoes. Of course, Mika would have explained that the shoes were of a time long ago, but she thought that some of the students probably attributed the explanation as being a politeness.

We were invited up to the house that night. A Catholic priest of the general area, along with a police chief plus another visitor was arriving. Peggy who did not want to negotiate the vertical path in the dark stayed aboard and missed a very stimulating conversation into which all were drawn.

We visited with the folks in the village as well throughout the days and met some members of the church of our affiliation. Visitors, much less foreign visitors arriving by yacht, were not an everyday occurrence during which individual villagers were sought out socially. We bought some eggs and that was about the only thing that there was available.

***

I always enjoyed our anchor windlass. It was very slow, retrieving only a few chain links at a time, which accounts for the power it generates. A crank handle, such as used to be needed to start the first auto engines is used to power

Chapter 5   Haiti

the windlass with me at the handle end. The clockwise turning is done while standing bent over behind the windlass. The turning is not of great effort, so the price of time is what one pays.

The original owner must have required the "hausepipes." None of the other Wiley-built yachts have them, and they did not work well. The chain links did not enjoy coming over the unrounded edge of the bottom of the end plate against the hull. So after trying for a while, I gave up their use in favor of the chain coming on deck from the bowsprit and then over the windlass to fall by gravity through the deck into the chain locker. But the gypsy [the part of the anchor windlass that engaged the chain links] was disadvantaged due to this change because the contact of the chain with the gypsy was severely reduced by it. The boat does look a little narrow eyed with those two "eyes," but that's better than not being able to see at all — I say with tongue in cheek.

Friendliness is not always the guarantor of total likewise reciprocation. We anchored again off a village about midday this time because from here we will be leaving Haiti and a good night's sleep is sought accordingly. There is no cove here, but the water was pleasantly quiet on the south side.

The folks saw us coming and since our anchorage spot was closer to the village than *Love Love's,* our number of outrigger canoes soon totaled about four; most of which were filled to capacity. I had a harmonica and Peggy had a guitar and soon the songs were heard all about. Peggy popped corn and a good time was being had by all, when Yusuki came up with his rubber dinghy and said that he saw one of the boys come out from our cabin with one of our large butcher knives and our binoculars and had hurried off in one of the canoes for ashore. I had remembered having placed a favorite butcher knife in the tray at the companionway ladder, which was no longer there; and I was furious. I told every one there what had been done — that we had opened our house in welcome to them, sung songs with them and eaten food with them, and that I was angry.

"Do you see this?" At the side of my bed close to the companionway ladder was a VHF radio which instead of a mike, had a telephone type hand set which I picked up saying, "I am the guest of Monsieur Duvalier!" I said with haughty drama, "I can call him with this radio phone. I am furious! I want you all to leave! I want the gendarme and the army sergeant to come here immediately! I want the knife and binoculars returned with the man who took them. I will take him to sea and cut off his hand!" Okay, their eyes were getting bigger with my staged indignation and I may have over-acted a bit.

They left, expressing shame over what had been done. I kept my guilt of over-acting from everyone, and maintained it when the gendarme came immediately rowing out in a dug-out canoe. He too was full of apologies and agreed to my demand that a guard be kept on the beach all night. The night was uninterrupted. The binoculars were brought back. The knife was said to have been dropped overboard. I dove around the boat but found nothing. Happily, the thief was not brought to me. At first light, we would be off westward.

CHAPTER 6

 PANAMA

Love Love has engine trouble, so we're going back to the anchorage. After all, if it's something disabling and parts need to be motored for, we don't want them marooned here without recourse.

At noon, we were off again. I see that they are choosing a course northward from ours. If they stay on that course we will lose sight of them. They, of course, are fully capable and may just be longing for some sights without the stern of the *Osprey* showing. He is after all a professional photographer.

Dusk of the first day crept into the western sky. The sailing had been very gentle with no heeling of the boat. The genoa and mainsail are full. The windvane is keeping the boat on her instructed course as it has since noon. The important job that I have is to sit back and enjoy it all. I am very good at my job.

Peggy just said those eternally pleasant words, "Food's ready." And I seem to have enough energy gained from the aromas from below that have launched me on the way toward the table.

In tropical climes we would not be comforted by the coal stove's added heat. We have a "gimbaling" kerosene stove which mounts atop the coal stove. By being able to swing from side to side, the stove and its burners, with the all important pots and pans for cooking food on a horizontal level, is maintained by gravity's perpetual requirement. Even when the boat is angled sideways due to the power of the wind heeling the vessel or waves cause the boat to roll about, the cooking surface remains horizontal.

Peggy had not announced what was for dinner, but I know what a beef stew smells like. One-pot meals are appropriate while sailing. I was hungry and stimulated. And although I was too enthralled with the night and the sailing to be willing to miss any of it by sleeping, this doesn't mean that the pleasures of expressed and experienced romance need be abandoned. The dinner was wonderful too.

Since the haze of dawn I have watched them. All in silent step, the mountain silhouettes of Haiti, harsh and huge, have moved toward the east. Again the lone flight of a big black frigate bird soars above watching the sea and the mountains moving eastward. The *Osprey* flies with him. Both of us fly toward the west and perhaps tomorrow pass the westerly-most earth of this land of mountains. Perhaps tomorrow, great Haiti will be astern, and her stark mountains be submerged into the sea.

The night is here with its blaze of stars. Oh what a sight. Many are becoming old friends even though I have not called them into my sextant as yet. The navigation so far has been straightforward dead reckoning. While they keep winking their assent to soon show their constant well-trod march across the darkness of sky, they repeated again their anxious willingness to show us the way.

"Peggy — come and look!"

"Oh wow!" She has a well-bound calendar notebook.

On the page of June 13 it says, "Saw the Southern Cross for the first time." I looked again at all that magnificence and recalled the poetic words, "and a star to steer her by." I smiled.

The second day was warmer. Hot actually. The sailing was a little slower but with enough breeze that the windvane continued to keep the Osprey's course.

I'm going to need more permanent shade over the cockpit. I've been thinking about it, and strange as it will sound from a wooden boat sailor, I've been thinking that I could quite easily and very strongly build a permanent shade over the cockpit using PVC pipe for framing. Now that sounds horrible, but I'm going to look into this in Panama.

Storm Petrels are fun to watch. I can't image how they earned the title of Storm to their name. When we see them, they are frolicking about always on gentle waves. They are generally quite dark brownish-grey colored top and bottom, showing some distinguishing white markings. For me, the fun part is their use of their feet.

As they move about, directly on the surface of the sea, they push themselves with a fast walking pace at the wave crest and glide to the next wave all this time watching for the movement of a small fish for lunch.

To fly under one's own power is a mind-boggling thing. To walk on water appears to be reserved for those in books of higher dedication than the one you are reading.

"Terns" are one of my favorites. They are very sleek, smaller than Shearwaters, and generally have variously deeper forked tails dependent on type. They dive beautifully for their dinner.

Shearwaters are open ocean birds, seen pretty much worldwide. What I like about seeing them is how they glide so close to the waves. They are much more sleek and streamlined than a gull and have quite narrow wings.

The Cory's Shearwater is grayish brown-backed with white under body and under wings, with a trailing dark edge around the entire wing as seen from below.

I didn't want to miss anything, but I did get my first three and a half hours sleep. The third and fourth days and nights were fast sailing. And at 2:30 AM I awakened Peggy to take the watch. I slept till 7:45.

Chapter 6 — Panama

We've seen lots of ships, but none going in our direction. I was expecting a steady line of ships going to the Panama Canal. It seems curious. Were it not for my absolute confidence in my navigation, I would be concerned about our course. I put the simple course selection through my head again and I simply cannot be wrong!

It rained most of the fifth day and night. The boat is sailing beautifully and the windvane "crewman" doesn't mind staying out there in all of this rain. Three cheers for the windvanes of the world. We've got to have a name for our crewman.

It's the sixth day. The rain has stopped. We're still sailing nicely with little heel of the boat making life aboard all that more pleasant. When I saw it, I thought just for fun I'd play the game of, *We're aboard a voyaging vessel from days long gone* – I called out, *"Land hooo!"*

The time was 6:40 AM. 12 hours later we were anchored in the waters of Colon, Panama.

Love Love arrived with equal smiles the following noon having captured the enjoyment of isolated horizons on a more leisurely sail a bit northward.

The Panama Canal! Talk about thinking outside of the box! You will remember that the French had built the Suez Canal, which by 1902 had brought two billion francs to France. They had anticipated a billion more than that from the Panama Canal, which is why they had begun the project.

But disasters mounted. They had put the equivalent of $109,000,000 into the project which primarily yellow fever was forcing them to give up, plus the fact that it had become politically untenable to continue. The death toll was unbearable, and it was all the way into the Americas, a long way from France.

Finally, on January 28, 1902 the US Congress authorized the purchase from France at $40,000,000, which purchased all maps, surveys, drawings, and records, plus the Panama Railroad, from the French Canal Company, and five million dollars to the titled landowners of a six-mile wide strip through the Isthmus.

So what made us think that we could do it? Or is the better question: who thought he could do it?

It was in 1903 that Panama had revolted against Colombia, and shortly after that the US and Panama entered into a treaty in which the US guaranteed its independence, agreed to pay 10 million dollars, and committed to pay a perpetual annuity starting in 1913.

Theodore Roosevelt was the US president. And we wanted a canal to give shipping an ease of joining the two halves of our country. Plus the fact that we had teams of medical researchers all of this time with the French to find a cure for yellow fever, which was anticipated. Workers, however, were not flocking to the jobs.

In 1914 the US signed a treaty with Colombia to settle differences because of Panama's revolt. Colombia was paid 25 million dollars. The US invested approximately three billion in the canal and by 1977 had recovered about two thirds of that amount.

One day ashore, Peggy met Hilda who had firsthand stories gleaned over the fifty years that she and her US Army husband had been there. This is, of course, well after the building time, and was during the army's protection of the canal. Hilda continued living up the hill on Tobago Island at the end of the canal after her husband's death.

We anchored at Tobago after our transit of the canal, which gave us the opportunity of becoming acquainted with her. There were perks for the army wives here.

The local workforce was as anxious for domestic work as any other. It is not difficult to become accustomed to a certain life style when most of your days are surrounded by such advantages.

Chapter 6 — Panama

The canal remains a marvel, which I was pleased to have viewed four times while we were there. The requirement for transit of a yacht is to have a minimum of four line handlers aboard to secure the boat while the water rushes in or out as the locks raise or lower the water level.

When one acquires authorization to transit, the date and time is issued to the yacht for same; the owner posts the info on the yacht club bulletin board, and volunteers sign up as line handlers for the event.

The owner gets his volunteers for only the expense of lunch and the volunteer crewmen gets firsthand knowledge of the procedures for their own upcoming transit. I added my name to a list and was contacted accordingly.

This transit was for a sailing trimaran. As we were going out, I learned that it had been built by the owner, and it seemed neither overpowered nor over-responsive to her steering as we left the yacht club area for the canal. We entered the open end of the first lock.

Our pilot had come aboard at the yacht club as all vessels have a licensed pilot aboard, and he had just advised the owner that he should increase the boat's speed. The yacht was about halfway into this lock. The owner looked back, saw the oncoming ship, looked forward to the lock gate ahead and said, "No, this is fast enough."

Picture a bread pan from which you have just removed a baked loaf of bread. Cut off one end of the pan, put the pan into a sink full of water so that the pan is about half full, and then while keeping the pan in the sink water at the same level, you push the loaf of bread back into the pan through the now open end.

The water will all rush toward the closed end of the pan, shoving anything in the way, toward the end of the pan (or gate of a lock) with gigantic force in the case of a ship, which in the case of this yacht would be a destroying force.

Some ships may have only a foot or two on each side to clear the lock. The advisor said nothing. The ship kept coming and the first thrust of the water had picked the boat up and thrust it forward and toward one side, which loomed up some 25 feet or more above the boat.

There were pilings lining the top edge of the lock walls. One of the volunteer crewmen already had a rope in his hand ready for use. He tied a large bowline in one end, coiled the rope with big loops, and with a full effort swing of his entire body, threw the rope for the piling, way up there some 20 odd feet upward, and 15 feet aft. It was a thing of beauty. The bowline opened fully, dropped over the short piling, the line was laid around a cleat on the boat, the line was let to drag outward, slowly snugging the boat so that the cleat was not be torn from the deck; and the yacht was saved from pending disaster. The volunteer crewman smiled. The owner, seeming oblivious of what had just occurred, looked at the slight scuff mark on his boat's side from having touched the wall, and glared at the fellow.

Once while at a marina in the ICW this same fellow needed a line out to a piling to hold the boat off the dock and had done the same thing. That throw from the dock was about thirty-some feet. Another yachtsman saw the throw and came to congratulate him. The yachtsman had been amazed by the throw. Pleasantries were exchanged in which it was confessed that the throw had really been just good luck. Peggy insists that I mention that it was her husband who had thrown both of those lines.

The two transits that followed were not at all similar to the first one. I don't know where that trimaran went, I never saw the owner again. I must say though, that the crew's reward for that full day's service, which was a peanut butter and jelly sandwich, was hungrily received. It had been a very, very long day aboard that trimaran.

I had been inquiring of various people where I might ask about Plath sextant parts. A yacht club member told me that he thought that if anyone would have it I should try a place that he knew about. He gave me directions.

Peggy and I took a bus to downtown Panama City and walked the rest of the way to the old part of town. The streets had become narrow and old. We were getting close. The business community in this area was housed in very narrow buildings two and three stories high; and there it was. We went in.

A receptionist sat at a desk just to the right of the front door. The long very narrow room was divided by a walkway between a row of desks on each side. The desks all faced toward the door. There were perhaps twenty desks all together. Three of them were occupied.

The ceiling was very high, making the long room seem even narrower. It was the sort of place in which green-shaded visors would be worn at the forehead and office sleeve covers worn from above the elbows to wrist.

"Pardon me but may I ask, could it be possible that you might have mirror replacements for a Plath sextant?"

"Mr. Roberts could tell you. He is at the last desk on the left." We approached the desk of Mr. Roberts. It was strewn with what appeared to be an unorganized hodgepodge of documents entirely swamping his desk.

"Mr. Roberts, we are Dan and Peggy Van Ginhoven. We are passing through going westward and one of the mirrors of my Plath sextant has begun desilvering. Might it be possible that you could have a replacement in stock?"

Mr. Roberts' eyes closed for a half millisecond. He pushed his chair slowly back and stood up. He was very tall. He was very gaunt and slightly stooped. I could not guess his age as being much less than 90.

He quietly said, "Come with me."

We followed obediently, not that he had given a command, but purely out of reverence.

We passed out of the office area into the stockroom behind of identically high ceiling, but it was much longer than the office. There were rows after rows of medal shelves not unlike a library in a very old town. He stopped. He had not shown any interest in anything to the right or left up to this point. He just stopped way down this aisle, turned to face the left, reached up to a shelf above his head, and brought down a small box. He lifted the lid and took a package out. In the wrapping was a mirror and an invoice.

We went back to his desk and we sat down in some very old chairs. While Mr. Roberts was unwrapping the mirror he quietly began asking questions. What type of vessel were we aboard; where had we come from; where were we going; were we going to Pitcairn Island?

I had answered each question conversationally, and explained that although we were interested in Pitcairn we were not going there because the anchorage is very insecure wherefore someone must stay on the boat all the time, and that Peggy's agility might not be up to her getting safely out of their long boat and onto the shore; but that we had planned to call them by radio in passing.

"Well, if you talk to Fletcher Christian, please pass on my best regards." Always one of the descendants is named after the original who mutinied on the Bounty. And in the fullness of time, we did talk with Fletcher Christian who said, "Wow, is Mr. Roberts still alive? He used to ship kerosene to us all the time for years." He also confirmed the anchorage problem. We did not go to Pitcairn Island.

But good Mr. Roberts seems to have always kept a certain place in his heart where the romance of sailing ships still voyage upon the private oceans of his very sharp mind.

Mr. Roberts looked at his invoice. He showed us the invoice date and amount. He had bought 4 mirrors and had this one left. "I'm sorry to have to charge you so much," he said. I didn't think it was much. Then he would ask another of the questions that you've just read and after hearing the answer he would again reduce his price. This happened several times. I was getting embarrassed. Finally I pressed the money to his hand as I continued our story. The gentle kindness of this man, whose life has been spent spanning the globe with his far flung reachings to bring merchandise to broad and to narrow places upon this planet, seems to have given him literal and vicarious pleasures. And has given to us a cherished remembrance of a noble man, gently lived.

Life was filled with all manner of happenings as we awaited our turn to go through the canal. We were all impressed with the efficiency of the canal operation. The water pumps are gigantic. Originally the ships were pulled into the locks by mules. The machinery now doing the job is still referred to as "the mules." I like tradition.

The yachtsmen kept coming. Not at all in droves, but the canal is a funnel point even for us. We met *Brown Palace* (named after the hotel) with Bob and Jane – folks with whom we have kept the closest contact to this day – and who have completed their circumnavigation at the time of this writing.

We never sailed together. Few people do. But they have graciously retained our friendship with mutual emailings back and forth. Many jokes have been shared by the Internet as well as some heart-wrenching news of losses of yachts and friends.

Brown Palace, though carefully grounded electronically, was struck by lightning while at anchor here and had all their electronics fried; from auto pilot to amateur radio, running lights to depth sounder. *Love Love* was also struck at the same time with the same result. Others, such as we who were not grounded, were for no known reason not struck though all anchored in the same area.

None of the anchorages shared over the 14 years of sailing within this book experience has ever seen another yacht struck. And I am unaware of a yacht sailing at sea being struck by lightning either. The *Osprey* did host a brief moment of St. Elmo's Fire among the ratlines once. That certainly is strange electro-magnetic stuff, if indeed that is its origin. No harm, of course, was resultant from the weird phenomena.

Sometimes it rains good fortune by accident. I had fallen into conversation with a fellow on the Panama train. This little train runs from Panama City at one end of the canal to Colon at the other end. He was studying on Barro

Colorado Island as a scientist and invited us to visit. When pre-arranged, the train stops there to bring scientists and supplies to the island, which the National Geographic Society has rented since 1923.

It has 30 miles of coastline and 40 miles of trails, all kept in the strictest pristine and unchanged natural habitat. We walked among the deafening sounds made by the Howler monkeys in the jungle canopy; and picking up a sloth which was covered by little winged crawling characters which spend their entire life cycle aboard this host.

I'm a bit hairy myself, but their invasion of my arms was found to have been done in error. These three-toed sloths move in extremely slow motion.

When one wishes to study something here, it may be brought to the laboratory. But it must be returned to the same spot at conclusion. Invitation to come here is very much sought after by those of the scientific community, and we accepted the liberty taken by this scientist in our behalf as a particular distinction for which we remain enriched.

To walk here is an experience such as the jungles of New Guinea have later afforded us with memories somewhat akin to the same feeling of awe while walking amongst the great trees of a stand of Redwood forest in the US west.

There is not a similarity of physical embodiment between these three areas, just an inner response that I would like to convey. But then, I can get carried away looking at a small flower with a magnifying glass, or by what's going on with the life of a small fish on a coral reef.

I was looking out the window of this train that was bringing us across the Isthmus of Panama. And my mind wandered in its usual manner. Time shifted in my thought to those Spanish seaman and soldiers who crossed this land with donkeys burdened by loads of gold and treasure, bound for Portobello, not all that far from our anchorage at Colon. Of course we went!

* * *

Chapter 6 — Panama

It was a perfect anchorage for those magnificent Spanish galleons. The cove had high walls, thick with jungle on each side. A small village now rests at the headland with its tall Catholic church looking incongruous as thirty vultures perched atop the roofline, the spire, and at the belfry.

Everything was stillness, as though the memory of these grounds, having seen such carnage have sought to turn away their face from the recollection.

Here, the protection of gold was priced by the sword. Here, just where we are anchored, once huge square-rigged ships lay awaiting great wealth which would bring praise and fame to those seamen upon their return to Spain. Perhaps the king and queen would personally come to the dock.

The pay received by that seaman standing over there, visible only within my mind, was already spending it in his head as he thought of his family. And the officers dreamed of greater things.

I don't believe that a place can hold a remembrance of times long past; yet there seemed to be a strangeness here. Perhaps the pause of my mind was due to those almost motionless black creatures festooned atop the church; creatures less acquainted with present life than with those whose life is but a memory.

Ashore, we went through the old fort built there to protect the ships while here, and the treasure it received before the ships got here. All spoke to us in hushed sounds it seemed. For yes, we had just come from the wild waters where pirates had lain in wait to chase and to plunder.

We too had entered here aboard a wooden sailing vessel. Did these trees look to see if a black flag with crossed bones moved aloft in our rigging?

I winched the anchor up. It naturally snugged into its spot on the anchor sprit extending a couple of feet beyond the bow. Ed, the designer, chose the arrangement perfectly with one CQR anchor fitting to one side and a bit aft of the other. We did not speak. I raised the main and genoa. As silently as we had arrived, our departure likewise sought not to bring awakening to this place, once bustling with hundreds of men and several square-rigged giants whose aft structures were embossed with much glitter of gold.

As the light breeze quietly filled our sails, a silent small wave moved from our bow. We left this place as it was – still and motionless in time.

***

Sailing eastward and then southward we came to the San Blas Islands where we had been advised to go when they were having congress.

Well, we didn't know when congress was convened, so upon arriving we asked; and "Oh yes, congress tonight" was the answer.

Next we said that we would like to see the chief to ask permission for us to come to the congress ourselves, which was answered, "Yes, I take to chief."

We went ashore. We brought a gift. The chief received us. We presented our gift. The chief smiled, though not very broadly, and asked what we wanted.

"We would like to ask you if we might be permitted to attend your congress."

We were so permitted and likewise given authority to go through the village and speak to whomever we wished. We thanked him for his generosity and took our leave of him. An appropriate gift had been given to our guide and we were on our own.

Armed with location and time, we awaited the unknown, happy that we were fortunate enough to have stumbled in here when congress was going to occur. At the appointed time we started for shore.

Everyone seems to already be here. We were on the Island of Tigre. Years ago the island chiefs had come together.

The question was, "Do we stay with our traditions and ways of our fathers, or do we enter the new world's ways like the mainland people?" Tigre was one with the group who chose to stay with the old ways.

We entered the building. It was the biggest thatch-roofed structure that we had seen. It reminded us of the big Ringling Brothers Circus tents by size. There were no walls or sides. The roof was held up at the edges by poles all around with really long poles holding the ridge line along the center. And most surprising was what appeared to be commercially-made baseball-type bleachers all the way around the perimeter with a very large area in the center which was covered with wooden folding chairs all facing toward the center which was to our left and filled three quarters of the space.

At the central area, and between two of the poles holding up the roof ridge, was tied a hammock in which the chief swung by pushing himself with one leg which hung out of the hammock; and between the next roof support poles another man was swinging in like manner.

All of the chairs on the ground level lined up faced the chief. These comfortless chairs were host to a couple hundred women all leaning forward sewing something. The men sat in the bleachers on similarly comfortable boards without back rests doing nothing.

The chief was taking a very deep breath and speaking in a very fast, totally monotone voice, making this noise until no breath was left and gasp another lung full with neither change of tone or speed. He went on – and on – and on for hours. Number two man began as he too exercised one leg a little, by swinging in like manner. He sounded slightly different from the chief but not by much.

The women had neither looked up, nor looked sideways, nor stopped. It was quite dark where they sat; hence the leaning forward as they each sewed decorative cloth strips on a piece of fabric appearing to be about 2 feet square. Their focus was intense. The men had not moved, except for the frequent nodding of their heads, which were trying to find sleep.

A sinister-looking man came. He entered opposite from where we both sat midway up one of the bleachers not quite midway from left to right.

He was dressed all in black. He walked back and forth at the bleachers opposite us and suddenly, and dare I say chillingly, shouted out, " IGEEE YAOOOO!" And then looked right at us.

Something ran bumping up our spine twice. This specter walked to several other places while the two center stage actors never interrupted either their sound or their swing.

Again he screamed, "IGEEE YAOOOO" from various places to which he had walked.

Congress went on, and on, for more hours. The bleachers felt as though they were producing blisters where they made somewhat less than joyous contact upon our persons. Nothing changed. When we were certain the fellow in black wasn't watching us, as unobtrusively as possible, we retreated to the boat.

The next day, the man who had been inclined to want to spend considerable time on the boat was with us again. We had spoken of many things during his visits, so upon his arrival, I told him that we had gone to congress last night. He nodded gravely. I told him that we did not understand what was going on.

He explained that the chief was talking in an ancient language which no one but the number two chief can understand. And that when he in turn spoke, he was translating what the chief had said.

"What did the chief say last night?"

Well it was instructions to wives. He said that when the wife's husband is out fishing or on the farm that she should not sit around doing nothing. That she should sweep the floor (which is bare soil) and that she should make the area look good. And, when he comes home, she should look at the bottom of his feet to see if there are any splinters and so on and on.

Chapter 6 — Panama

"We saw a man dressed all in black come to congress."

Oh yes, he was going around the congress and calling out, "They can hear you over here chief." Which speaks volumes as to the accuracy of our interpretation of things not understood.

He also explained that his job is to go to every house to see if anyone is hiding from congress or if they have a good excuse for being at home such as illness.

The Chief came out to the boat in his dugout canoe. He wanted to trade conch shells for socks. Peggy gave him ten pairs of socks and she was happy to have one of the shells in exchange but the chief insisted that she take all eight of the conch shells.

Peggy was preparing pancakes for breakfast at the time, and when one of the villagers came to the boat he and the chief were promptly invited to join us in the event.

The chief had not eaten anything like pancakes in his life. We know this because, although the chief stayed, the other fellow must have told one or two people when he went ashore, as witnessed by the fact that someone else came expectantly. In fact they kept coming. More and more men came. The chief was still aboard. He loved pancakes. Literally, almost the entire day was spent by Peggy cooking pancakes.

The houses are made of pole frames with coconut palm leaf thatch on the roof and sides. The folks sleep in hammocks tied between the poles supporting the ridge timber. No flooring is needed.

When a girl's eye falls upon a young man who finds favor in her glance, upon thinking of this matter, she will seek the ear of her father. And if he concurs with her choice in this matter, he will call upon the assistance of some of his friends who with him will chase the boy down, catch him, drag him kicking or not to this father's house, and throw the young man into the hammock of the girl.

If he jumps out, they will hunt him down again the next evening, and throw him into her hammock again. If again he *jumps hammock*, they will repeat this yet a third time. If this time he runs away, he will not be chased again.

If, however, he stays in the hammock any of these times, they are thereby married. And this is one of the excuses for a huge party after which the islands supply of home brew is immensely depleted.

The gentleman who had been most often present aboard was very anxious for us to see his wife, who by gesticulation it was explained had a toothache. This fact, could possibly explain his frequency aboard as being designed to create a bond of friendship. Was I going to pull a tooth?

We came to the house. She opened her mouth and showed me the area that hurt. Indeed the jaw was abscessed with an impacted wisdom tooth needing to be extracted. A loose baby tooth I might pull, but this, never.

"Where do you usually go for help with bad teeth?"

There was a place to go. His problem about solving his wife's terrible pain was his not having the money to pay for the service. I was greatly relieved upon hearing that the cost was 50 cents. The next day they were off by canoe to the dentist.

That's the day we went with someone else to his banana farm. We went with them in their long boat and outboard motor, way up a narrow jungle river and tied up to the bank where a trail led off. We climbed upward on this steep path for a seemingly very long time until finally getting to a cleared area planted with cocoa trees and banana trees.

That lovely hot beverage the world all enjoys called cocoa comes from a two inch stem holding a pod that grows directly out of the trunk of the tree, not unlike a papaya. The pod is about five inches long and seven or eight inches in diameter. Several huge bunches of banana were cut for transit back to the village. Each bunch was about a meter in length and enormously heavy.

Chapter 6   Panama

It was hot. Everybody was wet with perspiration and mud was visible in abundance, but lots of laughing accompanied the puffing. It was announced that we would stop on our way back for a bath at the swimming hole, where we got out of the boat and into the water -- clothes and all.

The water was quite swift and beautifully clear in the river. The swimming place was at a point where the river widened at one side. The depth here was from three to five feet. Oh my, it felt good! The mud was gone; the perspiration was gone. Everybody was laughing and jumping around.

Another boat came down stream and stopped, followed by two others, all full of people. Our host the farmer told me that these folks were returning from a burial up stream.

We had previously learned some of the customs of these people and knew that the important possessions of a deceased were always buried with him to use in his next life, be it a sewing machine or a trinket.

The new group by now was jovial, playfully joining the clowning around. I thought possibly this was with an aim of cheering the widow who was equally engaged in this tension release.

In the process of fooling around she had come in front of me. And when we found each other thus, and in mimic of what I had just done with someone else, I threw my arms into the air and with a burst of "Yeaaa!" I fell over backwards, followed without missing a beat, the widow in exact duplicate of my gesture followed mine to everyone's cheer of approval. Is there a better way to recover after burying the dead?

These were some of the women we had seen leaning forward at congress. They had been making molas. When the missionaries came and found the women topless, they were not content until they had changed the culture. The women had not been topless in reality.

They had always beautifully painted each other's upper body with colorfully painted decoration. So when it was insisted upon by the missionaries to cover themselves with cloth, it was of course, natural for them to make decorative cloth the same size as the previously painted areas and to attach such cloth to the required shirts. These cloth pieces are now named "Molas." They are sold all throughout the canal area and are prized as a remaining Folk Art of the world.

In many island areas money is not greatly sought after. Exchange of items is the more natural event. If you have something that I want, and I have something that you want, we can exchange these items. And if one is of more value that the other, a second or third item can be added to the deal. It was so here at Tigre.

We wanted to buy some molas from a traditional island such as this. We had mirrors. I had unsuccessfully tried to build a solar oven and had a considerable number of mirrors aboard. They were wildly fought over generally in great politeness. If a woman was wearing a shirt that had an attractive mola, at my slightest hand gesture, the shirt was off and a mirror gratefully received. But the women should not be thought of as unduly vain. The wealth of the family is worn on their bodies in the form of a gold ring through the center portion between the nostrils, and earrings are worn as daily dress as well as gold from the neck in the form of a breast plate, and gold bracelets rings are worn half way up the arms. Not all of the women wore decorations of gold. But all seemed to be adorned by some type of necklaces and arm and leg bracelets, with the nose ring never absent even in quite young girls. A red scarf with some white pattern often covered the head. It would seem natural that a woman would wish to see what she looked like.

We had good reason to have enjoyed our acquaintance with these Kuna Indians. They are a lovely group of people. Our brief five or six day stay with them shall be long remembered.

Our taking up of the anchor and setting sail was hailed by many at the beach with calls to us in words beyond our knowledge. But being accompanied by such enthusiastic friendliness of smiles and wavings, we felt assured that demons were not being called upon to darken our day. Apparently, Peggy's pancakes were not forgotten. I smiled.

We spent a strangely quiet night again in that cove where the shadow of those giant Spanish galleons had waited at the Fort of Portobello. That flickering shadow that moved over the great grey stones of the old fort was not the moon shadow of the mast of an ancient Spanish galleon, though some there be, who might say that it was so. The shadows moved.

The night vanished silently. And in that silence, our sails filled, while only the ripple of the bow wave of the sailing vessel *Osprey* whispered to the wind that we too were here no longer. Astern, nothing moved but for two black vultures that turned away from seeing us and looked again at the old fort. Now nothing moved.

* * *

Back at Colon, I was given the transit date by the Canal Company and phoned the church pastor to put the word out among the older teenagers that a canal transit was available for them to be part of if recommended by him. He was excited over the prospect. It's one thing to have lived next to it, but a big deal to be aboard a boat and go through the canal. I told him that I would need to know not later than two days ahead of time. He agreed.

The time arrived with no word from the minister and no answer on the phone either. With no contact, I went to *Love Love* and he and Hero, who could handle a line and belay it when told, would come. I got three others who also committed in time, so we were okay.

On the morning of transit the three men arrived, Yusuke and Hero came with Tomo and her mother as well. Then the four from church arrived, so counting Peggy and me, we had 13 people aboard instead of the required four. What a party!

At the yacht club we had met the captain of a US flag tugboat, which of all surprises was scheduled for the same time as we. Wherefore, at our pilot advisor's instruction, we tied to the side of the tug for our entire passage with no line handling required for our 13 hardies. The tug McChaffey and we entered all of the locks in front of our lock mate, the United States War Ship *Cushing*, a Destroyer, 564 feet in length.

We thought this a poetically protective display of power for us. We after all, we're the very last US flag yacht to pass through the Panama Canal while the

canal was still owned by the United States of America. The next day, Panama took possession and control.

At one of the locks while the tug and therefore we as well were already secured to the forward end of the lock waiting for the Cushing to enter, the tug captain came over and said, "Peggy, would you like to come up to the bridge and watch what goes on?"

"Yes!" was her instant reply.

She sat in the second of the high seats of rank way up there on the bridge and able to have a grand view of the beautiful surroundings of the canal. She went through two of the seven locks in this royal manner and then saw nothing else of the canal the rest of the way.

She was cooking for 13 people all the rest of the time. All aboard had a wonderful time.

The sights were great. The food abundant and delicious, and I'm sure that the boys from church were the envy of all. The transit ended with thanks all around; to the captain of the tug McChaffey, to the church boys and to the yachtsmen.

We were given a mooring at the Balboa Yacht Club. They run a constant shore boat for those on moorings and this massive crew of ours was brought to the club and taxis were arranged to get them to the train for Colon.

The cost of use of the canal is based on the cargo carrying cubic footage of the vessel. The fee for transit, (if measurement is previously done in the US with a certificate so given, as we had), for a yacht of our size, the cost was $12. That fee now for a yacht, soon became several hundred US dollars.

***

We were in the Pacific, or so it seemed, which is really what the Spanish gentleman Balboa thought when he named these quiet waters the "Pacific" Ocean. But he was seeing this huge protected gulf, not the ocean. We found the Pacific Ocean on many occasions anything but peaceful.

Waves are a product of wind, not geography. And the greater the distance the wind blows over water, the greater the size of the waves. And no water has greater distance than the Pacific. But why throw rocks at poor Balboa. As said by baseball umpires, "Ya calls em like ya sees em." Señor Balboa, it's okay.

We left the yacht club for Taboga, where we anchored while building the sunshade. It is a somewhat steep island. It actually looks very much like some steep Greek islands that I have seen pictured, dotted with houses perching up there, brushed by differing colors of brightness. Taboga makes a beautiful picture.

There were other yachts here. *Love Love* was there for most of the three months that we were there, as well as *Pursuit of Nantucket*, a perfectly lovely yawl of early wood construction with Dave and Annie aboard. We were to enjoy their company greatly while here and numerous other places throughout the Pacific.

We mourned the loss of such a beautiful boat on one of those far-off reefs. Dave and Annie were unscathed, but the picture of Dave's diving down into the boat and coming up with (for instance) a left shoe of a pair, while the local man had come up with the right one and refused to give the right one to him because he had found this shoe so it was his, disappoints me. Yet I can follow the primitive reasoning.

Chapter 6 — Panama

We went to the Russian circus in Panama City with Dick and Mary Ann Stresau of the yacht Sabot, which means wooden shoe in Dutch, very appropriate for a wooden sailboat. Peggy was very impressed by the circus bears.

The cockpit sunshade is a joy! PVC is made with more than one wall-thickness. I chose the thicker stronger product. The vertical framing is each attached with two bolts through the sides of the cockpit well, and the overhead frame is made directly above the verticals.

An extension frame port & starboard, as well as over the bridge deck forward, help shade us when the sun is not directly overhead.

The canvas cover sewn by Peggy, now has grommets as well, and I've used bungee cord to attach it so that it will remain tight at all times; even as the fabric changed size somewhat between wet and dry, hot and cool.

As a permanently rigged rain water catcher, I had bought male garden hose fittings placed through the canvas from the top and secured there to prevent spin when a hose is attached from the under side. The hose is fed into the two fresh water tanks' intake openings in the bridge deck, and gravity does the rest.

This is our underway system. At anchor we have a sunshade, which covers the house from the mast aft, also with two hose attachments. Our two water tanks hold one hundred gallons each. The fuel tank holds one hundred gallons and I carried fifty gallons more fuel in plastic jugs.

While at Taboga, we met Jan who worked for the Inter American Tropical Tuna Commission. It was her job to go aboard the big tuna clippers with those gigantic nets, to try to determine where and when the tuna were found during their migrations.

Patrick, a single hander aboard the sloop *Juggernaut*, a 27-foot Catalina that subsequently completed a circumnavigation, became acquainted with Jan. She had a large rubber inflatable dinghy with a big powerful outboard engine which she permitted the use of to Patrick and me to take in hot pursuit of the thief of the *Osprey*'s dinghy, reported last seen making toward Panama City.

The city in some areas is much like Venice with its canals running between walled buildings. These places were dimly lit. We went farther, still no dinghy. It was getting spooky.

I was walking to a special store in Colon. The street in that culturally declining area was abandoned of pedestrian traffic. Unbeknownst to me, someone was matching my footsteps and gaining closer position to me as he came.

Without the slightest sound being detected, two hands went into my front pockets from behind. Instantly I jabbed my elbows backward, knocking his arms and thereby his hands out of my pockets as I spun around in righteous indignation to do battle. He too had spun around and was heading away. In mid turn, I saw four men running in our direction about a block and a half away. I did not think that they were coming to my assistance. I continued my spin to full circle and strode broad-shoulderedly on without a backward look.

The store supplied my need. A taxi supplied my transport back. From that time forward, when going either to Colon of Panama City, I wore two pairs of trousers. The inner one carried all items of value and the outer a tight belt.

One of our yachting friends was a practiced long-distance runner whose pocket was picked of his wallet. There were two of them. They both turned and ran with him right behind them.

They went through an alley, over a fence, down a street for three blocks, into a private yard, through the front door of a house and out the back door with our friend right behind them.

The people of the house were sitting in the living room and our friend said that he was running too fast to take notice of the facial expressions of the house owners as the three of them burst in and ran through.

Now he yelled in fluent Spanish, that there is no money in the wallet – only papers important to me but of no value. I have money in this envelope. Give me the wallet and I give you the envelope. Finally the exchange was made on the run and the chase was over.

Two minutes later a police car came by. He hailed them, told them what had happened. They had him get in the back seat and started out. But it was instantly obvious to him that they were not going after the two guys.

When the car stopped for a traffic light he jumped out in fear that the police were taking him perhaps to a dark alley as well. Of course, we must attribute that to what – paranoia?

We gave up the canal search. I was armed, but we didn't want a war if our way was blocked getting out.

It was a unique ride back. We saved two drunks who had fallen into the water, and recognized two separate dinghies floating away, which we returned to the proper owners. This has been one crazy night.

Was it Christmas? "When what to my wondering eye does appear but a miniature sleigh and" – a dinghy? – with – *what's that smell?*

The dinghy was back at the *Osprey*! It had been taken from the dock where we had left it while going to a Chinese restaurant with other yachtsmen, and here it was again.

Peggy was awaiting my return when a fellow came up with the dinghy saying that he had found it and he wanted $100 for bringing it to her, which then came down to $50 which Peggy settled at $20.

The dinghy stank of fish. It was smeared with fish oil, lots of beans and rice were dropped all over it. Jan was certain that one of the tuna boats had been robbed of stores from the galley. It was a mess.

We showed the police who with a shrug had concluded no likelihood of arrest. We weren't after a pound of flesh after all. So we felt that our duty had been satisfied. The cleanup job took time.

One of the very happy facts by which we were benefited greatly was the zero value to the tuna boat people of their inadvertent catch of mahi-mahi which also went into the salted storage holds with the tuna. These Mahi were given freely to us as the tuna were off-loaded onto the bigger transport ships. This was being done here at Taboga, a few hundred yards from us. We ate salted Mahi across the Pacific as far as the Marquises Islands. Thanks folks.

Jan was permitted to bring Patrick, plus the Nishikawa family from Love Love, and Peggy and me, to one of her tuna transport ships for a Korean dinner of rice, kim chi and fish, served with stimulating conversation. Another fun evening was enjoyed by all.

We were three months at Taboga, and the time had arrived to take up the anchors and bid a very fond farewell to this historic place. But let's not rush away! We'll anchor at the Perlis Islands before leaving the Gulf of Panama. I might catch us some fresh fish on the way.

I don't use a fishing pole for two reasons. It not only would be a bother to store it, but a hand line is more efficient. The flexing of the pole which benefits the problem of fish breaking the line or the hook is nicely overcome with a hand line by one of those thick rubber cargo tensioners with an attachment hook at both ends.

The fishing line is all nylon except for the last twenty feet ahead of the lure, which is of the customary plastic filament. But aboard the boat I belay the line on a cleat on the house at the bridge deck. And I have two small loops tied, into which I hook the rubber. The length of line between the loops is a foot longer than the length of the rubber so that the force of the fish is taken up by the stretch of the heavy-duty rubber before coming up hard against the belayed line. The usual hand line spool is used to take up the entire line when not in use.

Peggy remembers this fish, I don't. She remembers it because, as she says, "It wouldn't fit across the bridge deck." If her memory is correct, it would have been a little over six feet long, pretty big for a Mahi Mahi. Suffice it to say that it was of some considerable size.

However long it was, when we got to the Perlis shortly thereafter, some local folks came out to the boat with whom we were able to share most of the fish. Peggy has a fantastic recipe for pickled fish, which makes for great d'oeuvres. So we were able to keep some of it after a hardy meal for ourselves.

I am not one who is oblivious regarding dispatching the life of a fish. I seek to have it done quickly.

I have found that placing a wet towel over the fish starting at the mouth and ending at the tail, after which I slid my hand from the head to the tail, the fish instantly stops thrashing. It must think that it has been swallowed. A screwdriver through its brain dispatches all sensation.

Tomorrow we would be off for what would become an 11-day sail to the Galapagos Islands. Some camaraderie with the Perlis Islanders, some laughter and smiles, aids well the digestion and the sleep. Peggy and I slept well.

CHAPTER 7

 THE GALAPAGOS ISLANDS

The anchor found its way back aboard, the mainsail and drifter took their place, and upon Peggy's smile (which is the official signal to begin) we sailed out of the Gulf of Panama and into the Pacific Ocean where the *Osprey* would spend many wild and many gentle years to come.

I still felt as though I had not yet left home and years had passed. Our country still lay due north of us. Thousands of miles would yet be sailed before we were out from under the US. This is not prompted by disaffection of the country. It's just that I was amused by Alaska reaching so far westward as the longitude lines squeeze together toward the Arctic Circle.

Upon arriving back to the states 23 years after having started this voyage, we bought an RV coach in Florida and drove up into the Arctic Circle to see yet another world. The North Country is a spectacle of its own. Looking southward from there, we saw glaciers of ice with no hint of these lovely waters where now we sail.

There was no wind as we left the Gulf of Panama. Only a breeze stirred the heat of the day. It was the middle of winter, a secret apparently too well kept from the friends of Neptune.

Cocas Island was way to the north. Our good friend Emmett had gotten almost to Cocas when with mixed emotions he brought the good ketch

Zephyrus about, abandoning what had been a commencement toward a circumnavigation. They were undone by several things, but these doldrums were a contributing factor.

The Cocas Islands are where friends of ours aboard *Brown Palace* were when Jane fell ill. Bob had a helicopter flown to pick her up for a medical evacuation. Well afterward, they were to continue their fine voyage.

I raised the iron mainsail (started the engine). Steering can be a real drudgery if it has to be done 24 hours a day. With no wind, the windvane steering doesn't function. Fortunately, in Jacksonville Florida, we had bought an electric autopilot to hold course for us in just such circumstances. The man who sold and serviced that particular make of autopilot patiently endured my questions, which I'm sure seemed to go on forever.

I bought the Cetrec Autopilot. And with his last words of assurance, I was indeed happy to see yet another "crewman" aboard who wanted nothing other than to steer while motoring. He held course wonderfully and even permitting dodging around something floating on the water, after which the touch of a button would reassume the previous course.

Voyaging should be fun, not drudgery. If it becomes drudgery, one often is inclined to not continue. It was an absolute joy until we had arrived several years ago in the Bahamas. I called Jacksonville and with no hostility at all in my voice, I reported the symptoms of its behavior. His immediate response was, "I'll be on the next plane" and he was.

Not until years later in New Zealand, after enormous hours of perfect service to the boat, it was necessary that I send the unit back for its well-deserved maintenance service. I applaud the manufacturer.

We were motoring onward one day. Peggy was in the cockpit. I emerged from below with the most grave of announcements. I was properly attired for the occasion. I said, "I am King, and Neptune is my name." My wig was of brightly colored wool, which Peggy was using to make an afghan.

An appropriate ceremony was conducted by which mere mortals are eternally changed by The King of the Clan of The Sea. Only those hardy souls who have braved the crossing of the Equator are ever so greatly honored as to be presented into this hallowed Association. "Fare thee well, ye honored seamen of the world."

The King grabbed the virgin by the hair and [these words of the author may have been deleted by the editor].

We powered our way through the doldrums. The breeze returned, followed shortly by the wind, followed shortly by his two brothers. It started to blow. But that family was not long winded, and we missed their departure but only briefly for they returned again -- with gusto, yet no sooner had they done so, than they were off again. For days it was so.

These islands were once called the Enchanted Islands, for the mystery of thickest fog has oft times hurled its cloak as though to have plucked the Galapagos Islands from out the sea. It is reported that long ago, the Ecuadorian Navy once returned home declaring that the islands had vanished; for though they searched for them, the islands could not be found.

This results from the cold Humboldt Current, which sweeps up from the frozen south, and then meets the sun-baked islands so close to the Equator.

Yet, on December 31, we spotted one of the islands of the Galapagos. On the second of January, when darkness was descending, we heard a loud unfamiliar ruckus. It was a honking sort of animal noise, which surrounded us upon entering our first anchorage in these fabled islands. I turned on the spot light and could see nothing but eyes in all directions. The sound was a shockingly loud cacophony. There was a show of splashing into the water and back out again. Almost deafening were the sounds.

They were sea lions. But beyond all of that, or perhaps better said in the midst of all of that, the landscape stood stark in its stillness. Unworldly were the shore shapes. Nothing alive and green was seen above the water's edge. Were

Chapter 7 — The Galapagos Islands

we on planet earth? How could anything look so strange? What were those things? They looked like weird cactus, big as trees. And the rocks seemed formed by a sculptor who had lingered too long at the wine press. It was strange. It looked like the moon!

The anchor added another splash to the cacophony surrounding us. The chain rumbled out. The sea lions decided to forgive our intrusion. Where they snoring? I think Peggy did.

Even here, day followed night. We were at Plaza Island. Outward from the island and 90% from it, and beginning a couple of hundred feet from shore, were two rock jetties both several hundred feet in length. They were entirely possessed by sea lions. The huge bulls were bossy guys! The females would be playing together happily and wander off a little farther than their bullying protector thought it safe to go, and he would start bellowing his commands probably saying,

"Get over here. How can I protect you from a shark when you're that far away!? I've got 11 of you to take care of, so get over here!" And with an appearance of annoyance they would go back.

There was a yacht that came a day or so later. Their dinghy was afloat behind the boat, and the youngsters of the sea lion clan would jump into the dinghy over the stern. And as the next one came into it in like manner, the first one was forced forward. This continued until the dinghy was full, which meant that when the next one came in, the one farthest forward would have to dive out of the boat, and so the game continued. I think we had more fun from the game then they did.

The birds had their own games. A yellow warbler flew into the cockpit. We remained motionless as it explored this new find. Not yet content with the entirety of its exploration, it went into the cabin and

looked around. Standing regally, cloaked within its golden vestment, a thorough stock was taken of the surroundings before rejecting the house as unsuitable, and it flew away. But not before being willing to pose for the ubiquitous photo op. Royalty can at times acquiesce.

Royalty aside, other formalities beckoned, and we made for Academy Bay to face the customs authorities entirely void of the necessary documentation permitting our presence. We had no visa. Such matters are very darkly looked upon. I flew the Q flag stating that the vessel was quarantined. No one may approach the vessel and no one may enter the country by coming ashore.

Someone came and informed us to go to the customs office where we claimed entry due to the emergency of sail damage and an engine fan belt having stretched to maximum adjustment.

Entry was granted for 7 days. I ordered fan belts from Guayaquil, Ecuador and a few days later found a tailor. The tailor spoke Spanish. I spoke English. He had understandable difficulty with my conveyance of specific service required. I wanted certain areas of the sail sewn over top of the stitches that were there, due to some thread being chafed. The tailor saw stitches. Why would anyone want more? They were holding the fabric together. He was confused but efficient. Where the panel stitching had torn loose was obvious. After all, he possessed the monopoly of his trade for many, many miles beyond the horizon. And when understanding the requirement, he commenced accordingly.

Patrick, a single hander, arrived with his boat the *Juggernaut*. We had met him in Panama. He came over and shared his experience upon his earlier arrival here in the Galapagos. It was not at a customs official port of entry, but although not going ashore, he was interested in seeing the native wild life.

It was different somewhat from our experience. He had anchored no more than a hundred feet off shore, and had no sooner awakened the next morning when he saw an apparition approaching on the beach. Or so was his first millisecond reaction, followed immediately with another. Oh yes! She was real and she wore tennis shoes! Only tennis shoes. And as it turned out, she

Chapter 7 — The Galapagos Islands

really wanted to have conversations with Patrick because he was her own age. The scientist whom she was assisting was very much older. Patrick stayed several days talking to this lovely young woman. Patrick had a large collection of shark's teeth and always gave one to the young women who came aboard for conversations with him.

Patrick met a young woman living with her family here at Academy Bay, whom he felt certain would like to have one of these shark teeth. They had spoken a number of times, but she had not yet visited with him. There was to be a fiesta party of games and food advertised for the following Saturday night. Tickets were being sold.

Now Patrick was traveling without funds of any great quantity, so two tickets represented a major investment. Nonetheless, he inquired if she would like to join him by attending the event and his invitation was enthusiastically accepted. He arrived at her residence at the appointed time and was startled by her being accompanied by her father as chaperone. However, upon arriving at the fiesta to be required to also buy a ticket for her chaperone was a monumental shock. Ah, such are the trials of a bachelor.

Peggy felt sorry for him, and Patrick was often found at our table throughout many ports of the Pacific. He completed a fine circumnavigation.

The belts came. They were the wrong size. We showed customs the belts and the orders. Our time was extended, first due to delivery time of the belts and now again due to error. We were a month in the Galapagos instead of a week. We loved every minute of the time. Had we not had problems, we may not have been granted entry at all.

We expected other yachts to be there. Only the red boat with the black dog was here. These Austrian folks had been aboard the *Osprey* at Taboga, and it was great to see them again.

That same day a lady was passing by in a lovely dinghy, of which I praised her. And it was such good fortune for us that she returned the next day with her husband. They so graciously enriched our experience of the Galapagos Islands and bestowed upon us the greater gift of their friendship, residing forever undimmed in the treasure store of our minds.

Andre and Jacquelyn De Roy had lived through the terrible times, the times of the Second World War in Belgium. When it was over, they longed for a place beyond such reach. And upon hearing that "Homestead Land" in the Galapagos was being offered, they did not hesitate a moment.

It was necessary that Andre take a long bus trip when they got to Ecuador. He did not speak Spanish. He got the correct bus with help, and was very interested to see people traveling with a couple of chickens in a cage or a pig on the roof. Folks with lunches ready to eat and other vendors were selling food on the way.

He was hungry but had not brought any food with him and was delighted to have someone offer to share. But they would not take his money, nor would those who were selling. They always turned away with an odd expression. It was not until sometime after the bus ride that he learned what was being said, "No Father, no money from you."

Andre had looked to their eyes as being a tall skinny underfed holy man, such as a monk. And if truth be known, money was not his most abundant resource. But a new life into which they could devote themselves was within their firm grasp. A pioneer life of boundless expectation had brought wondrous light pouring into every corner of the dark shadows of their prior world! What excitement!

They marked their intended claim for homestead land up in the highlands above where Academy Bay is now. They found that they had a Norwegian family as neighbors not a great distance away. They were a hardy lot with five burly sons.

Water is a precious resource up there. Banana plants are grown for water content with which to feed the cattle. Years later, that family found an open water spring a few hundred yards from their house in the midst of so thick a jungle that even five robust boys had not penetrated to the spot.

This was up where the giant turtles roam and graze, where the land needed to be cleared of jungle in order to farm. One can only dimly cast an eye to such times that caused our friends to yearn for so remote a place upon the earth as this.

To this Belgian family, a son and daughter decided to be born, joining their parents in this wild place. The world turned. Opportunities pounded upon their door. And when they joined us aboard the *Osprey* that day, they had already built a yacht, making even the fastening nails by hand out of heavy gauge wire. (Had they thought it an avenue of escape if needed? I don't suggest this as a motive.)

They had used a ball peen hammer to form the nail heads. These are resourceful people. When we were there, their son was a tour guide for the islands and their daughter was a published photographer for National Geographic Magazine.

* * *

These are volcanic islands. When one becomes active and starts erupting, everyone is evacuated by the government of Ecuador. But Andre and his daughter Tui, head for the island with her cameras.

The islands are strangely formed and can be inhospitable. It is said, that a company of army men were landed on one of the islands and told to cross to the other side where they would be picked up by the ship, which dropped them off. Only one man made it. Others either fell into various deep crevices and thus into the jagged depths below or were otherwise killed or died of starvation trying to get across the island.

Tui didn't have any pictures of wild dogs for which her publisher had asked, so the film hunt was on. They had covered an exhausting distance and seen nothing. Climbing atop one of the many very pointed lava cones about eight feet high and 30 feet in diameter, they looked for wild dogs in all directions with binoculars. Still nothing. They threw a rock way over that way and an entire pack of wild dogs jumped up from the brush. Not only jumped up, but attacked. The three of them, Andre, Tui and her brother, were back to back beating the dogs off in a fight for their lives when the alpha dog gave a sound and instantly they all were gone.

Tui had taken some pictures, as only a photographer would dare. What she got was a hindquarter here and a few other parts there but alas, nothing was usable. At the time of our conversation, they had not tried again. This is not a tame place.

Peggy and I had caught a ride on a truck going up into the highlands. The driver was kind and pointed out interesting birds along the way. We saw several kinds of Darwin Finches, as well as a bird using a thorn tree as a bug killing device and storage area since the bug was left impaled on the thorn.

There are three enormously different climatic zones on many of the islands such as Santa Cruz Island where we were at Academy Bay. The coastal area is arid, wind swept, and unique in appearance; while upward in elevation, green grew the land where the backs of mankind had cleared its jungle. And third, at the upper reaches of the islands, lava formations were eroded by strong winds, which seem to have twisted the island yet again into strange appearance.

We were walking a trail where we were judged intruders, and perhaps invaders into someone else's territory. It was a very large bull with his head down pawing the ground. His neck seemed as broad as his body and his horns more than capable of any task to which he might choose to engage them. Wild cattle roam here. The bull was up on a ledge somewhat above us. But this was not a barrier to prevent his joining us. Peggy followed my request of her to continue walking with me and not to look at the bull, which snorted around a bit more but concluded that we were not a threat to his domain. No more accurate conclusion has ever been made by man or beast.

We came upon a turtle. The area here was of rolling hillsides. It had been lightly raining occasionally. We were slightly down slope of the turtle. Up from where we stood, bright green grass grew lushly up the gentle slope. An old gnarled wooden fence of rough-hewn timber stretched unevenly to the left and right about ten feet in front of us. Another ten feet beyond the fence stood a giant turtle grazing. His shell was all ashen from the rain and lightly landed at the top most of this giant's shell stood a delicate little yellow warbler. Although my camera functioned properly, the picture in my mind can much more readily be brought forth without search, and perhaps with greater pleasure. The contrasts of the sky, at the moment brightly blue, having waved a wand of sparkles upon the damp green of the grass on the hill before us; with this ancient crudely hewn wood fence in the foreground; beyond which grazed this magnificent creature of wondrous ages past, hosting a tiny and frail yellow feathered warbler upon his back, is a printed picture forever present upon the mind of even so unpoetic a fellow such as I.

We had brought lunch. And what one does when in the area of these giant Galapagos Turtles is simply to walk up to one and sit down on top of it

to rest or in our case to have lunch. We each chose a seat. The turtle, which is only briefly interrupted in its slow grazing, just retraces its head and legs, exhaling loudly in the process and awaits its return to normalcy with no other expression.

If I were asked to blindly estimate the likely frequency of such interruptions to their grazing, I would hazard a guess that an individual turtle might be sat upon as frequently as perhaps once in every several years. We never saw another person when we walked amongst these giants. Tourists who come here see the turtles too, but they see them in the "zoo" of Academy Bay.

We were surprised to note that the digestive system of these turtles is not of the greatest efficiency. They were eating grass exclusively, and after it's being processed through the digestive system, the grass did not appear much changed by any of these turtles, but only twisted up somewhat upon being discharged. Obviously, enough is enough as the saying goes. These marvelous creatures were some of the ones that Darwin had lunch with that day when he went ashore.

André and Jacquelyn spent a couple of hours aboard the *Osprey* with us. They were charming, gracious, informative folks, who invited us to join them for dinner. Both of their offspring had flown the coop for a month or two on assignments, so it was just the four of us.

They had built their house here just off the beach at Academy Bay with stones that were picked up in its vicinity. No iguanas had occupied the immediate area before them. Had they done so as was the case with several houses we saw, the iguanas assumed that the house was just an up-growth of the rocks upon which they were accustomed to sunbathe after sea ventures, and had continued sunbathing on the same spot; in such case, atop the roof.

The De Roy's house was just lovely. Some would call it small of room size but totally efficient indeed. For years there were no windows, which was greatly appreciated by the bustling community of birds, which flew about at will inside of it. So much so that Andre and Jacquelyn began to recognize certain individual birds. And a couple of these birds began recognizing their habits as well.

A specific male and female, which they recognized due to the male having one of his toes damaged, and the female by a mark on her beak, were observed as being mates. They remained so for many years. Other finches incessantly bickered noisily at each other, while these two never did. Harmony continued until for unknowable reason they chose other mates and squabbling was their daily routine for a few years, until the two of them reunited. The squabbling ended and peace reigned supreme. These two birds seemed to feel that Andre and Jacquelyn were leftover parents or sponsors of some kind, because they were not above pulling a chair up to the dinner table, as it were.

They would individually land on Andre's head and wait for him to bring up some food in his hand. If this didn't happen, they would lean up side down over his forehead and look in one of his eyes to make sure that they had been seen. If Andre brought up his hand, opened it with nothing in it, acceptance of this fact was immediate, and the male would fly away. The female had not yet learned that particular trick when the windows were installed.

As you can see, these good folks lived close to the habitat of which they were indeed likewise a part.

They are the first time discoverers and therefore the ones who named one of a red fish of the area. They like wise discovered numerous shelled creatures, which they have officially named and cataloged. How grandly educational it must have been for their son and daughter, who were entirely home schooled in this truly unique area of the earth. I doff my cap.

We received a warm letter from them when we were in Tahiti years later. They were well.

CHAPTER 8

The Vast Pacific Ocean

Such a fine day! To be underway again felt good. The weather was beautiful, though it still felt brisk due to the cold Humboldt Current. We were not permitted to stop at any island on our way from Academy Bay on the Island of Isabella. But, oh how I wanted to stop at Post Office Bay! Such long tradition is not easily disrespected.

The old sailing ships and the whalers centuries ago used to stop here without fail. A barrel had been mounted on a pile of rocks into which sailors would put letters for home. When a ship came in here, it would take all the letters addressed to the places where it was bound and leave mail to other countries to be picked up by a vessel going there. Letters would often spend years awaiting its homeward bound sailing vessel. It would have been fun to address an envelope to one's self, such as:

From: Dan Van Ginhoven, aboard the sailing vessel *Osprey*
         Westward bound from Galapagos Isles
         Homeward bound in 12 years

To: My wife, P.A. Van Ginhoven
         The Americas, North
         Colony: Carolina, North
         Hamlet: Salisbury, Oak Tree Lane, # 147

Chapter 8 — *The Vast Pacific Ocean*

Thanks to any ship of commerce or navy, bound for
The Americas – Carolina Colonies

But alas, we complied with the laws of these islands. We did not stop.

Thousands of miles of trackless ocean stretched beyond our horizon. We saw no other yacht while making this westing. But one small ship happened our way. It was great to see it. We had seen no evidence for quite some time, which could prove that we were not the only persons living on this planet. The ship changed course toward us and I noticed that I was unclad.

If one must go to the foredeck to handle sail where salt spray may drench one, it is much more efficient to leave one's apparel in the cockpit where it is dry than to have wet salty clothes that may take days to dry out again. I quickly dressed as social grace requires. She was a lovely little thing. Just off the ways; she looked all bright and Bristol fashion, having just been out of the water for painting and looked just perfect.

She was a really small freighter, carrying cargo plus perhaps a couple dozen passengers; all of whom were lining the rail to see this little yacht with two jibs set out on poles being pulled at the nose by the tradewinds right here in the middle of thousands of miles of ocean.

I put up flag signals saying that I wanted to speak via channel 16, which is VHF radio. I called. No answer. So much for modern day flag recognition. They came within hailing distance and asked if we needed anything. Peggy wanted to ask for chocolate ice cream but I vetoed it. They may have been concerned that we might need food or water, which would have been a completely different matter.

They asked if I wanted them to report our position to Papeete radio. I told them that I would be putting in at the Marquises Island and was uncertain as to when we would enter at Tahiti. I did not want to cause concern or a search for us. They understood and resumed speed as the passengers got their last pictures of boat, the lady, and the guy with such a wild beard.

Enthusiastic waves were exchanged. I regret not asking for a photo or two to be left for us at the American Express Office in Papette, Tahiti.

The old sailing ship captains over many years of sailing the oceans of the world kept logs of their passages. Weather was not the least of the important data. These logs have been studied in recent history and compiled in a book, which no prudent sailor is without. It is called "Ocean Passages of the World."

When referring to the conditions of the sea, which we are presently sailing, and the time of this sailing; the weather is referred to by the captains of those great sailing ships as being "salubrious." And indeed it was so!

Constant steady tradewinds were perpetually with us. It was wonderful! With Ruth, the name given to our windvane steering system, caring for our course, and the down wind running rig that "Kismet" had insisted I needed; we were effortlessly carried across the sea by the two jibs foreword of the mast. It was marvelously wonderful!

Sleep was great and an unhurried inclination to "break the fast" since last night's dinner, prompted the question, "What's for breakfast?"

Not knowing if we would be granted entry into the Galapagos, in Panama we had stocked the boat for our South Pacific crossing. We had been given entry, however, by which our experience was immeasurably enriched, while our cash was reduced by the departure fees at the customs office which cost us $40.00, leaving us with $80.05 which was to care for necessities in the Marquises where we would be for three months.

We would come to our next American Express office in Tahiti, through which our funds are accessed.

The clearing fees of customs is why one of the yachts with even fewer funds than we, had taken the opportunity to remove his passport from the drawer where he knew it to be, while the officer was away from his desk and took leave of the area with some degree of haste.

In Panama we had bought several dozens of eggs. Each egg was covered by us with a heavy film of Vaseline to keep air from entering the pores of the shell too quick. The carrots and cabbages were wrapped in newspaper. The potatoes and onions were swung in net hammocks and as one spoiled it was thrown overboard. Oranges were wrapped in aluminum foil. The sharp cheese was "plastic" and better than nothing because it didn't mold.

For breakfast today, we had oatmeal with margarine and raisins, and really excellent tinned crackers. They come in a square tin about 7 inches in size with a round opening pry-up lid. They are named SkyFlakes, by Monde M. Y. San Corporation, Cainta, Rizal 1900 Philippines (www.mysan.com.ph). I love these things! They are always crisp and fresh at sea. I am not a paid sponsor, but whole-heartedly recommend them to you.

Catching fresh fish in mid-ocean very seldom happens. There are the occasional migration schools that you may notice. We noticed only a few. Canned meats supplied our protein and variety. And our dehydrated vegetables were without limit.

In the Bahamas I had installed a salt water pump at the sink which was foot activated, making dish washing easy, and efficient by saving fresh water.

Try to imagine the nights without another light for a thousand miles in any direction. What a show! And when the moon is full, one actually can easily read in the cockpit. Celestial navigation is done at dusk and dawn, when the stars are still bright enough, and the horizon distinct enough. But on nights without a moon, the stars *blaze* in the sky, and the planets shine as though they have been polished by a New York shoeshine man.

Doing navigation in the evening using the stars or planets or by the sun or moon in the daytime is not a complicated process. Primarily, the sextant work must be a bit quickly when the seas are up somewhat; such as with this long passage because you can only see the horizon when atop the crests. So to increase that time as much as possible, I would sit on the dinghy with my feet stuck in the handrail along the house edge. I would have already identified the name of the star, I would get it into the sextant at zero angle which means that I'm looking directly at it rather than at its image in one of the mirrors, and as the boat starts coming up toward the crest I would be dropping the image down toward where the horizon is expected. And when the horizon is in view, I would adjust the angle, rocking the sextant to just caress the horizon with the image of the star. When getting close to it I would call out to Peggy, "Readyyyyy...Mark!"

Peggy would be in the cockpit with the boxed clock in her lap watching the second hand, and at my call "mark" she would write down the second, and then look carefully to determine and write the minute to which that second belongs, and then record the hour. She next would ask the name of the star and record that.

This is repeated three or four more times with different stars or combination of planets and or moon with added note of upper or lower limb in the case of the moon. At the equator, for every 4 seconds of time error, the navigation plot is one nautical mile from the correct position. Care is taken in each aspect of the process, all of which is of equal importance. This is followed by the calculations and plotting which I do below. It is not at all difficult.

Ruth, our name for the windvane, is very accurate. But to find a small island 3000 miles away would require steering accuracy to the hundredth of a degree, which obviously is impossible. So for the first couple of weeks my navigation is no more than dead reckoning.

I continued on course until the location of the first of two ocean currents that we would be crossing and changed course to ride this conveyor belt for several days. Here, it was going almost in our direction, and though we would be going somewhat on a longer track this way than holding course, the time would be benefited by the speed of the current. I left the current at the point at which it no longer aided our crossing. The second one never materialized, or it was too slow to notice, or I just missed it, I don't know which. Some days I needed to adjust sails for wind conditions or slight wind changes, but basically the trades stayed steady in speed and in direction. This is trade wind sailing at its best!

A bull Mahi joined us one day. We could easily tell that it was a male. The head is much blunter than a female's. What a sight! He was surfing across an ocean! That still blows my mind. What a way to travel!

The wind and sea were coming from aftward. The waves were no more than twenty some feet (which was not threatening in any way, nor uncomfortable). And this Mahi would surf down the face of the wave, catch up to the boat about at our mid section, continue forward almost to the bow; and then would move a little to his right away from the boat a few feet as the boat continued forward and let the next wave catch up to him which he would surf the face of repeating his progression. We would watch him from the starboard deck, looking straight down on him, he was that close.

It was especially beautiful in the mornings. The colors of the wave varies from ultra deep cobalt blue at the base, as we looked back eastward toward the sun, to ever gently changing lighter shades of blues as the thickness of the body of the wave narrowed, until below the crest it was changing through glorious hues of turquoise. The crest itself was completely clear.

Now place on such a wave, a big Mahi Mahi with his silvers and yellows and blues and greens, effortlessly surfing the face of such a wave. What a sight! For three days he kept company with us. And with the wonders of mental playback, that same Mahi accompanies us today.

As with so many interesting creatures, the Mahi mate for life. In this case, his mate may have become prey to one of the denizens of the deep, or the ravages of age, or a commercial fishing net from a tuna boat.

The last day he was with us, we had sighted the island of our destination. The island was directly ahead as my sextant had expected. There were reefs south of it, wherefore I turned slightly to the right. The Mahi carried on straight ahead, surfing as he went.

Earlier that day a huge marlin burst into the air shaking his catch wildly as you have seen them behave when trying to free themselves from a sport fisherman's line.

Wow, what a fish that was! It's always a unique experience to suddenly see a creature from another world. To you Sir Mahi, fare thee well. We enjoyed the time we spent together! We will miss you.

The entire month of February had passed while we were at sea. It remains my most pleasant of all passages. I could not stop smiling. Yet landfall is an excitement of its own. Especially when arriving from a long ocean passage.

There was a very beautiful and inviting cove we passed coming around the northwest of this island, but we were so close to the point of proper entry that I carried on. I unbelayed the anchor, lifted the windlass stop, let the anchor drop, backed away and set the anchor.

A great voyage, seamanly done, though by no marvel from my hand, has passed into the small history of a couple of lone sailors aboard their wooden ship. Well done ye men of Oxford Maryland, ye good men who birthed her. Royal Neptune acknowledges you each.

And you oh *Osprey*, the ocean who has cast its eye upon many sails these long centuries passed, has bade you be named with those giants great, who have gone before. Not as their equal, they who were huge of sail and size who bore those folks of fame, but you too have done well for these two frail and insignificant folks who were entrusted to your care. Your job has won you praise.

CHAPTER 9

 THE MARQUISES ISLANDS

Dusk brought us over the northern portion of Hiva Oa Island, and it was already dark as I choose to anchor southward at Tehu Ata Bay. I thought that I could make out some slight silhouette of palms to the port and starboard as I entered very slowly. I judged the distance that I could enter to anchor by the distance of the apparent harbor opening which I could dimly see and multiplied that distance by guesswork into the black cove ahead.

Forward, I could not see where the water ended and the island began. The obvious intent was to go as far as possible for the quietest motion of the water without putting her on the beach. I felt really comfortable with the proportions even though it was pitch black. I set the anchor. I looked at Peggy. I smiled. It was a superb voyage.

How quiet it all seemed, both of sound and movement. We have sailed for perhaps 4000 continuous miles and have arrived to an invisible anchorage. Deep was my sleep. Yet, even in the non-reality world to which I was transported, I heard the sea. I smelled the air. And upon my lips lingered that oh so slight savor of salt.

Morning was formally announced by a lordly rooster dutifully commanding the sun to be brought forth, and it was so. My first pleasure of the day was to look out at the perfection of my choice of location where I dropped the anchor. I was rather shocked to find how close we were to the beach!

Wow how the proportions of this little cove had shrunk during the night. This was a very small cove! But all was well. We had come close to no hazards. But alas, the surprise was shocking.

It is well, however, that we chose as we did, enabling us to enter Tahauku Bay of Hiva Oa daring no hazards in broad day light. We enjoyed our arrival refreshed, and excited to officially arrive in the Marquises Islands.

The Marquises were named by Captain Alvaro de Mendana de Neira after his patron the Marquis of Canete in 1595. These are one of the most remote islands in the world, lying 1300 miles NE of Tahiti and 3000 miles from the nearest continental country, Mexico.

There were four yachts at anchor ahead of us; three French and one US. By the time I got the anchor down and set, Philippe Robard had rowed over in his tinny dinghy. He welcomed us to the neighborhood and gave us two wonderful oranges. Philippe was aboard a yacht of 23 feet in length, which he had singlehanded from France. To do so, he needed to leave his harbor very quietly. France qualifies their countrymen's vessels by categories.

In the case of Philippe's yacht, he was restricted from going beyond the boundaries of the harbor, but here he was, very far indeed from his home port in France. The smaller the yacht, the less swiftly she will sail. And his passage to the Marquises had taken 72 days.

Moments after Philippe's welcome another of his countrymen rowed over with a gift that quickly came to hand. It was a delicious half cantaloupe. We so enjoyed this display of camaraderie and fresh food that thereafter, I took up the ownership of being the welcoming committee.

Years later a young lady came up to me, in a subsequent land which memory evades me, saying, "You won't remember me, but we came into Hiva Oa from a very long sea voyage and you came to us bringing a loaf of fresh bread and fresh fruit. That was absolutely wonderful. Thank you again for that."

The Marquises Islands   *Chapter 9*

I would have taken enormous pleasure from thanking these two Frenchmen likewise, were I to have had such an encounter years later. It was most memorable to us as well as to the young lady who came to us. We had all been somewhat changed by the vastness of our solitude.

Denny and Maureen invited us to the Finisterreiu for the enjoyment of dining with them the night of our arrival. We felt caught up in a social whirl!

And yes, as others arrived from their epic voyage, I would jump into the dinghy with whatever fresh food I could grab, I would row over to praise and welcome them. There was only once when I was not met with ear-to-ear smiles. And that was from a single hander who was already below deck when I arrived at his boat.

It was perhaps 27 feet in length, remarkable due to the quantity of growth just below his water line. The tub worms and grass were, with absolutely no exaggeration, 10 inches in length. We all had some, always on the port side, which faced the sun. When he answered my call and my knock on his hull and came on deck, he wore farmer's overalls and a beard. All of us gentlemen had beards. Yet he didn't answer my greeting. Although he didn't utter a word, he was not at all hostile. Some days later when he spoke to me, among other things, he said that he had been 79 days in his passage.

I also saw that he was using an octant, very different from a sextant and has numbers so small that a magnifying scope is attached to read them. It is the same as used by Captain Cook whose last voyage ended in 1792. I concluded that his failure to speak when first I came, was due to his having gone so far back in time within his mind that the return to reality was being forced upon him too quickly.

In another harbor a little farther north, a really big yacht of old style came in. I don't recall if she wore a square sail or not, but I greeted their arrival in what had become my custom and told them that the event of the week was occurring this evening. There was a small hotel that an Australian couple had recently started with little thatch-roofed huts as guest rooms. The poles used had new branches growing out of them. Once a week they put on a dinner for the yachtsmen and these new people came. The skipper of the new boat and I were sitting on the floor together. Almost everybody was on the floor because not much furniture was there. And as we talked he told me that the owner of their yacht was a well-known personality of some kind, singer if memory serves, and as we spoke his girlfriend, sitting on the other side of him was talking to someone beside her and put her hand on his thigh. He turned toward her. She had not turned toward him. This took half a second in total and he was back talking to me. We both knew what had just happened.

She needed a physical assurance that this was real. To touch something she trusted; that they were actually in this place with people doing familiar things. She needed to know that this was actually real. Is this what the man alone at sea for 79 days was experiencing when I called to him? I can only ask. I know that there is a uniqueness of experience to those who go down to the sea in ships.

We met a fellow church member. Louise and her son Patrick had come from Tahiti to work their copra. We tried. There's this knife that is used to make a scooping action with one hand while you hold a half coconut with the other. We respected the knife. And fortune guided against any blood offerings of the day.

Actually, it was very much less than a day. And as always with long labor invested by great numbers of people, very great respect is bound to result from the experience of that proverbial stroll in someone else's sandals.

Patrick became our tour guide. Now there's a title not often heard in an area such as this. The very early history and culture of these islands, still to this day, appears to be somewhat shrouded in mystery. But Patrick knew where there were some old ruins of stone foundations called paepaes, where the king lived high on the mountain. He showed us the red bananas reserved only for the king. The area of the "refrigerator" was still discernible from the rocks surrounding the pit. Primarily such things as breadfruit, but other foods as well, were put in a floored and walled pit and covered for the three months time when breadfruit cannot be harvested. During this time the *refrigerator* supplied the food needs.

Breadfruit is that wonderful staple food for so many of the South Pacific Islands. It grows on a large tree, is a green colored fruit, with a rough and prickly exterior, and has a mealy edible pulp, which is cooked. We have often had breadfruit, but in non-copious amounts.

On one of our non-guided, very challenging assaults toward a mountaintop, I noticed a bulge in the undergrowth. It was an ancient wooden saddle. Some conquistador had ridden upon this wooden horse saddle! I lugged it down from the mountain and put it in our engine compartment in spite of my fear of termites even after spraying it numerous times. No termites were ever found.

The socializing with these hard-working friends was memorable. "And of course Louise, we will be more than happy to bring whatever you wish to your relatives in Tahiti," we said, as we were departing her cherished land upon this far-flung speck upon the sea.

* * *

Thor Heyerdahl of the raft Kon Tiki fame, spent considerable time here in the Marquises Islands; specifically the island of Fatu Hiva which held an allure to me as well.

The day came. An anchor suddenly thrust its ponderous way through that watery world of hidden mystery. It grabbed hold of the sea bottom in its possessive way. We were anchored in a cove, which seemed eternally gazing shoreward. For shoreward the valley began its slow march upward into the hills.

Had some ancient creatures burst from the sea? Had they been so gigantic that in their thrashings about they had formed all of this? I am not one disposed to think so. But those who have lived upon the land of this island have thought this valley, reaching up into the hills, to be a holy place. They called it the Valley of the Gods, and with slightly squinted eye, there were shapes of strange and unearthly wind-eroded sculptures to cause pause.

But alas, the blinded soul of this seaman saw only a uniqueness of beauty here with cause to enter (not to flee), to climb (not to bow), to explore (not to tremble)!

And the pamplemousse, as called here, were absolutely heavenly! We simply call them grapefruit. There were grapefruit trees in abundance. I have always thoroughly enjoyed grapefruit, especially the pink ones; I've always found them the sweeter. There were both pink and white ones here. But the white ones here were sweeter than the pinks and were even sweeter than any pink one that I have ever eaten in my life. Beyond a doubt the most wonderful grapefruit in the world! I wanted to send seeds back home! I was an instant disciple. A fervent convert to the Religion of Grapefruitism, as it were. Or perhaps more pointedly expressed, I was hooked.

Too bad that I knew seeds were not permitted to be mailed into our country from abroad. And yes, I agree that our agriculture needs to be protected from possible carriers of disease.

The locals found that they were adversely affected digestively by the grapefruit, so they were perfectly happy to have us take as many as we wished. I loaded the boat and was never digestively challenged. Oh they were good! No wonder good old Thor Heyerdahl hung around here so long.

The seaward approach also presented peaks which time and erosion had left standing such forms that fishermen, especially with cataracts, may have seen as godly. We shortly were to take a swift departure.

We were asleep. It was night. There was loud fast knocking on the hull. Who would be here before daylight? Well, actually the first light of dawn was here. It was my mind that could not see through my closed eyelids. Again the knocking. I got up. There were several grim faced men in one of the large canoes. "A child is very sick. She must go to hospital on Hiva Oa. Will you take them?" This was being spoken in French. I asked, "How sick is the child?" I wanted to stay here a few days longer.

They had thought that the child might have died last night. It was an emergency. And, of course, we agreed. They brought the child with her mother and sister and many boxes and bags. We were off.

The child was of an age that it was not yet walking. It was held by its mother who became seasick while still in sight of Fatu Hiva. The sister took over for a few minutes and also became ill. So Peggy held the child the rest of the time. It would cough so hard and so long that with each spasm we wondered if she could get another breath. We anchored, launched the dinghy and got them to the hospital.

At Hiva Oa the chickens were dying. What had Peggy been exposed to? She had held that child for 9 hours.

* * *

That afternoon, a yacht arrived here to formally enter and I talked to them from the dinghy as I brought some fresh food to them. They were having difficulty with the steering system. It was the same as ours, so I told them that if they wished, I'd take a look at it. After their clearing-in with customs I came over again.

We spent a long time with it, and after an overhaul and greasing, we stayed and spoke of many things, of fools and kings (as the song says) and the sun seemed to move faster than time, because darkness had covered the seascape. Upon coming on deck we saw that another yacht had arrived. The lights were out except for a flashing strobe light. Was there an emergency aboard? I knocked on the hull. There was no response. We carried on to the *Osprey*. The next morning the strobe was still flashing. I went to the boat and knocked again. This time there was an answer. And yes, there was a problem. He couldn't walk. He had hurt himself. It didn't require an explanation as to how. "Do you want to go to the hospital?"

"Yes."

I got another fellow from a boat and we managed to get him ashore. The police had a vehicle. I don't remember if it was the only vehicle on the island or not. Suffice it to say that traffic was not a problem. The police car took him to the hospital.

Here, as well as at most other island places where we have been recently, the hospital supplies the place and the treatment; the family supplies the food and comfort for the patient. Peggy and I were the family. We were responsible for him. All of which was perfectly acceptable to us. However, they told us there was no x-ray machine here and we would have to sail him to Nuku Hiva or wait here until a plane came six days from now to fly him to Tahiti.

For all we knew, such a delay could cause a deformity that might impair his sailing, which is why he was here. We sailed him to Nuka Hiva. It was found that his foot was indeed broken but there was nothing that they could do for him and non-use of the foot was the only treatment needed. So he needed to get back to his boat for the boat's safety, one-leggedly or not.

But by now Peggy has become terribly sick. I described our unknown encounter with the child and the chickens dying, but the diagnosis of this clinic was that she had Dengue Fever, also called "breakbone fever" due to the pain involved. Peggy felt terrible in the extreme.

A new boat came in here. I asked if they were going south. They said that they were and that they would happily bring our patient back to his boat at Hiva Oa. We told them about the chickens dying but they were intending to go there anyway.

In the fullness of time, Peggy began feeling better. And we sailed back to Hiva Oa again.

It seemed that our friend with the broken foot had gone ashore at Tahuata and gotten lost. He climbed up a tree to try to orient himself, was attacked by bees and broke his foot when he fell out of the tree. The sea is one thing! But to go on land—and then actually climb off the ground up into a tree—well that is really asking for it, don't you think?

We saw him again in Tahiti some several months later. His foot was fine. But his aversion to trees and bees lingers properly.

Tahuata is really close to our Hiva Oa anchorage, and it's such a lovely little spot that when the idea of a picnic popped into someone's head, we all agreed that was the place to go.

Peggy made a big pot of soup in the pressure cooker. I stuck a matchstick into the pressure relief valve opening to keep the soup hot and we motored off. For our next trick, we needed to get ashore from the *Osprey*.

Everything was loaded into the dinghy for the short row. There was a little surf at the beach, but no problem, the others made it okay. The idea is to get on the back of an incoming wave and row like mad to keep up with it and you are always landed on the beach without incident accordingly.

I don't know what happened! We came rushing in as expected, made contact with the beach as expected, but that next wave was not expected! It picked up the aft end of the dinghy, Peggy and all, and she and the dinghy came right over me in a perfect display which in some quarters is described as, "Arse over tea kettle," and while completely upside down in mid air Peggy yelled "I got the soup!" And thanks to the matchstick, no salt water savored the soup. We all had a great time. We built a bond fire, and with a half moon, talked half the night away.

The beach wave was harder on the dinghy than on us. Her stern seat was torn from the boat and needed its mounts replaced. We had named the dinghy, "Ah Spray," but this had somewhat surpassed her name.

We had Thor Heyerdahl's book aboard about the Marquises. He speaks of giant Tikis here on Hiva Oa. They are still here. They must be known by someone other than TH. Denny of Finisterreiu not only had found someone who knew about them, but also knew where to go, and had a jeep with which to get there. Of course, properly, there was a fee for the service of transport. The fee was beyond our horde of money, which started out here as $80.05.

The thoughts of, "Oh my! Oh despair! Oh disappointment!" changed to "Oh yes yes Denny, we will happily accept your advance of sixty dollars to be replaced in Tahiti! If you will not be undone by this, let's tell your driver to get ready. We're ready whenever you say!"

What a jeep ride followed! We are told that no development of any kind occurred here until ten years ago. And prior to only six years ago it was only possible to walk this path or to take a horse. The "road" in a few places had such steep and sharp turns as it climbed the mountains, that the jeep could not turn sharply enough and had to back up using two maneuvers to get around the turn.

The jeep gained the summit by digging its way upward with all four wheels spinning on occasions, aided immensely by the white-knuckled grasp of our fingers on any hopefully strong part of the Jeep.

Here too, plate tectonics pushed up mountain ridges that erosion has swept away to knife-like stretches of mountaintops (if six to ten feet can be referred to as knife-edged). It certainly felt like it when the jeep went on and on over such edges where it seemed as though less than a foot of space separated the outer edge of the tires from an abyss a thousand feet below us on each side.

As we descended off the ridges and breathing was possible again and one's eyes opened again to enable the jungle majesty to be seen as the vastness of untouched, impenetrable glory which it is, the contrasts within our minds of our "concrete jungles" is startling and small by comparison.

We traveled over three mountains, passed several very small villages of a few families each, and then, we arrived.

The Marquises Islands   *Chapter 9*

There was not a museum found here. There was no bronze embossed plaque of announcement. I had expected none. "Where do we go?"

"It's close over that way."

I was the one who went a little to the left, and further into this temple green. I pushed aside some thick live foliage and as though a thousand heralds silently blew their horns and beat their drums, *here,* right here still stand these gods, carved hundreds of years before European man had ever sailed amongst these islands of the Pacific.

Carved of stone, eight feet tall they stand; huge, ponderous and impressive to any eye that dared a glance upon them. They stand unaware of the passage of peoples or the passage of time. They stand at the foot of a valley. Mountain ranges crisscross in increasing heights behind them, amongst the rich and varied greens of this vibrantly living jungle through which we pressed our way. They stand in silent stillness as only Father Time records their way.

This place, where ancient priests had chosen, is a flat area about a hundred feet square. About three feet lower was another square, almost flat where people worshiped in reverence deep and devout as looming beyond, the gods' mountains reached their arms into the clouds.

There is no sign that today anyone had worshiped here, nor yesterday. But someone cares. Always someone has fought the jungle over the centuries. Always the jungle reaches. And only a sharp blade can strike it back. Today, the jungle is very close.

It is always an odd experience to return from another time. Thank you Denny, we couldn't have done it without you. And I wouldn't have missed it for the world! See you in Tahiti.

We seem to stay longer in places than most. And some seem to really be flying onward. We have shared anchorages with many boats but please know that "paradise" is by no means crowded. Although we find absolute enrichment from the glories of beautiful peaceful coves of quiet waters where no foot print disturbs the sand (and may not have done so for decades of time), the camaraderie of fellow seamen has its own enjoyment.

We have shared anchorages with, to list some of the larger ones first; a three-masted Baltic Trader about 125 feet, converted to a yacht with 16 people aboard. She is a US flag vessel owned by all aboard. Then arrived was a new 79 footer from England, with a paid crew of eight plus the fellow and his sister. Upon his father's passing, he will become a Lord of England. A new 65 foot Swan (the manufacturer's company name), owned by an Italian couple with one paid hand who also is an MD and great cook. They have hotels. They keep the boat in France, live in Switzerland and fly a Swiss flag of registry. The US yacht *Myonia* has been cruising 20 years and are on their fourth intended circumnavigation. And the smallest is the yacht *Mortai*, a French flagged vessel of 23 feet who took 73 days to get here from the Galapagos. That's the spread of size, from 125 feet to 23. Well done all.

Others we have already spoken of, and there are many friends whom we have yet to meet.

CHAPTER 10

 TAHITI

The word cannot be heard without the simultaneous swaying sound of music played enticingly within your mind, as those undulating motions dance wistfully before your eyes.

Ah Tahiti, so many and basic are the delights offered to the world by your advertising; so many have come, so many have stayed. We are on our way.

Strongly blew Tahiti's god of wind as though impatient to see us arrive. The *Osprey* shook her sails once and then let them stretch out happily as though to say, "Ahh. How good that feels."

We were zooming along. She threw spray from her bow as though in irreverent jest, to splash water onto the face of Tahiti's god by saying, "Is that all you've got?"

It could be described as a bit stormy. No chance for a celestial navigation fix. I reefed again and we rushed on. I may have to heave-to well before dawn if I don't get a fix.

I slept. Peggy shouted my name and I was braced for danger. She hadn't called me when the motion had thrown bilge water up onto her bed. This had never happened before. With a shallow bilge and soft chins the bilge can throw water right on up the inside of the hull all the way beside the bed. She knew that the boat was not at risk. "The moon! I see the moon!"

Chapter 10 — Tahiti

The light had awakened her. She grabbed a note pad, pencil, and the chronometer (clock). I grabbed the sextant from its box, dashed on deck and there they were. Three beautiful stars to shoot and the moon to show me the horizon! Wow! I knew these three, I called "mark" to Peggy for each one, and the sky went black as quickly as the moon had peeked through the blackness to see where we were. I was delighted. The sailing had been so good. The *Osprey* had been flying over these waters, and I needed this fix or I needed to slow her down even more. I could not risk the hazard which is on our course.

I opened the requisite couple of books, did a little simple math, plotted the results on a universal plotting sheet, and there we were. No, not close to where expected, but exactly where we were expected, a fact that is never poorly received.

We had been sailing beautifully, too fast actually. It was night and the taffrail log had warned of fetching the atoll before dawn. The fix now confirmed that we would have been secure without the fix because I was intending to come about and backtrack for a while rather than stop.

The boat's motion is more comfortable that way. But dead reckoning never feels as good as absolute knowledge feels regarding one's position in closing quarters. We could never have seen the atoll with its low trees in this totally black night before disaster. I could have gone down to storm jib size, but it was nice to see her sail like this.

This was the right amount of sail for the wind. It was fun.

So at the appointed time as previously decided and now proven by the fix, I came about and retraced our way. I came about again on the original course, setting us again toward our hazard. I was secure in the knowledge that she would not come up on the island before dawn. Shortly after first light and right on queue the atoll brought herself in view. We had originally been sailing on a beam reach. The run back on our course was also a fun ride. The *Osprey* had continued her play with Tahiti's main wind guy, laughing all the way, and the atoll ruffled her low palm trees to greet the morning exactly where she had done so, from time immemorial, and exactly where I had known her to be; thanks to charts and good fortune.

We altered course, sped past the island, and set a new course. It became apparent that to gain the harbor at Papette would be a long hard slog to windward, whereas the course that we were sailing would bring Moorea to us. I held course. Conditions remained steady and harsh. We were still flying along. We could see Tahiti well by now. And our long absent mail beckoned loudly to us, but "gentlemen do not sail to windward."

Not only did Moorea present herself before us, but she chose to open her beautiful bay of favored anchorage directly on our course. It was an amazement to roar across this long space and have the steering system, without so much as a nudge from me, bring us zooming into this quiet anchorage.

I had watched it all happen. And as I sat well forward of the wheel watching its ceaseless course adjustments left and right, in full knowledge of what was going on, I mused only in half question, "Whose hand is that on my wheel that brought us thusly here?"

The profile of Moorea is what a fertile mind at best artistic flourish would conjure forth. She is formed in perfect frame and garbed in garments green indistinct in the twilight. She is want to cast a net of spell upon all who see her. She calls in whispered voice to all the world. She calls just behind the sounds of all the songs Tahiti sings. She is a beauty.

We slept there. We smiled there. And easy was the laughter over the smallest excuse. Such is Moorea.

Chapter 10 — Tahiti

It's still blowing like mad! But we can almost see the mail from here, so let's go to Papette!

In the harbor, boats were lined up at the city marina with nice easy boarding from finger pears between the boats, with steps up to the sidewalk. But the $80.05 that we had when leaving the Galapagos Islands had been somewhat depleted in our three months amongst the Marquises Islands!

We arrived in Tahiti with exactly 18 cents US. We looked at those boats with their convenience only by way of noticing them. The boats to which we looked more closely were those in the low rent district. They had a couple of anchors off the bow and a couple of lines ashore. We picked out a spot in front of an old church that had enough space and a place to secure shorelines. We had hailed a couple on one of the boats already set up and confirmed that no arrangements were required with anyone for permission to moor here so we followed suit.

It was four o'clock when we got to customs. "Not a problem. Come back tomorrow. We are closing soon."

With a line to shore with a block having a becket to secure it with, and lines through the block to the boat, the dinghy could snap her painter to one of the block lines, and the dinghy could be pulled out of the way from both the boat and the rocks on the bank of the shore.

We came back the next morning and new adventures lay at our feet! But first, to the American Express Office. We could cash a check for up to two thousand dollars at a time and use the card to buy traveler's checks. Finisterreiu wasn't here yet, but we were ready with the $60 upon their arrival.

There were 40 letters for us and four boxes. The calendar may have said, June 02, but it was Christmas aboard the *Osprey*!

We contacted by our two-watt radio, the amateur radio operator in Florida USA whose call sign we had recorded, and yes he was very willing to make a phone patch for us with our son David. But again we missed him. So the man agreed to call on his own until he could pass our message to him. Then Dave tried to contact us and missed us, leaving a message to phone him direct. We called collect. Parents can do that too you know.

It was great fun to hear him and know that he is well and for him to hear from our own voice that we are well and in fabled Tahiti.

***

Louise, our friend in the Marquises, had asked us to bring letters, honey and bananas to certain friends and relatives. When we get to some of the church people, we must ask our way for these deliveries.

The second place we went to was the office of our church and met instant friends. There were several of our churches on the island and suddenly the numbers of our friends were jumping in numbers like popcorn. The islands of the Tahiti group on many maps are called the Society Islands. And the society with these boundlessly enthusiastic friends simply took over our lives.

Marcel Millaud wanted to show us Tahiti. What a kind and generous person. I bet he's a great teacher. He drove us entirely around the island. Showed gardens to us, cascading waterfalls, even his mother's lovely beach home with lots of beautiful grounds around it. He invited us to stay there if we wished, but contrary to the comprehension of most, we actually preferred to stay aboard the boat.

He asked if we thought that a rock could float. The answer was supposed to be no. After which he had many times in the past put a rock of lava into the water and to the shock of the observer, have it float. Everybody should have a few parlor tricks. Marcel is an extremely interesting person, interested enough in astronomy to have chosen his son's name from that shining host. He pronounced his name Oreo, as the cookie is pronounced in the US. After all, that is the French pronunciation of Orion, great hunter that he is. Marcel is a wonderful asset to his church, the public schools, and his unofficial ambassadorship for Tahiti, though he is more hesitant than the PR advertiser's referencing to the island as paradise.

Another teacher with whom we became very well acquainted is John Reynaud. His good wife had her feet in the limelight as a ballerina in France. As a boy John lived with his family in Vietnam. One of the stories that certainly impressed us occurred during dinner one evening in his childhood. Their dog had let out a yelp of fear, came running at full maximum speed through the open front door of the house with a tiger not far behind him. Neither one slowing down as they passed through the dinning room where the family sat. The dog and the tiger went right through the house and out the back door! The talented dog escaped.

John's English was perfect and the rest of the family was comfortable in two or three languages as well. Great fun to be with them, as their generosity was extended frequently to us and ours to them. The stimulating conversations were endowed by the adroitness of John's quickness of intellect; of which the acceptance of his doctoral dissertation may give evidence. This event occurred while we were there. As with most teachers, I'm just a country boy who is accepted in a crowd of others who are likewise endured.

Tahitians love to get together. And when they do, there is always food. And where there is food, there is French bread. And it seems that we were passed around like butter. It was like seeing long-lost family never before known. Hardly a day went by without someone either being aboard with us or our being home with them. None of us ever stopped eating.

The first weekend we spent with one of the families, we couldn't sleep! We kept laughing about it as quietly as possible. I can't imagine what they must have thought the Americans were doing! You know how those sailors are. It was the noise!

I had thought that after being aboard for several years without ever sleeping ashore during that time, that perhaps the motionless of it would be difficult. But it was the noise!

Crickets shook their legs, frogs must have been hopping into things head first in the darkness and yelling out, "I saw that!" while 20 others laughed at him. We had no idea what the other 90% of the noisemakers were, but it was a circus! What a strange world the land is.

Bleary-eyed morning came and our gracious hostess asked me if I preferred fresh bread or stale bread for breakfast. Well, I had no idea why this wasn't an odd question. So I thought the safest thing would be to say fresh. Where upon our hostess was off like a shot to the bakery. Breakfast was lovely and informative, because although I did indeed eat that lovely bread still hot from the baker's oven, and many other delights, I learned that the stale bread was dunked in the hot coffee with all ceremony and enjoyment.

It's a very practical solution for stale bread and a pleasurable tradition indeed.

We were in Papette for eight months over all and in the general area for eighteen months. There are people whom I will want you to meet, and events that I will want you to enjoy, but to give you some idea of our daily life you might read Peggy's Notes II (See Appendix C).

＊＊

There was a weekly gathering of yachtsmen and others who are called by the sea. These unstructured food and gab fests occurred at the Acajou [cashew] restaurant. It is said by some, that the tales heard within such circles around the world, oft times lean beyond the inconvenient restrictions of not only historical fact but even yesterday's witnessed reality.

I do not tread such paths, but an acquaintance reported to me that next week a Tahitian *traditional* navigator would be there, who was the assigned navigator aboard a rafting re-enactment from Hawaii to Tahiti. I very much wanted to hear what this man would have to say.

It seems that one school of thought, as quoted from www.janesoceania.com/oceania_polynesians/index.htm presented a very succinct history of

Polynesian migrations. I quote: "The achievements of the navigators were remarkable, but not mysterious, given their pilotage system, passed from generation to generation.

Micronesia and eastern Polynesia were colonized within the last 2000 years, originating in Fiji AD 1. Tahiti was settled by AD 800, Hawaii by 600, Easter Island possibly between 300 and 400, New Zealand by AD 1000. With these voyages the last chapter of the 150,000-year spread of modern humans across the world ended."

I do agree that the Hokule'a, a double-hulled canoe that carried two lateen-type sails, has had replicas built, which proved very capable indeed.

The gentleman did identify himself as I had been lead to believe. He confirmed his use of lattice charts. A chase boat was equipped with GPS. There were various problems which he declined to discuss, enjoyed his dessert and bade us all good day. However, I felt that there was no BS about the man.

A few days ago, I read an article written by Jan Prince in the Tahiti Sun Press, which Peggy had saved, in which Rodo was featured. I had wondered about his rather non-Tahitian last name of Williams.

It reports that his family comes from Katiu, an atoll 300 miles east of Tahiti in the Tuamotus where a pirate ship came aground. All the crew except Harris Williams were eaten. Harris was declared "tapu," married to the chief's daughter, as well as to the daughters of two other chiefs. Rodo's full name is Rodolphe Tuko Harry Williams. He learned navigation from his Tahitian father, "Who never broke a boat."

I had not known how far back in time his traditional navigation was going to be, so I was not disappointed by the encounter. He seemed to me a stalwart fellow and a man with whom I might willingly be shipmate. I do not always find myself thusly inclined. My exposure to information about the original Polynesian Navigators was not yet complete, and likely never will be. However, what I later learned is disturbing.

***

One of the memorable feasts at which we were honored guests, was for about thirty-some folks, all seated at a long table made of planks. The boards groaned at the weight of the food, which kept emerging from the kitchen. The aromas of these delicacies new and unfamiliar rushed unrestrained through our welcoming senses and conversations whirled about until someone said the word fafaru and everyone got very quiet.

There was a glass jar with a tight lid on it. In it was fafaru. The women would hardly look at it as it was passed around. Some of the men just shook their heads no and passed it emphatically on. One slightly opened the lid just fractionally, jammed it closed shaking his head no as he pulled at his nose as though attempting to force a bee from his nostrils. Another took a small piece out and ate it. Some actually shuddered at the sight. Was this all a sham to frighten these two poor delicate pampered souls or was this as bad as the show was presenting?

The glass jar came to me, tightly closed. All eyes were now on me as they had been on each prior recipient. It couldn't be all that bad! I opened the jar just slightly with great suspicion, and my stomach muscles convulsed at the smell; but I could not let it be seen. Rightly or wrongly I felt that I needed to be initiated by passing the test of sportsmanship or be diminished before our hosts.

The name is translated simply as salt fish. A fish is immersed in seawater and then left to rot. The stench is over powering! I will never know what it tastes like, though I lifted my fork from the table and very slowly watched it enter this mire that was glazing my eyes. I saw the fork extracting a very small quantity of the fish, as I pleaded for strength to adequately enable my capacity to hold my breath. I was horrified to look closely at what my fork had obediently removed from the jar, whose top I had swiftly reattached.

As tightly closed as my mind had shouted to my mouth muscles to refuse entry of this substance, social grace demanded that I either fall upon my sword or follow this dance of death that my mind had been seeing and permit entry of this substance and swallow it with a smile. All eyes were still silently upon me. And being too cowardly to fall upon my sword, I completed the travel of this substance to its intended destination, and smiled. I am immodest enough to say that no greater sacrifice of one's self for one's country has ever occurred in the annals of ancient or recent history.

I ate copious quantities of other real food attempting to expunge the physical memory of this event, while some small nod of approval hopefully may have occurred. No recognized ill effects have resulted, though I intend the blame of any future dementia or erectile dysfunction on Fafaru. It was a great party, a wonderful feast, and a most memorable experience.

* * *

Let's go to Bora Bora for Christmas! And of course, we stopped at a couple islands on the way. Going into Raiatea I was blinded by the sun's reflection on the waters of the rather narrow harbor. My sunglasses were not sufficient for the job and we would have needed to lay-off until the angle of sun to the harbor changed enough to remove the glare.

I needed to be able to see where the reefs were and was pleased to put my goggles to use for the first time. Welding hood masks and goggles can be selected with varying darkness of glass. I had been trying these on one day back in time and had chosen the lightest shade made, for just such an extreme event. And here was the spot for which I needed them. I love it when a plan comes together (eventually).

Being now securely anchored we were interested to meet a brother of one of our new Tahitian friends. John had worked diligently through the normal politics of any state school administration with a constant eye toward getting an appointment to teach on the island of Raiatea.

He is a very interesting person. He and his wife visited aboard and ate with us as we with them in their lovely house on the mountain, where I saw that he was awarded a number of impressive plaques by Award Committees of France for free diving to 90 feet of water.

John very properly is a proud Tahitian. Among other reasons for this pride is that from childhood he had heard the stories of his ancestors whose heroic navigation skills had brought mankind throughout the Pacific Ocean.

Raiatea was the island of the school for navigators. And he longed to find out all there was to learn about this so that he could publish to the world these facts, whereby giving homage to these men as their exploits properly deserved.

He came to teach in the public school system. And he came to learn, as a student of these things, which were so honored in the mind of that young boy John, which memory never dimmed in all of these passing years.

I have taken pains to show you the immense sincerity with which John came to this study, so that you may indeed know that he was not easily turned aside from his quest.

John was concerned. One of his students seemed to be somewhat unwell for a while and then was not coming to classes any more. He went to the boy's house.

The reason for John's concern came from what he had learned. He told us that certain islands in days past were the center of professional study. If you wanted to excel in fishing you would go to one island. If you were to want to excel in healing, you would go to another island because those men who were honored and recognized as being the greats in that realm were there.

John explained that what was required was simply to have a spirit indebted to you, so that when you need something, you need only to inform the spirit and he would have no choice but to make it happen. Those persons to whom a student had come for such learning would teach the students how to successfully indebt a spirit to them. Such teachers were paid large amounts for their learning, which is why not everyone could afford to learn at such level.

Chapter 10   Tahiti

The primary way of accomplishing this is to give the spirit the life of your eldest son. And if you make this contract, the spirit takes the life. You are not required to kill him. One's knowledge that a contract has been accepted is evidenced by the dying of your son.

I asked if a son were told of this gift. John, who is not a believer in the spirits, feels that it is resignation that kills the child. "John, is this still going on?"

"Oh yes! That's why I was so worried about my student."

If you have concluded that I am not a believer in the spirits, you would be entirely correct. John found nothing praise-worthy in this and has not published his findings. I, of course, have no direct personal knowledge regarding spirit indebtedness.

We took our dinghy up one of the little rivers of Raiatea. This is something we like doing. We often get up into extremely remote and beautiful places this way, and Raiatea was no exception.

The river was not very deep. The banks were thick with lush jungle-type green from huge leaf plants to delicate ferns, and trees that reached skyward from one bank leaned over toward the other bank, which likewise leaned toward them. They crossed like this, creating an avenue arcade, a tunnel, an arbor seeking to exclude the sun from seeing this private waterway enshrined by secrets only whispered of by the trees.

It meandered around one gorgeous scene to the next one trying to outdo it. I was determined to see farther, but alas, there was an absolute jumble of fallen trees completely blocking the way. The banks could not be scaled to bring the dinghy around this mess. And the water wasn't deep enough for me to sink the dinghy by filling it with water to get under it, so nothing for it but to climb through the trees with the dinghy. What a picture that would have been with all of those branches and trunks to hall the dink over and through. We must have gotten fifteen feet in the air with the dinghy and it half full of leaves before getting over the last barricade. Yes we had kept in mind that we had to come back that way later on. But neither sleet nor snow will keep the postman from his appointed rounds or a seaman from his intended course.

We saw spotted eels with up-standing ears and some that were a little smaller without spots and with no visible ears at all. But what fed our need and wish with such satisfaction, was that glow within our being from the sights and sounds; the feel of the scent of flowers and touch of shaded sun beneath this endless arbor of wood and of leaf and of sky. For all of this was experienced by something other than this crude nose, this calloused hand, these wanton eyes. For here strode the soul. And I smiled.

* * *

Bora Bora came to us over the horizon, first showing us her peaks, stark against the sky, followed by her broad shoulders. She seemed waist deep in her private pool of the ocean. Coral had grown a magnificently colored girdle to retain her appearance for she was no longer a youth as islands go. But what one can see will take one's breath away. And, oh my, I have seen her coral too!

Will you think unduly dark thoughts of me? The breeze had been blowing extremely light but constant all day. I dropped the anchor between the wind and a beach inside the lagoon. The lagoon was very deep and swung upward to the beach as a steep cliff. As the boat would drift shoreward the anchor would grab at a very efficient angle. The usual procedure is to put down a second anchor shoreward in case the wind was to change. That would give me two forty-five pound anchors down, one with all chain of about a 150 pounds at least and the second with forty pounds of chain plus rope. That's about 280 pounds of ground tackle in super light breeze in a protected lagoon. I didn't put down my second anchor, the one with chain and rope. The island is far too small to make its own weather, which would require another set of considerations. Many places have offshore wind during the day and on shore wind during the night.

If the wind made up it would awaken me and if it changed directions I would care for it when it occurred.

The onshore light breeze slowed and died; and turned 180 degrees. The boat lazily drifted over top of her anchor as I slept and it kept going, picking up her anchor from the opposite direction to its holding ability and onward over deep water, where it just hung straight down with forty-five pounds of anchor and about 150 pounds or more of chain.

Peggy awakened me. "We're drifting," she said.

"Oh we can't be!" There was no hazard of any kind, but I did not save myself any energy by not having put down that second anchor. A couple hundred pounds to bring on deck by hand is not totally without some small effort in the middle of a quiet night. Yet I must admit that the dark silhouettes of the peaks of Bora Bora and the palm trees along her shoulders and her shore, with the night flowers wafting scent on the breeze and the sky adorned in her most sparkling gown, was not entirely wasted on the foredeck of the *Osprey* who slept on.

We joined the Bora Bora Yacht Club, which may be unique amongst like-named prestigious organizations. Only foreign flag vessels qualify for membership. Now there's a twist for you. This club has not come upon the scene from antiquity. In fact, I designed the club flag. It hardly matters if it was ever made by anyone or not. It is that kind of place.

The membership dues covered the possible use of a mooring as available, though all were full while we were there for a month. It's nice to have a dinghy dock to come to for convenience and the restaurant and bar to hang out in with the owners. The business also had a few thatch-covered guest cottages for those arriving by airplane, and showers for the bodies, and machines for the washing of clothes for yachtsmen, were also available and happily used.

I moved the boat to various locations for snorkeling or for quiet waters. Some of the coral areas were truly magnificent. The fish shimmered in all their glory as the giant purple sea fans bowed approval. One place especially which is just off the other small hotel close to the yacht club, was an absolute marvel of glorious coral growth. Sea fan presence was crowded with an amazement of hordes and hordes of swirling fish. There were yellows, blues, reds, oranges and mixed-colored fish with a few green and spotted moray eels. They all seemed to call out, "Hey! Don't leave without seeing this neighborhood before you go! We're great!" It was a magic world of under sea marvel. It was absolutely fantastic in all respects!

I hesitate to tell you, but it shows that even here things change. When we returned some months later, all of the sea fans were destroyed, as was part of the reef. Apparently a storm had come through. Severe wave action can destroy the fans. And maybe something man-made was ground into the coral, or trees uprooted can do the same thing, if hurled into them. I don't like being too quick to damn mankind for all ills. It was a terrible sadness to see. I mention it only to point out that this too can mend. And such sadness is properly tempered by this knowledge.

As we were wont to do, we went to church. As always we were warmly received and met each person with interest and pleasure. It is immeasurably rewarding to us when we are granted that wonderful gift of permission to glimpse beyond the social mask, which hides us from each other.

In this event, it undoubtedly was due to Tamanihi's experience of being on the sea, and our being seafarers, that so quickly opened that door which upon our departure had Tamanihi and his sons carrying seven stalks of bananas on poles, each one three or up to four feet in length and about three or four feet around, plus huge numbers of drinking coconuts loaded onto the boat. Coconuts to be opened for drinking are always brought throughout the islands as departure gifts because not all

those bringing such gifts realize that water can be brought to sea in any other sufficient quantity.

Tamanihi and his sons would have been in the hills days in advance of our departure looking for appropriate stalks to bring so that they could cut them in just the right stage and huge size, to properly show their esteem of our persons.

My esteem of the kindness and hospitality of Tamanihi, his wife Pani and their family, and for reasons here following, is without peer. But before I tell you that part of the story, I must tell you more about Tamanahi. He was known about the island as a great fisherman and included us in the stone fishing as well as fishing on the reef.

I was a bit hesitant when we went reef fishing, because he and two or three of his sons all started out onto the reef calling me to follow them. When I say, *on* the reef, which in my prior circles was never ever done, I mean they were walking on top of the reef each with a bamboo pole waving me to follow as I had stopped short.

I stopped for two reasons. Number one to not damage the reef and number two to not damage myself! I got the first problem eliminated quickly enough seeing that a prior foot pathway had already been made by numbers of others, leaving the second problem. I was wearing push-alongs as I call thong shoes. And I could envision them sliding from one side to the other exposing my bare feet to sea urchin spines.

Out I went. Tamanihi never said, but I have reason to believe, that he gave me the use of his very favorite bamboo pole. It was amazingly light though just as long as the others. Each pole was matched in length by the same amount of fishing line. And we each had a bag to carry the catch. I started out.

I used the butt end of the pole to help balance my way as the coral cut my feet and the sea urchins shot spears of pain all the way up my legs. It was all such great fun, a show that required my very best actor's performance. By now I had broken several feet of Tamanahi's wonderful bamboo pole! I was cut, bleeding, and impaled by sea urchins, and feeling so bad for having damaged Tamanahi's pole, which no amount of fishing diversion could possibly keep my undisclosed mind from wishing to be elsewhere. One is, however, always aware of the overall requirement placed especially on the recipient of hospitality, that such hospitality is indeed not only noticed but deeply appreciated. A good time was had by all.

The word went out to the local church of our attendance and Tamanihi invited both of us to participate. Each year there is a special joint gathering of the church. Everybody who can muster the fee to get there, goes to Papeete for ten days of camp meeting time. Families are together again, friends are seen again since last year, singing and fellowship is enjoyed like the feast that it is.

The sale of the catch was going to pay for passages from Bora Bora to Papeete and back, plus expenses while there. The day arrived. The people arrived, maybe forty or fifty strong. Canoes were the dominant boat, but some runabouts were there too. Nets could be seen piled in the sterns.

The air crackled from the electric charge of excitement with people calling out here and others shouting to friends over there. This was carnival at its best. It was immense fun and hadn't even started yet. But then, I didn't know what we were starting!

Tamanihi was the man in charge. He called out someone's name and said go over there, and he was off, his boat, his net and his stones and his group with him. And so it went until I could see something beginning to take shape.

The nets were strung out from a narrow point at a corral made of chicken wire that reached the bottom and the water surface, which had a narrow opening. One long, long line of nets lead to the opening from one side and another long, long line of nets lead from the other side of the opening; and thereby opened widely to the corral.

People were in the shallow water walking with large rocks tied to a short length of rope and everyone at Tamanahi's signal started swinging these rocks from side to side making an immense *kaboom* sound which underwater had a concussion effect. The result was that of herding the fish into a narrower and narrower area. When the water became too deep to walk in, the boats were used for the people to continue doing the same thing.

I too was hurling my rock to exhaustion and changed to a lesser efficiency to bashing a swim fin into the water, causing nearly as much concussion. This continued for nearly an hour as we, the fish cowboys and girls, herded the fish toward the corral!

The corral was at a shallower place and could be walked around. It was full of fish by now and at the moment before more fish were getting out the door than into it, a wire door was securely closed.

The stone fishing was a great success! Huge numbers of fish now needed to be bailed out with wire nets on poles by people inside the corral and taken ashore at the rate for which sales could be arranged. Often those either inside or outside the wire corral would grab a fish by hand (there were that many splashing all about), then bite the fish by putting its head into their mouth from the top of it, and thus killing it. This enables one to eat most of it where they stood, the remainder of which will be dined upon by the crabs.

***

Before this time, Tamanihi had lived for some time on the Island of Maupiti. An American had been on Maupiti for several years and had built a boat while he was there. Upon this man's departure, he had given it to Tamanahi's friend. The time came when Tamanahi's friend wanted to go back to Bora Bora and he decided to use the boat to get there. Tamanahi agreed to go with him. This was a distance of about thirty miles. They had plenty of fuel and they had three outboard motors made by Segal Outboard Motor Company, all mounted on the transom. The boat was loaded and they started out.

The trouble came about due to the sea action. It was lifting the engine water-cooling intake ports out of the water when the boat pitched upward at the stern. This gradually over-heated the engines and ultimately seized their internal parts together. All three engines became useless. They were well offshore by this time, and they were now adrift at sea.

They took stock of what they had: A bag of mangoes, some water, an oilcloth kitchen table cover, some matches, kitchen ware, a kettle and some clothing, a length of fishing line and some very small hooks.

Rank in most island societies where nothing else distinguished, is based on age and rank rules. In this case, Tamanihi being the younger automatically complied with the decisions of his friend who did his best. He was responsible for their lives.

They had gotten closer to Bora Bora than to Maupiti. They started rowing. They were going into the wind, so in an attempt to reduce windage, they removed several of the bow planks from the boat. They bailed water and rowed to no perceptible success.

They had read in the newspaper about a tour ship coming by their area that night. So a fire was prepared as a signal to the ship of their distress. They were ready when the ship was sighted. They lit the fire. They waved frantically. The ship did not turn nor slow down. It disappeared over the horizon. Oh what a disappointment! They rowed more. They rowed to exhaustion. The effort was futile. They gave up.

Nights followed days. They eat the mangoes. The water had not lasted long. The boat had become a place providing shadow in the water under the boat where a perpetual number of fish of various sizes hid from their larger toothed predators. So far, hunger was staved off by carefully presenting a baited hook to a fish small enough not to break the line or the hook. They caught small fish that had become their food source. Of course, one at a time the larger fish took away one hook at a time until all were gone.

They faced all weather conditions of calms and storms, sun and rain. Weeks had gone by as they drifted. They found that they could catch rainwater nice-

Chapter 10   *Tahiti*

ly with the oilcloth kitchen table cover. They could keep water in the kettle and some other kitchenware. But they needed food.

They had watched Mahi approach the boat on the surface, turn on their side as they came to the boat, pass under the boat still on their side and straighten again to their normal upright position once past. They tried to catch them by hand but it just never happened.

"Let's hit them with something. That way we can stun them and then grab them." They had taken the outboard engines apart in an attempt to repair them. They each took one of the long straight drive shafts from the outboard engines.

One man stood on one side of the boat, the second man stood on the other side. And when a Mahi approached and turned sideways, the first man would try to jab the fish with the steel rod, throw the rod inboard and grab the fish by the tail with both hands and heave it into the boat. If the first man missed, the second man would try on the other side. It worked! They had food! More food than they could eat. They tried sun drying the fish, but it never worked. They got sick from spoiled meat, but survived it. Mahi were not there every day. Their hunger grew intense between times.

More weeks passed. The friend of Tamanihi was responsible as the older person. He had failed. And being thus dejected, lingered for quite some time before succumbing to despair. He died.

Tamanihi buried him into the sea and was alone.

He carried on the routine of his life. One is able to accept one's circumstance whatever they are and the daily survival skills continue. This is my life now. I go on. Thus moved the natural progression within the mind of Tamanahi.

Days became weeks, weeks became months, and months became unidentified lives unto themselves. He took no interest in these passings. Time had no meaning. It was normal living now. This is where I am. This is what I do. This boat, this sky, these fish are my world. Time as a concept no longer existed. These are not words that Tamanihi spoke to himself of which I am aware. These are words that depict the story as he told it to me.

Suddenly he came alive with anticipation!

There's an island down-wind. Excitement mounted to ecstasy until it became absolutely clear that he could not make a landfall. The wind was blowing him past it. He watched it for every moment, before the hungry horizon devoured it as he watched it disappearing. Then, it was gone.

Time passed unidentified and then one morning another island had come up out of the sea. He was going to be close to this one. He rowed. It was working. There was a cove. He could get into it! But there was a cliff there. He would wreck the boat on the cliff and drown! Row that way!! Get around that corner beyond the cove entrance!! He gave all he had. He made it. I'm almost there!!

He could see now around the corner from the cove! There was a lagoon beyond the reef!! I can get on the reef!!!

He did. The boat hit the reef. He kept hold of the line from the boat. He was so weak! He tried to pull the boat along on the reef!

But he had been seen. Others came. They took the boat. They got it from the reef and across the lagoon to the shore. They carried him to a native house. He couldn't walk by himself. They reported his arrival and how he had come. This became an official police record showing the date of his coming ashore. They fed him, housed him, and clothed him. He was with very kind people of this American Samoa Island.

The people of Maupiti were able to match his known departure with the precise date in the newspaper record of the tour ship's being there, so that both the date of his beginning of this survival episode, and the ending of it, was recorded in police records of the ending. Tamanihi had survived six months at sea in an open boat with practically no supplies.

This epic survival matches any such event in the annals of modern history of which I have awareness. You are a far better man than I, Tamanihi. I salute you!

Please know that although I have not personally seen these records, I'm sure that the Tepa family has retained them. If anyone connected with an official oceanic record-keeping organization wishes to enter this name into such records, please contact the family who at my last knowledge still resides on the Tahitian Island of Bora Bora in French Polynesia.

CHAPTER 11

⚓ THE DAY FISH ⚓
RAINED FROM THE SKY

It was time to reach toward that western horizon. We were ready for our departure, but Tahiti seems to have forgotten to awaken that sleeping giant whose winged flight hurls the wind about. We waited for several days. And finally he awakened! Rather sleepily I might say, but enough for us to bring the anchors aboard.

The US flag was moved from the stern and raised to the mainsail gaff peak (or rather to its location on a Marconi rig), the French flag stood at the starboard spreader as I took a glance up to the cannons mounted on the high point of the steep face of the Bora Bora mountain. We had climbed up there to look at those cannon and found them maintained and oiled! These are they who have stood guard duty over the entrance to these isles. These guns now hold silent sentinel upon our way, yet tradition speaks in voices from the past.

"A SHIP!" — —

"What flag?" — —

"She shows a French flag at the starboard yard!" — —

"Hold fire men, she's OK."

Chapter 11   *The Day Fish Rained From The Sky*

"Her name is *Osprey*," whispers the sea, as Bora Bora echoes the words, "Fair winds to thee."

Life settled comfortably into the embrace of those two persons in the care of this vessel. Their world, which moments ago encompassed an entire island, is now pressed within a few square yards of space. The people are completely unaware of this. They stalk about upon this deck and see an entire ocean with horizons unending. They even feel as though the vastness filled by countless stars is their universe as well. What strange creatures these mortals be!

The first day out, I came up from lunch, sat down on the port cockpit seat and stiffened to a silent gasp! I quietly said, "Peg, come here and look."

It was a tornado such as I have never heard of before or since. It was absolutely immense. The funnel had a gigantic diameter! As it spun, the lower third threw a curving fountain of water off the immense funnel.

The distance the water was being thrown showed the huge speed of its turning. I can't judge how close it is, but with absolute clarity we can see the water that is being thrown off.

The black cloud the color of tar to which it is attached was very low. The height of the funnel from sea to cloud was only about three times the diameter of the funnel. There is not the slightest possibility of survival if we are caught by this thing. The rest of the sky is cloudless. Only this towering blackness filled one spot. Upward, the bottom of the cloud was flat. We were looking directly into the face of disaster.

Which direction will it go? It doesn't seem to be moving at all. I looked forward. Again I silently took in another involuntary gasp. Way off, but directly on our course, a feeding frenzy of big fish was going on. I watched. They were orca. I said nothing to Peggy.

Many years ago, I had been scuba diving off the Florida Keys when the atmosphere felt strange. There were tightly schooled bait fish in various places; each one had a couple of barracuda beneath them as though they had selected their private territory. I went around these groups.

But an especially large school out-maneuvered me just by moving in mass and I was surrounded by them.

I was almost at the surface. The fish were ten inches from my body in all directions, and into this space moved a four-foot long barracuda on one side of me and two smaller ones on the other side. There was nothing gentle about their action. Their pectoral fins were jittering in agitation.

The point here is that, just as tornadoes can move in direction, so do schools of fish – especially big fish on which orca would be feeding. In a feeding frenzy, predators seem to go crazy, leaping out of the water in all directions. If an orca were to come down on us, the boat would be destroyed.

So which way shall I go? I chose to hold course and watch both hazards very carefully to see if anything changed. The orca were well in front of us, perhaps two miles. I could easily see that they were orca. Being in full frenzy, leaping out of the water, they are easily identified by their black and white markings.

The tornado still seemed not to have moved. I was using a part of the boat in front of me from where I sat as a range line between my eyes, the boat part, and the tornado. I had my left foot against the forward end of the cockpit well, to know that my eye position wasn't changing and thereby give a false indication of the tornado's movement. It still seemed planted there.

The orcas were no longer showing themselves at the moment. Were they gone or had the school moved to a new slaughter point? Were we at that point?

Still no movement of the tornado! I had seen "water spouts" many times. Just narrow little snake things curing way up skyward, but nothing like this great grandfather of all weirdly powerful twisters of which I have ever heard. Then the thought of one possible reason for never having heard of it became chillingly obvious. No others ever survived.

Chapter 11 — *The Day Fish Rained From The Sky*

We carried on. We slowly gained distance on our course, which ever so slowly moved the position of the monster farther from us. It never seemed to move. The orcas were never seen again. And one very unusual memory is eternally enshrined.

So ended, "The day it rained fish from the sky."

* * *

I had thought that it would be fun to stop at the Island of Suwarrow, to see the place where Tom Neale lived as a hermit. Tom was a sailor aboard a ship that stopped there in 1945. In 1952 he received permission to live there.

He was the only inhabitant of the island until a year before his death in 1978. Treasure had been found there in the 1800s, and was remarked by Mrs. Robert Louis Stevenson that Suwarrow was "the most romantic island in the world." However, it was not the treasure island of his book by that name.

Today, the island has been declared a nature preserve by the Cook Island Government and is reported to be home to a million sea birds, thousands of coconut crabs, hundreds of sharks and a few rare species of turtle.

Its anchorage can be rather exposed in some weather, but the primary reason that I chose not to go there is due to our having waited so long in Bora Bora for enough wind with which to be sailing westward. I did not want to be held in Suwarrow's reef area for favorable weather. Unfavorable weather cannot only bring delays and inconvenience, but can also cause a genuine problem if it blows in unexpectedly from the south.

Eleven times our planet turned before showing us the way into the Pago Pago Harbor (pronounced as though it were spelled Pango). The passage was not entirely uneventful.

For the next ten days you're going to get wet more than once, tired more than once, and you will remember the taste of salt on your lips. Let's keep sailing!

The Day Fish Rained From The Sky   *Chapter 11*

We are aboard a timber forty-one foot sloop (one mast and one headsail—or "jib"). The mast is timber, built of four planks, like a long hollow box. There is no roller ferruling of headsails or mainsail.

The voyage originally began with eleven bags of jibs in good condition of various ages. I refer you to the notes on reefing (See Appendix A Page 268), which system I have used aboard the *Osprey* and found both safe and efficient. I set the boat up this way to enable me to single-hand the vessel, which is how I have sailed for some time.

Peggy was seasick for the first five and a half years of this voyage, not to the point of losing her breakfast, but being exceedingly unwell most of the time. Wherefore, during those early days, she also survived my cooking which actually may have compared less favorably to seasickness. She most assuredly has my nomination as providing true grit in this non-Hollywood production.

Jolly Old England, from whence cometh our language and the carry-over language of the early sailors, results in a confusing hodgepodge that I shall make little attempt to clarify. To illustrate the problem, however, here are a few examples: The word starboard, the right side of the boat when facing forward is pronounced starbid, and all sailors still say it that way. The main sail is pronounced mainsal.

Then there is a myriad of confusing words such as, going to the head, wherein head refers to a toilet. And here again, it's still called the head. Let me explain that one.

There was no indoor plumbing in the grand old sailing galleons. Some arrangement needed to exist for 40 or so crewmen's function. Buckets could fill too quickly and the sides of the boat were often awash by waves, so that clearly would not do either.

You can see in your mind's eye the stern of a galleon with its great room's glass windows across the entire back of the ship. This is where the captain and officers congregated and where they have a full view of anything dropping off the stern. So this area would not be highly favorable for locating the necessary facility.

That leaves only one remaining area, at the bow of the ship called by the sailors, the head of the vessel. These ships all had bowsprits, which are of timber extending forward of the vessel, permitting sails (headsails or jibs) to be used farther forward than the vessel actually is in length.

Thereby she is given power greater than her size could otherwise provide. Planks were attached to the bowsprit with the prerequisite holes, accordingly.

So there was logic to the old language of the sea. Lives depended on a sailor learning that language, because if he in error let go the topsail yard brace when he was told something else, seamen may well be hurled from aloft into the sea to their death.

They had to learn the ropes and is the meaning of the term. But now we have kept it alive because sailing to some of us is itself, a look cast backward in time. But I shall do my best to translate my speech into 21st century ease, though apology is due to you present day seamen and due also to the traditions from that time not really so long ago.

Ocean sailing is certainly no chest-beating bravado. There is no thought of need to get psyched somehow as though this is in any way a breath holding white-knuckled event. It is something one does after breakfast.

After being freed from the reach of that tornado, which by landsman's rules is called a waterspout, we continued motoring through the night until 11 the next morning, thanks to the steering ability of our autopilot. I thought that we might have enough breezes to sail and thereby to have the windvane steer the boat. But now the autopilot would not release the steering even though it was turned off.

This was another first. The helm (steering wheel of the vessel) could not be turned at all, even by hand. I disconnected the wires — still no release. Finally, after hours trying everything else, I removed the drive chain from the helm's drive shaft and that solved the problem. The autopilot was now no longer available by throwing a switch. If we were to motor any other time during the next week, I would need to reconnect everything that I had just disconnected.

But now the windvane system needed a pat on its head. This system has a piece of plywood, ten inches wide and three feet long, and mounts in an upright position. The base mount is turned until the up right edge of the plywood is facing into the wing. This "blade" is mounted on a pivoting axis.

If the boat turns off course to the left, the wind blows against one side of the plywood and blows it over. This movement turns a gear, which causes a rudder in the water to pivot. That rudder when turned into the water flow of the boat speed is very powerful. Therefore, if a line is attached to the windvane's rudder and brought up to a drum on the steering shaft, the helm is returned and the boat returns to her chosen course.

What had happened is that this rudder's pulling line attachment had broken off and needed to be repaired. The difficulty presents itself in the fact that this part is well aft of the transom and in the water and is well and truly out of reach. As mentioned before, there is a two-foot square platform extending out the back of the boat. The windvane is attached to that, and what needed to be repaired is behind that!

By a little balancing act on my part, I got the job done before long. This had required my pushing myself out of the boat on my stomach onto the little platform aft, with only my knees and feet on the boat and the rest of me dangling out and over the stern on that platform The boat was rolling so I had that to contend with as well.

Peggy was steering. She was also giving me strongly phrased vocal suggestions that I should proceed with caution or words to that effect.

Peggy is not to be criticized for her concern. Beyond her proven interest in her husband, when one remembers that she is not really a sailor and defi-

Chapter 11 — *The Day Fish Rained From The Sky*

nitely not a navigator; as the only other person aboard, my non-overboard loss is of some interest to her. And I try to remember to take as few unessential risks as possible for the ease of her mind, as well as personal inclination.

While in the Bahamas, I built a down wind running rig. These poles, to hold out two jibs for the boat to be pulled downwind by the bow, were not built out of perfect material. I had used galvanized iron pipe on which the poles ride.

Today, one of these pipes rusted through and broke. I lashed the pole down, and used the mainsail boom instead. We had been very benefited by this rig, enough so that we had given these poles endearing names. We always referred to them as our tusks.

With our motoring last night, due to little breeze from the east, it was just enough to bring the exhaust of the diesel engine hovering over the boat and dropping sooty oil all over the place. The entire boat needed to be scrubbed clean along with some body bathing as well.

We went to bed at 6:30, but I was up and down a lot. Peggy slept better than the night before because we are now clear of those islands. We had passed between two atolls and had been unable to see either one of them during the night. She has been a bit nervous. She always feels better with lots of open ocean around us.

*　*　*

The Cook Islands are well to the south of us now.

It rained a bit last night. The temporary fix of the windvane rudder broke five times during the night. Each time I needed to wiggle my way extending myself overboard to work on it. I also steered the boat by hand from 10:00 last night till 3:00 this morning. But now, we're barreling along.

At 3 o'clock I called Peggy up to steer while I took the genny down and set a smaller jib. I used the spreader lights to see by, because the night was dark due to some cloud cover hiding the moon and half the stars. The windvane steered for a while. I slept some, but steered the rest of the night till dawn. In her notes about this night Peggy says, "When I was steering, all I could see was the compass, but out of the corner of my eye I saw white water everywhere with big waves and wild wind."

It's time for a fix. Star shots with the sextant are done while the stars are still bright and the rising sun has lit the horizon enough for it also to be clear. I'm not a compulsive navigator. Some skippers require a daily fixed position at sea. The thinking behind that may stem from the concern of not being able to get one when you need it, and that's good thinking. However, I seldom fix our position before about halfway to our destination.

I like star shots in the morning best. If I am up during parts of the night, it holds a certain pleasure for me to look about and decide which stars I will use. At dawn, a star should be neither close to the horizon nor close to directly overhead. I prefer first magnitude stars because they are the brightest ones and will be most visible when the sun is coming up to light the horizon for me.

As the horizon is getting brighter, the stars are getting dimmer. If clouds are moving around the sky I can't plan on just which one I will "shoot." This is a term referring to sighting through the eyepiece of the sextant and with its mirrors, bring a particular star to touch the horizon. The sextant in this process permits you to read the angle.

Celestial navigation requires knowing the degrees of angle at which a particular star is above the horizon at a specific second in time. This angle changes as the world turns. So this is done with some precision. Peggy is a critical part of this. She records the time when I have measured the star's angle.

When I have it just right I call out to her, "Mark." And she writes the second, minute and hour of the time in Greenwich, England where the zero meridian is located. All calculations are based from that point, and makes for ease of solutions. The boat is still rolling quite badly, but we are sailing fast. We are at about mid-point of this passage.

Chapter 11 — The Day Fish Rained From The Sky

Peggy's notes say for this date that she has been okay for the past two days but that I am still cooking the meals and that I had repaired the windvane again.

We're losing the wind now. But we both had a great night's sleep, though we are still rolling due to waves not yet easing after the blow.

Both Peggy and I read most of the day today. I wanted us to have something special for dinner. So at 2 this after noon, I had opened a large can of roast beef from France. At sea, we try just to heat precooked stuff to indulge our inclination of work-free time, plus protection from the greater risk of permitting my skills full rein in such an endeavor. The dinner was really good!

Peggy changed the clocks back another hour. It's always good to see these events, which mark our movements across the planet.

Last night, winds were light and waves were still up, so we spent the night rolling. The sails were flapping and sometimes sounded like the crack of a whip. The night, however, was lovely to watch with the moon over half full and the planets in full dance with the stars.

At 8:30 this morning we saw a yacht! Wow! After all these years, that's a first. We could see the mast clearly and most of the hull. I called them on channel 16 but no answer. They were ahead of us and to starboard. They were too far away for us to identify them. But later in the day contact was made! It was Martha and Chip on *Nerissa*. They had seen our lights last night too.

The wind has almost entirely gone now. I'd better start the engine. The engine didn't start. It wasn't turning over properly. I sprayed the starter motor. Nothing yet! I'll let the oil penetrate awhile. At 4:00 in the afternoon the starter engaged properly and started the engine.

Peggy's passage notes of this night say, "We had to steer due to the autopilot being broken. Dan steered longer than I, but once I steered three hours straight – it was awful! At 10:00 last night Dan awakened me. He had seen a green flare!"

A green flare is not a distress signal – unless it's your last flare! I called on channel 16. "CQ, CQ, CQ I have seen a green flare. Vessel having fired a green flare identify and state cause for flare. Over." I listened carefully with the engine off. No response. I repeated several times with no response, and restarted the engine.

The flare had come from the right and well forward, first arching upward and ending at the horizon toward the left and was still lit. I had not seen the flare until it was almost to its highest point, so I could not know where it was launched from with any precision.

We turned toward my best guess. We watched the waves ahead. We saw nothing. We called on channel 16 again. Still nothing was heard. We kept searching. I climbed the ratlines (the steps up the rigging) but I could see nothing from there. No lights, no shapes against the starry sky were seen either.

We carried on for a couple of hours with no success at all. I finally decided to make for Pago Pago as quickly as possible. We were very close, and there would be a Coast Guard station there since this was US Territory. They could send a plane or ships to do a proper search. I changed course for Pago.

The night continues. An hour or so later, zoom – it flashed past us. We instantly knew what they were. Do you remember the dolphins we had seen all alight from phosphorous in the water? Well, these were bigger than dolphins. These were pilot whales and they are about fourteen feet long. Tonight they were zooming around us in all directions. The whales obviously could see each other all lit up, and we may have added to their play. Our underwater shape was probably glowing just as they were. We couldn't see far enough over the side to see ourselves glowing, but oh what a sight they made!! Even though we had a lot of moonlight right now, to see these big guys darting around each other, over and under each other, and zooming under the boat and around the boat was such a glorious thing to see!! They played around us for half an hour or so! It was easily the highlight of this passage!

We had a hazard ahead. It was Ross Island, and stands only 60 feet tall at the treetops. We never saw it. At 10 am we saw Manua Island and were able to start sailing again.

Peggy's notes say, "Hard night. Large waves and hard wind. About dark Dan put up smaller jib. Sailing fast. We stayed up all night. Bad night!"

At 7:00 the next morning I spotted Tutuila Island where Pago Pago is located. It kept disappearing as the rain squalls swept our course. The wind was strong and the waves were up again.

This harbor entrance must be used with some care, as the rusting commercial fishing vessel on the reef at the entrance side gives witness. If the seas had been really bad, with a full keeled sailboat, I would have needed to stand off until conditions eased over the sand bar, but at 11:30 I rode the back of a wave into the harbor.

CHAPTER 12

 Samoa

I was really apprehensive when I did not see *Nerrisa* in the harbor. They had been ahead of us. To add to my dismay, the Coast Guard station had been closed. But to my very great relief, Martha and Chip came in later the same day!

I had considered that instead of a flare gun signal, it might have been a meteor burning green as it was entering and possibly leaving our atmosphere; but at sea, one cannot ignore the possibility of distress just because you think it could be a meteor. My present conclusion of the event is that it indeed was a meteor. Our friends had not shot a flare signal.

This turned out to be a much lumpier passage than I had hoped for, but even so, Peggy did very well.

It's great fun to have friends sailing into the harbor. We always get together after we have seen them up and about after a period of rest. New friends are always met ashore, many of whom are interested to come out to see these little worlds that we inhabit.

There was somber news on the amateur radio net this morning. There were three yachts at Suwarrow yesterday when a force nine hit from the south (Beauford Wind Scale 9 is a "strong gale" 47 to 54 miles per hour). All three went up on the reef. Only the yacht *Myonie* got off. *Saturn* and *Pacific Mariner* were both lost.

Chapter 12 — Samoa

It's a gut-wrenching thing to commiserate with folks whose boat is lost like this. The other side of the coin, of course, is that the people were not lost as well. They salvaged some things which they brought to Pago aboard *Myonie*. We all bought what we could to enable plane fares, etc.

For quite some time we had kept a list of boats who indicated their intent to circumnavigate. We seemed always in less of a hurry than everybody else so we started a list to keep track of them. But there were so many who were not heard of again, that we discontinued the list.

The huge bulk of those, we can be assured, turned back for home ports. Many also change direction toward other destinations. Yet, some yachts did not survive. Those of whom we have direct knowledge were themselves picked up from either remote places or were on islands with airports.

The *Osprey* too came to grief. She survived an idyllic dismasting off New Zealand, but was destroyed by a typhoon in the North Pacific as related to you toward the end of Book 2.

Just across the harbor from us is the big Starkist Tuna cannery. I don't know where the source of the water condition came from to cause the fouling growth on the underside of all of the boats, but it was terrible. We were there for six weeks in total, and had to scrape the bottom two or three times to rid it of its growth.

The *Osprey* is a timber boat. And if the bottom paint is scraped off, the wood is exposed to the boring of teredo worms. These critters destroyed the planking of ships throughout the ages. Some yachtsmen used a garden rake, borrowed from shore, to scrap their bottoms, which may have been fine for steel or fiberglass hulls, but was not fine for us.

The entire bottom of the boat was covered in a super tight growth of tubeworms that looked like icicles, all of them up to six inches long in just two weeks. With snorkel, mask and fins, I scraped these things off and was surprised by how easily my process worked.

The underwater sound was a surprise too. It sounded just like small icicles being broken off. For those who have not endured the freezing of winter and do not know this interesting sound, it is rather like a gentle breeze softly moving a crystal wind chime.

I had bought some auto-body plastic applicators intended for dent filling, which I found here. These are about four inches square with one edge sharpened. Being made of flexible plastic I was not running the risk of gouging into the wood. It worked great!

We were invited to a feast at the chief's house. At the appointed time, folks brought us to the house. The house had been built for large occasions though not overly large itself. There was a very large room, however, with ten, three-person couches, end to end along each of the facing two walls. We were directed to a couch and sat comfortably talking to our closest neighbors. The room was full. Peggy was the only woman.

There was a banana leaf on the floor about five feet in front of each person as a tablecloth. When the chief moved from the couch to sit cross-legged on the floor at his place at his "table cloth", everyone followed to do likewise at theirs.

Women began bringing food to each person on a full sized turkey platter entirely filled with food! It was all wonderfully and beautifully prepared including its colors and differing textures, and gigantic in its abundance. The food was mounded in its immensity.

Heroic was my attempt to honor our host by not leaving any food on the platter for to do so might have perhaps shown disdain for his dinner. Much preparation had obviously been extended by many people to present such an enormous feast. But Peggy kept removing food from her platter and putting it on mine! I ate more.

At last I had managed by previously unknown expansion of my person, to finish the food, and a woman was there to immediately offer to bring more!

Chapter 12 — Samoa

The dessert came. Oh my, what could I do now? I ate. I tried! But the pain was so great that I could not perform my required etiquette and told the good man who had been our assigned social guide for the feast, that I begged to be forgiven but I simply could not continue eating this wonderful feast because I could not eat one bite more even though the joy of this food has been marvelous!

"Oh, that's OK," he said nonchalantly. "The food that's left on the platters, the women and children eat in the other room." Oh my! My etiquette requirements were very misunderstood. I have no fear that anyone went hungry because of my blunder, but that fact somehow failed to ease my pain at all.

We meet folks afloat and ashore who have granted us the gift of sharing with us their personal aspirations. One fellow gave his boat a biblical name. I hold every person in high esteem who actually begins his personal voyage and the reasons need not seem the same as mine. Mine are simply because I had the boat and the time, the inclination and the capacity to do so. I remember, however, as a child, tracing maps because they were interesting, especially of Indonesia with all those islands.

I had no firm grasp of reality before my teens, when I first heard about the international rates of monetary exchange. I found that I could take 100,000 dollars to China and at a ten to one exchange in 1940s, come away with what in the US would have cost one million dollars.

At age eight or nine, I knew by its name that Chinese junks (sailing vessels) came from China, and that's about all I knew about the subject. It is this odd beginning which first brought sailing into my mind.

Long were my pleasant thoughts about personally going to China for the building of such a craft. I enjoyed envisioning the oriental carvings on the bulkheads, etc. And at the completion of such a vessel, I had thought to sail it from China to Hawaii via the Indian Ocean, the Atlantic and then the Pacific My childhood thoughts, being completely unencumbered by the reality of monetary needs, permitted me to assume that I could then use Hawaii as a base from which to sail throughout the Pacific. I found great variety in the reasons people chose to undertake these ventures.

The master of a certain small yacht felt called to go to Fiji where no one had yet heard the name of Jesus Christ. He felt that he should go there to spread the gospel. As gently as possible, I informed him that there was probably one church at every corner of the streets of all of the towns in Fiji.

I remember him as a kind-hearted fellow. We had met him in Panama. He had just towed some other vessel from the Bahamas to Panama. I never asked about the circumstances of that, but this can be a very dangerous feat were there to be following winds and seas, as the one being towed can overtake the other, ram and sink it.

I mention this motivation of missionary endeavor at this point, due to meeting someone here who was building a huge trimaran in the jungles of American Samoa for the purpose of sailing the world to bring the gospel to those who have never heard the news. However, it would take an enormous flood or some miracle to get this boat launched into the sea. The boat was perhaps three quarters complete when we saw her.

The gentleman who had previously felt called to Fiji, tried to get a permit here in American Samoa to start a missionary radio station, but was not granted a permit.

Can any of these intended ventures be much less endowed with wisdom than my own? I don't think so.

Late in the day tomorrow, we will be making for Western Samoa via an overnight sail.

After the departure proceedings, getting underway was leisurely. During the night we saw the lights of another yacht, which is very unusual. I called on VHF radio channel 16 but got no answer. None of the boats in Pago were leaving when we did and none came into Western Samoa the day we did, so those folks were passing by without stopping. Being right at the front door, it's really unfortunate for them not to have stopped, but many are limited in their time.

* * *

Western Samoa is a totally different country, so after entry formalities, and after motoring through the anchorage area to choose a secure spot, we lowered and set our anchors. Next we launched the dinghy, put up our sunshade awning, and rowed past some of our friends on the way to shore.

We went to the American Express office to cash a check, went to the market for a few things, and had tea at Aggie Grey's Hotel. This is the Aggie Grey famous throughout the Pacific from Australia to the US.

This pretty village girl married an English migrant chemist, and through the beauty of charming friendliness welcomed people to their hotel. The fame of the idyllic Tropical Island cultural show put on at the hotel was shared throughout the Pacific during the Second World War and after.

I think it may be revealing for you to see how much the shore life enjoyment is a real part of cruising. So let's follow these few days here in Western Samoa to see what we are doing and to glimpse the lives and culture while we are privileged to be here.

July 2, we mailed five letters and walked to the headquarters of our denomination's church. We met Pastor Adams, the Mission President, and William Miller, the school principal.

He gave us a tour of the school and grounds. One of the teachers, Mishason, a Japanese American, drove us back to the market to help us transport some heavy things like a large bunch of bananas, yams and other things.

We went to the Prime Minister's office, but he was away attending a police graduation. We had wanted to pay a courtesy call, as low-key as possible, and show him the letter and watch which had been given to us by one of Robert Lewis Stevenson's descendants but were entirely satisfied that we had made the gesture and were not going to return.

While still at work, one of Peggy's friends there had accepted a boarder in her house. He was an older gentleman who, hearing of our pending sailing trip, had wanted to meet us. The four of us met at a local restaurant for dinner and talk.

He soon revealed that he was the "great grandson" of Robert Louis Stevenson, and indicated the number of "greats" that would be required to indicate him. He told us that one of the two leading families of Western Samoa were always chosen as the primary chief and that he had written a letter introducing us to the chief and asked us to present this letter to him. We thanked him for such a great kindness, and promised to do so. If truth be known, though not overly shy, we prefer to watch a parade than to walk in it, so to speak.

But the great kindness of good Mr. Stevenson's wish to bestow distinction upon us, to be formally greeted thusly, was given to us with such abounding warmth of good will, reemphasized at the conclusion of the dinner by his pressing into my hand a pocket watch that had passed to him from his famous "great grandfather"; and was so heart felt, with such immense sincerity that this protocol itself was enough to require our follow through with a call on the chief, much more so, being the fact of being honor bound by his kindness.

Robert Louis Stevenson lived in Western Samoa for all of his later years. Upon his death, all of the men of the island spent the entire night by torchlight cutting a wider walking path, and smoothing the way from his house all the way up the mountaintop where he spent so much time. This was done so that all of the islanders could be attendees, as the body of "Tusitala" (the story teller), Robert Louis Stevenson, was carried up the mountain to his final resting place.

We visited his house on the third of July. We walked up to the top of the hill where he used to sit looking far out over the land and over the sea. A plaque there now bears these words: "Home is the sailor, home from the sea; and the hunter, home from the hill."

His home and its grounds are very lovingly still well maintained. Water flows down from the hill and curves back from the house encased as sparkling jewelry by the big boulders that contain it where it opens to a grotto. The water was as clear as diamonds and almost icy on the hot day that Peggy and I splashed about as irreverently as the family used to do with the kids before dinner.

For those such as I, whose eye of remembrance is moistened by recollections of gentle family and of fondest friend, I raise my glass of praise to all ye whose lives were well lived, whose loves were well cherished, whose honor stands enshrined by time.

***

We ate at Aggie Grey's again and saw a great show at which her daughter participated with gay abandon. Aggie became eminently well known during the Second World War, and was indeed the most renowned hotelier throughout the South Seas.

On the fourth day of our stay here we took a taxi to church. Bill Mitten and his family invited us home with them for dinner. Bill and his son drove us back to the harbor and came out with us to see the boat for awhile. The day was packed with pleasurable pursuits and copious quantities of food and conversation.

The next two days started out with Peggy up at 5:30 to get bread pudding made for a church picnic. We went to Lefago and swam at "Return to Paradise Beach" where the picnic was gathered. We were taken on a car tour of half the island. What a wonderful time.

The Western Samoan fale (house) is a thing of beauty and simplicity. Several layers of rocks form the area on which the house is built. This gives elevation to the floor over the surrounding grounds securing much drainage for rain run off. The roof and its structure is a work of artistry as the thatch is weaved magnificently and ornately. There are no enclosing walls. How about that for air circulation?

The house is furnished with a modern bed and a few other things. Privacy is supplied by a few roll down mats at the sides of the house. Beyond question, my favorite villages in the entire Pacific are those of Western Samoa. They were lovely of architecture and construction.

A village is generally made up of fales in a circle with the chief's fale somewhat toward the center. His house is also dignified by being built on a higher rock foundation.

In early days, when the chief's food was served, all the men stood around the house with their spears and shields guarding the chief from attack by neighboring tribes. Then the men returned to their own fale to eat their meal, and would be off as a group for a hunt or for fishing; leaving time for the women and children to eat an unhurried meal.

The tour by car was a significant gift to us, as so many other experiences were which enriched our enjoyment and edification while we were here. And dinner at Aggie's was as much fun as each time prior. Again, her daughter was there and danced beautifully with the others in the show. Everything was great.

On the sixth day, we were taken around the other half of the island. We swam in the ocean and in a pool into which cascaded a magnificent waterfall, crashing white along a rugged rock face. With a loud roar it slammed into our pool. This entire spectacle was embraced by glorious greens of jungle trees and giant leaf plants draped with vines, which must have been planted for Tarzan.

We were back to the boat at 5:30 and had a pizza worth writing home about!

July 7: We will be leaving tomorrow. So I'm going to run the generator to charge the batteries while Peggy goes into town to the bank and post office. I scrubbed the bottom of the hull again. No boat likes to start out with a sea-grass-encumbered hull.

Bill Miller was taking our five-gallon diesel fuel jugs and us to a gas station. We brought home seventeen and a half gallons of diesel fuel, which topped off our capacity.

At about six o'clock, John Ryan came to take us to his house for dinner. They live up above Vailima, high up in the mountains. Dinner for eleven people is an event. And to have nineteen items on the table is a feast!

What lovely gracious people the Samoans are; who have laughed, and loved, and enjoyed their lives surrounded by the beauty of these islands, as eons of time has passed gently by. Great wooden ships with clouds of sails have dropped their anchor here, and lingered long as copra was bought from the islanders and repairs were done aboard these ships.

Many young women were interested to see these men who came ashore from such great ships, and shy glances in time flourished into moments of intimacy. True and joyous love was often changed to heartbreak and anguish, as the ship of one's loved one sailed over the horizon, taking him forever away.

No village of the island was spared this agony. Mothers have looked into the face of their little child and seen there, the face of their lover. It remains clear in memory even to this day.

But here, in the house of Ellen and John, and with their friends, not one face was to be seen without a radiant smile or outright laughter. It had turned into a party and was great and wholehearted fun. Yet even such a day and such an evening must bow to the inevitable turning of the planet, as copied by the hands of the clock.

Everyone stood and was forming a circle. We didn't know what this was about, but we too started to join the circle as it was forming. People were joining hands in the circle but we were excluded and gestured toward the area inside the circle. We complied. The people of the circle started quietly singing a song in their language as they in slow rhythm all took small steps in unison to their right. It was a long song. It was sung slowly. It was sung in great sorrow. We were mystified.

At certain parts of the song, everyone while still holding hands, would close in toward us and touch our heads with their hands still held together; and then while still singing they would move out again into a wider circle and slowly and rhythmically continue stepping to the right. Some of the women were softly crying.

They continued the song now in English. And each time they closed the circle to us and touched our heads with their hands they sang, "Goodbye my friend. We will never see you again." The song came straight out of the time of the great square-rigged sailing vessels. It came straight out of heart of those who walked here before. It came to us with a tear.

The next day the *Osprey*, another wooden sailing vessel, sail quietly out of the harbor. She too disappeared over the horizon. Sadly, Peggy and I "will never see them again."

It takes considerably longer for a boat's departure than an airplane due to personally being required to present oneself at the customs office before we take off. But by 11:30 I had the deck ready for sea by stowing the sun awning, securing the dinghy upside down on the house, and getting the anchors up. Peggy had put everything in its place in the galley, which by so doing prepared it for sea.

The weather was pleasant but the breeze was light, so we motor-sailed in order to be well clear of the islands during the remainder of the light. We always find ourselves looking back to the place we leave behind.

The eye of our mind saw the hill where a sailor was home from the sea, we saw friends whose lives moved gently through their span of time, we saw a land of rugged beauty thrust up out of the sea whose moon still saw shadows whose memories it now garbed in stillness. We saw flowered garlands freshly picked by loving hands so very long ago, each flower chosen by moistened eyes.

The tears of our friends, who had sung our farewell, were not for us who were known but for these few days. But for a moment, we had been seen as those others who had come from the sea who had stepped from a sailing ship and stepped into the hearts of their families.

And their tears were in saddened homage to those persons, those lives, those loves, living still in cherished memory and honored lineage; and whose children's children stand now grown, whose children all knew of those days now lost from their hearts.

Did you notice that? I can't quite identify it. The aroma was too swiftly gone. The breeze had brought a brief sweetness in its passing. *Ah*, it was just the faint loveliness of *today's* blossoms that had graced the island. It really wasn't brought to us—from another time.

***

We motor-sailed the rest of the day and sailed slowly through the night and so sailed the next 24 hours. The boat was rolling without much pleasure all the following day. At three in the afternoon I started the engine and we motored through the night. Dawn was announced with such magnificence of beauty in its color that I raised all light sails and turned off the sound of our engine to have no such interference with the glorious portrait of the personage of this coming day.

Peggy still slept. But before long those always welcome aromas of breakfast joined the rest of this gorgeous day. Suddenly, I interrupted her by calling out, "Peggy! Whale!" She was up in a flash and in time enough to see the eye of the whale still out of the water, as his body was slightly turned. The whale was no more than a meter from the side of the boat. It's always an event to see a whale. To see one within reach of one's hand is something special.

There was an island directly ahead. Beyond it and a little to the right, was an atoll painted on our close horizon as though posed there for a picture post card with just the right number of palm trees leaning out over the sandy beach. The proportions of the island and its contrasting colors of varying shades of green from her trees, whiteness of her sand, and the turquoise of her lagoon, were perfection.

We had just enjoyed a lovely breakfast and already I must have been looking forward to lunch because I thought that I would sail us toward that atoll, and if the coral permitted a close approach, I would put us there at least long enough for lunch.

But let's first drink deeply of the cup at hand! What a sight this is! This island directly before us had leaped out of the sea. She was tall as she reached into the sky. Volcanic turmoil from deep beneath the sea had birthed her some eons ago. The smoke that still curled upward was from her last eruption. Her face was of broad sheer rock jutting vertically out of the sea before us. A breeze was cooling her face. It came from Samoa, and rustled the leaves that framed her crown.

But life was brought to this Island of the Kingdom of Tonga. It came vibrant and filled with a raucous laughter like the shouting of birds, white ones, black ones, big ones and small. *Thousands* of birds sailed up the long stone face of the island, all the way to the top, and then they fell off the updraft, gliding back down to the sea and immediately again push the up button of the elevator, cavorting about in loud delight as they mingled together in the play.

White birds seemed jostling with black ones, small ones darting amongst the big ones, all of them zooming effortlessly about. There were big black frigate birds. There were small white terns of many kinds, and sea gulls of many kinds followed after them. Thousands of birds were there. It was a circus!

It was a scene so overflowing with life and joy as to bring to wonderment what a new creation of life must have been like. Movement, just at the edge of my visibility, caused my head to turn. I did not want to leave this magical sight and I saw nothing in that direction. But a moment later, I turned again. Something had moved. This time I saw the last half of the movement.

It was a whale! It had just crashed back into the sea. Today, everyone has seen TV events of humpback whales breaching. We had never heard of such a thing at this time, much less been present at such an event!

I turned to Peggy and said, "Did you see that?" And no sooner had I said it than I turned again to the spot and saw another whale lift his head straight up from the sea and swim himself out of the water up to his knees, as though whales had knees. What a sight!! What an event to see! All I could say was, "Wow!!"

An adult male humpback whale can be fifty feet long! And he can weigh 50 tons! He reached up to the top of our mast! What a majestic creature! To be so close to such an undreamed of spectacle rooted us in astonishment!

I had no sooner heard myself say, "Wow," when another whale came up out of the sea; followed by another; and another. One at a time they filled the sky, hurling the sea in a gigantic burst of water in all directions when they came crashing down again. We were struck with awe, speechless before such a spectacle!!

We were overcome by what we had just seen when another whale swam himself up out of the sea and threw himself sideways into a huge bursting of the ocean surface. All together, we saw thirteen whales come out of the sea nearly to their flukes. The last one too was gigantic. And he was the show-stopper. Because when he brought himself up to that standing position, he did not throw himself over.

Instead he leaned slightly, and then he started moving across the surface of the sea, tail-dancing across the water in a jubilant joie de vivre (joy of life), and then finally hurled himself back to the sea with a crashing explosion of water, to, as it were, place an exclamation mark with which to end the show!

I have told this experience to some few audiences and have almost always concluded by saying, "And to this day, I have felt myself, brother to the whale."

I, who while hiking on a mountain trail have marveled at the close look at a beetle wiggling in my hand as I looked through a magnifying glass, can only say of this spectacle, "Wow!!!"

CHAPTER 13

⚘ TONGA ⚘

We had come to the northerly most island of The Kingdom of Tonga, and dare I say it? "What a whale of a welcome it has been!"

We almost forgot that beautiful little island just close southward with the artist's placement of its palm trees leaning outward over the spotless sands. It was another of these places on earth where no other foot prints than your own mark the sand. "How long ago was the last person here? Was it weeks, was it months, was it ………?"

But alas, two considerations won the day, and we did not go ashore. Firstly, one is required to properly enter a country by presenting oneself to the customs office with formal papers, after which going ashore is legal. And that fact trumped the second reason, which is that shallow rocks are known to lay quite some distance off the surrounding reef here. Their hidden location poses a lurking danger. The temptation of walking, touching, breathing, seeing, smelling, and briefly living the reality of that storybook marvel of the South Pacific Paradise has cast many a sailor out to sea. It is compelling, even when we have done just that these many, many times.

Ah, how softly and how sweetly are these siren songs still "sung by the pines of the forest." Surely Longfellow won't begrudge me those couple of words, and perhaps I might be forgiven the mix of types of trees, for we too have cast a look backward in time.

Chapter 13 — Tonga

We sailed on. And soon we were captured by this new horizon. Tonga's embrace was to become a romance.

The Kingdom of Tonga is now comprised only of three island groups; the Vavqa'u, Ha'apai, and Tongatapu, the first of which is our wish to explore. Ours was not the first European-type sailing vessel to arrive. Dutchmen named Scrouten and Lemaire arrived in 1616.

In 1773 Captain James Cook arrived here as well, and called it, *The Friendly Islands*. The name is still used today, even on some of the postage stamps. Patricia Ledyard titled her worthy book, "The Friendly Island," written after her many years of living here. She graciously accepted our visit to her home at Utulei point, where it overlooks the harbor of Vavau. As she said, her view is "enhanced by a thousand memories."

The entry into the harbor is from the south and carries onward into the island until finally having made a turn to the east, completely excluding all waves from this grandly secure sanctuary. To have the boat motionless, be it while awake or asleep, is more than just of mild notice.

And what a surprise! An entire *fleet* of friends was here. Jack and Sheila aboard *Argyle* (NZ), Bob and Jane aboard *Brown Palace* (US), Russ and Jodie aboard *Cats Paw* (US), Franz, Peneke and their two daughters Maryn and Arjen aboard *Rampetamper* (Netherlands), *Renaissance* (US), *Taku* (US), Fred aboard *Tangarora* (US), Bill and Carol aboard *Shammy* (US); wow what a party! And they were all hanging out here because everybody was having so much fun! This is a great place!

One of the frequented events was published over VHF radio by a yacht chartering company here. They had a number of CSY sailboats, which are a modern fiberglass, 41-foot cutter rigged yacht such as *The Brown Palace*, which is owned by our friends, Bob and Jane. The company prints a chart for its yacht-chartering customers, which has all of the interesting anchorages marked and numbered. If a customer needs something, they can radio the company and a fast motorboat is dispatched to the numbered location on the customer's chart, accordingly. The company may broadcast an announcement that at 2 o'clock at number 18, the village there will begin an entertainment followed by a feast.

Several of the charter yachts may arrive at these fee-required events, as well as most of us cruisers. This is the income source for the village and individually for those who weave those wonderful baskets.

Upon arriving, one sets an anchor, sees the banana-leafed roof ready with its inviting shade, sees the women gathering, and sees the under-ground-oven mounded with its heat-retaining banana leaves. And when the rush of activity is over and the appointed time has arrived, we all start rowing ashore.

A smiling welcome is extended to each person and we are escorted toward a place on one of the lovely mats placed on the ground for us to sit in the provided shade where our food will later be brought.

A line of women from this village sat on mats. Each woman had several baskets in front of her, which she was proudly displaying for sale. As we were escorted to our place, we were not being rushed along. We could greet any of these folks and leisurely inspect her baskets, look at others, and return to the woman whose work we were most impressed with and buy from her, before proceeding to the shade pavilion, which had been erected for us.

Russ and Jodie had come ashore when we did, and after Peggy had bought a couple of baskets, Jodie heard Peggy say to herself, "Oh, I wish I had more cash. I love these baskets." Whereupon Jodie said, "Well here, take some of this. You can give it back when we get to Fiji." She knew that we used American Express to cash our checks. They too are friends with whom we have retained contact, since concluding our voyages. They have visited our land home and we theirs. Peggy was delighted. And as most of the cruisers, Peggy too sent baskets homeward as gifts.

Next came the Hawaiian-styled dancers, who were a delight. They made no attempt to hide the fact that they were having a wonderful time. Their costumes were exceeded in radiance only by their smiles. There was one marked difference between them and the Hawaiian dancers though.

The skin of these girls was shining with oil, sticky oil at that. The purpose of which was the fact that the audience was able to place dollar bills directly upon the skin of the dancer, an event which caused them to be even more vigorously possessed by the rhythm of the drum beats.

The music was great, the girls were plastered with money, and the feast began. It continued until dusk was finding its way. Our conversations too were wending. Never in history has a person left a Polynesian feast with anything remotely resembling hunger. It is an event!

So with care, we helped each other up, moved our dinghies off the beach and into the water, and while filled with the contentment which camaraderie, framed by the elegance which South Pacific Isles endow, Peggy and I glide across these still waters, step up onto the teak deck of this ocean sailing yacht (baskets first), we sit down on the cushioned seats of this cockpit, look at each other and smilingly take each other's hand as we step into the cabin with unrestrained pleasant urgency, to gently bring together the fullness of our day.

Such is the living aboard an ocean sailing yacht where a south sea island night has dressed its palm trees in the sequins of myriads of stars, and where moonbeams flow downward from the mountains to bring ripples across the water. Yet as time through eons has seen, the hand of a man when reaching for his woman, demands no such enhancement of surrounding by which to taste more fully the exquisite joy of life's fulfillment. However, *it does not hinder.*

Another day has dawned and we all kept our VHF radios tuned to the charter company's frequency to hear what was going on, as well as calling each other to say, "I'm going to #8 this morning, but I'm spending the night at #4," or whatever the plan happened to be. Always, only the number was used as indicated by the company chart. For us who are so used to latitude and longitude designations, it was fun to say, "I'm at 20, where are you?"

Several of us met one day at the "cave," referred to in the guide. The entrance is about ten or fifteen feet under water. Followed by a horizontal swim of about eight feet, plus another ten or fifteen feet up, brought us into the cave.

Coming up for air, we saw the cave was truly high and broad. The edges had shelves a few feet wide, which were above the water line area. There are stalactites and stalagmites of impressive numbers where a bridal couple are said to have hidden.

Their marriage had been forbidden. But even in paradise, Romeo and Juliet might cast wistful eyes upon each other, even though no authorization has been proclaimed. Stories of romance can even make an interesting cave more fun.

* * *

It's always a pleasure to buy things from those who come out to the boat in their dugout canoes. The favored things for us are either fruits or vegetables.

We saw a fellow paddling toward us. We thought it probable that he had something to sell. But alas, we had a really great quantity of what he had and I explained this to him. The fellow seemed extraordinarily anxious to sell something to us, so I asked him if he had a chicken. His face brightened as he assured me that he did. We settled on a price. I carefully explained that the chicken was to be cleaned, and that I wanted no feathers left on it.

At the agreed upon time I rowed ashore. The man was there. The chicken was there. My money was there. And a terrible problem was there, due to a misunderstanding. The chicken had indeed been plucked featherless; however, it was still alive. Oh my!

I was horrified for the poor creature. But nothing could reverse the event, so nothing could be done but to have the fellow take it back with him. And afterward clean the inside, etc.

He returned later in the afternoon. We were hosting folks from another yacht for dinner, which Peggy prepared. Our guests were not told of the reason why my appetite had abandoned me. I was seen greatly enjoying the fresh vegetables. A shudder convulses up my spine whenever I recall that terrible event.

* * *

There are coral reefs that lie within the protected waters of the island as well as a *maze* of coral reefs off shore northward of the islands as well as to the south and east. Here again came our good friend Fred, who found after the fact that he had passed through them blindly at night and had once again done so unscathed.

I knocked on the hull of Fred's boat from my dinghy. "Fred, may I come aboard?"

"Yes, yes, come up!"

I told him that I was worried about the possibility of his having a compass error, which might be causing his non-arrivals at his planned destinations. One of these errors could be in his deviation table. A compass does not point directly north. This "error" is called variation and alters in intensity throughout the globe.

But the compass is also affected by the iron in the boat. This is called deviation and varies differently on the various headings (directions of compass courses) of the boat, for which a listing or table is calculated by swinging (turning) the boat through 360 degrees and comparing the readings to a known source.

I offered to lash his boat to ours, swing them together through 360 degrees and compare the results. Fred however, felt his deviation table was sacrosanct. Someone whom he held as unchallengeable authority had calculated his deviation table. Yet in deference to me, he permitted the exercise. The resulting figures differed from each other in an erratic way. Always the gentleman, Fred accepted the results with expressions of gratitude, which I took to mean, were for my misguided concern rather than for the evidence it presented. One does what one can.

* * *

Peggy likes shells. But even as she had not gone underwater to get into the cave, likewise finding shells in anything other than wading water is only a slight inconvenience for her. It only requires her verbal entry to the "Honey Do List," and off I go with fins, mask and snorkel.

Certain kinds of shells travel an inch or two below the sand surface of the sea bottom in search of their food. They usually go in rather straight lines. And as they push forward, the sand drops off the trailing end of their shell. A shallow trench is left behind them as they continue forward.

When the sun is at a lowered angle in the sky, such as at about 9 in the morning and again at 3 in the afternoon, this slight shadow marks the trail where a shell is to be found at one end or the other. Danger may lie here.

Upon coming to the end of one of these slight trenches, one dares not just grab a hand full of sand and lift the shell out. Some of these shells fire a poison-tipped dart deadly enough to kill a small person, or so it is declared. Though not a small person, I chose not to test this postulate. And certainly gentlemen of caution do not carry such creatures in the front pockets of their swimming shorts, which also happen to be the standard deck wear aboard. Attire specially designed as bathing suits frequently fail the endurance of long-time sailing. I scoop these shells out of the sand with a vegetable strainer.

It was here, in the Kingdom of Tonga, that I attended my most memorable ballet. It was performed underwater. The ballerina was magnificently costumed in delicately flowing purple. She was only about the size of my thumbnail. She was a bivalve, pure bright white in color, with purple hairlike veil trailing the entire length of both of her shell opening edges. This purple skirt was one and a half times the length of her body.

She opened her shell and the music began. For as she thrust her shells together it was as though gravity had released its demand upon her, for she darted upward with the loveliness of her purple skirt fetchingly fluttering the water in her meteoric moment of ascent. This followed by her moment of falling, all done with purple fanning in her trail.

She fell perhaps one third the distance of her ascent, and then again she hurled her shells closed; once, followed by a pause, then again, followed with a pause, followed by a third; each done with utmost grace and fanfare.

This was repeated in fives and threes and sevens. The grandeur of the music, though created only by my mind swelled toward heaven. As it increased in pitch, the ballerina followed as though possessed by the music, as she went – "da da de dum—de dum," with each increasing crescendos. It was a thing of exquisite beauty. And from my snorkel, Neptune heard my most sincere praise as I whispered, "Bravo!"

I was moved of spirit, perhaps as deeply by this little shell, as I was by the immensity of the power of the whale that walked upon the face of the sea. Residing still, in our shore home, and nestles comfortably in an appropriate Tongan basket, rest some shells who found their way aboard the *Osprey* and into Peggy's hand. Ah what creatures here thar be.

The first stonefish that I had seen was here in Tonga. It was in very shallow water and I brought Peggy to see it for her interest and for her awareness. The stonefish is easily stepped on, and with devastating results. Tonga is also the first place where I met a lionfish. The turkey fish is much like it but with broader fins and therefore is even more stunning and interesting to see than the lionfish.

***

A knock was heard on the hull. It was answered with the same pleasureful anticipation as always. We are all popping in and out of our boats to share all manner of conversation, be it with news or concerns or just fun in general.

This time it was Fred. He had a flexible and collapsible dinghy, which folded down to about a foot in thickness to stow on his cabin top when under way. It was very practical from that standpoint, but Fred hated the thing with a passion. He was frugal enough to not get rid of it for a different one, but kept hoping to wear it out somehow. It did not row well. It was not immensely stable to stand up in while getting up aboard our boat but he made it.

He came aft into the cockpit and we sat to hear Fred disavow himself of what we knew was a problem based on the seriousness of his expression. Fred could not get his engine started. We talked about various obvious solutions such as having fuel, or charging batteries to turn the engine faster, or bleeding the injectors, but Fred was here to ask for a tow out of the harbor.

Of course, I was perfectly happy to tow him to where he would have more sea room in which to maneuver. We too were leaving shortly, which means in a couple of days, so Fred seemed more relaxed. I'm sure that he knew there was not the slightest likelihood of being rejected.

The conversation went to various things including everyone's amazement that a bank robbery had occurred a few days ago right here in these gentle surroundings. Especially because Fred said that someone had approached him a day or so afterward saying that he wanted a yacht to take him to Fiji and that he would pay reeeealy biiig money for the trip.

Now Fred was not financially deprived. He did complain that his father always wanted to know why he needed the money that he was asking to have sent, "Because it's not like it's his money, it's mine!" Knowing this, we were not concerned that Fred was going to do something stupid, and he continued by saying, "There's no way that I would take this guy, but the fellow's eyes were so big when he spoke of this really big money which he would pay that I said, 'Well, how much money are you talking about?'"

"I'll give you two hundred dollars!" Fred said that his eyes were huge in reverence of just the sound of such great wealth. I am happy to be contentedly assured that even had the sum been impressive, Fred would not have been tempted to actually do it. And just beyond the horizon of time, there awaited a disastrous end to Fred's sailing, were this fellow to have been aboard.

***

It is not unusual for us to feel a twinge of regret to leave the places we visit. We had again become friends with many local folks, especially from church. Many folks had come aboard, frequently to a slight jealousy on the part of our fellow cruisers. These isles are universally known as The Friendly Isles with good cause.

We enjoyed many of the feasts planned for the sailors. To eat in moderation is a talent not well honed in Tonga. And the snorkeling and shelling was captivating. Nowhere have we found such an abundance of cowry shells. In the shallow water where flat rocks can be lifted, an entire colony of cowries can be found clinging upside down on the rock's bottom. Perhaps one or so would be taken by us and the rock carefully returned to its original place.

Life of all kinds seemed to be in harmony with its neighbor. The people too seemed content, as seen from our admittedly detached view. And if it is true, and I believe it to be, perhaps this speaks high praise of the King.

He is a direct descendant of George Tupou IV. King Taufa'ahau Tupou rules his kingdom from Tonga's capitol city, Nuku'alofa, where he and Queen Halaevalu Mata'aho and their family live in a white Victorian palace, which dates back to 1867. The king not only respects tradition, but is also a forward-looking monarch as his two university degrees gives testimony. The understated elegance of the palace is not to be taken as informality. No Tongan may have his head higher than that of the king, a fact not taken as demeaning by anyone here.

***

Yet the earth keeps whirling about, actually over 1000 miles per hour at the equator, and our departure, as that of our friends, is approaching. Bob rowed over. We had seen him at a couple of other boats as well. "Be sure to come to the captain's meeting tomorrow!"

I'm not very big on "captain's meetings." I thought that somebody wanted to talk about the new islands. In a matter of days the ocean's volcanic depths can shove an island above the water surface where no island had ever been before and therefore would not be on any charts.

We had been hearing the warning to mariners over the radio that three new islands had appeared between Tonga and Fiji toward which we all were sailing. They were said to be a little north of our course and I felt no concern beyond normal cautions.

However, when three have just been shoved up, others may arrive tomorrow and be on our course that requires night sailing as well as daylight. Nonetheless, I said, "Sure Bob, I'll be there."

All seven or eight of us packed aboard one of the boats and half the people were talking at the same time, not about the islands, but about the navigation problem. For the first time we will be needing to use the designation *Eastward of Greenwich England* instead of westward in our calculations and everybody seemed to have his own idea as to how we should do this. This was not just a definitive difference. A different calculation is required.

Not seeking in anyway to denigrate my fellow skippers, but some of the ideas seemed, at least to me, to be "way out there," as street jargon goes.

I tend not to try to use voice volume to get a word in edgewise, as the expression goes, but I finally was heard saying, "I know the answer!"

And finally Bob hollered out, "Let's hear what Dan has to say."

My source of this confidence came not from the fathomless depths of my innate wisdom. It had something to do with the old expression, "When all else fails, read the instructions."

But in defense of my fellow skippers, I should point out that most were using the sight reduction tables for aviation because they are somewhat easier than those used for ships. And therefore, such information may not have been available to them.

I use the HO 229 reduction tables for my celestial navigation. And in the forward section, this is clearly discussed; so I knew what the required change of procedure was. I had looked it up days ago, and I finally resolved everyone's uncertainty. That, of course, did not mean that our group all suddenly leaped into their dinghies and rushed away. Nothing requires rushing unless you are at sea and conditions warrant. A couple of hours later I was back to Peggy and the *Osprey*.

***

The word was out. The church folks knew that we were leaving soon, and these lovely people started streaming down to the water's edge. I would row over, happily bring them to the *Osprey* and welcome them aboard. Many had not been to see our small world before, while others had. Many came with farewell gifts of tapa or baskets or food and fruit, telling us how their kids had come home during the week with bubbling accounts of the schoolboat bringing them out to us and their happy consumption of great quantities of ice cream.

One of the charter yacht customers from the US had bought a quantity of wonderful cheese that had been shipped in to Tonga, and they invited all of the cruisers who were in that anchorage to a pizza plunder party. Wow, it has been a long time since many of us had enjoyed pizza. It was just as good as we had remembered!

So we checked with Fred to see if he too was ready to leave, we processed the documentation of departure with the customs and immigration offices, raised the dinghy to her sea birth atop the cabin roof, brought up the one anchor which was well set in the soil of the Tongan harbor, took Fred's tow line, and waved good bye to Charley, Rose, and their son Peter. We took up the slack of Fred's line and we were off again. Perhaps we may meet the Gavel missionary family again somewhere. They know that we applaud them and wish them well.

A couple of hours later, at Fred's radio call expressing his contentment to begin his sail to Fiji, I cast him free. I had told him that when he had Suva in sight that he should call me. I would monitor channel 16 for his call. And when he was close enough, we would motor the *Osprey* out to tow him into Suva harbor.

We sailed on. And yes, the forming of uncharted islands was not beyond evidence. To my surprise, we saw waves breaking where no waves of this nature should be found. I sailed well around the spot. Peggy's vigilance of scanning the horizon (which was already on heightened alert) seemed now to be galvanized to the task. She is great!

CHAPTER 14

Fiji

We left Tonga on the eleventh of August and arrived in Fiji on the fifteenth. The sailing was with light winds and straight forward. Suva Harbor presented its entry where and when the navigation projected it should. Except for the last day, the sky had been overcast making celestial navigation difficult. As it was, we arrived at the harbor at three in the morning, sailed back toward Tonga for a couple of hours and returned for a secure entry with the required Q flag flying. The harbor certainly can be sailed into at night, but it is always my preference to not do so.

Approaching the quarantine buoy, we picked up its slimy barnacled end of the mooring line, which I did not want to bring aboard. Having used the boat hook to bring it within reach, I passed a line through it to keep it off the boat and secured our own line on the boat. It was about three in the afternoon when *Spellbinder* came in. We had met them almost two years previously in Fatu Hiva, of Thor Heyerdahl fame. We put out some fenders and they rafted to us. It was fun to see them again and to hear their news and wanderings, but everybody was tired. Keeping watch for newly-born islands through the night had taken its toll.

When we were cleared for entry I passed by a couple of yachts to ask if the yacht club had any restrictions as to visitors anchoring location; was told that there were no restrictions, chose a spot secure from the swing of other boats, and set our anchors by backing down on them. By 5 o'clock we were asleep. We called for Fred on the VHF radio with no response.

Chapter 14 Fiji

We slept soundly. Upon awakening I called for Fred again and got an answer. "When should we come out to meet you Fred?"

"Well, actually, you won't have to. I'm on a reef on an island east of you, but I don't need any help. I've gotten the boat off and am not taking on water [as might have been the case were his hull to have been damaged]. But my rudder is gone."

Fred had tiller steering and the weighted rudder's pintles can be lifted out of the gudgeons on the transom. Fred was getting ready to launch his search for the rudder. Oh Fred! Not on another reef, Fred!

We launched our dinghy to go ashore. The yacht club had a proper dinghy dock. We had learned from the boats in the anchorage that the dock and club were available to us if we joined the club as associate members. It required only a small fee. We needed to find the American Express office to get some money. We had been told where the bus stop was, so off we went.

We were surprised to see a small prison directly across the street from the yacht club. Fellows with black and white striped shirts were inside the fenced prison compound where they were cutting grass with machetes.

It is tradition here in Fiji that men wear skirts. Trousers are very common but skirts are more the norm. About which I hasten to point out, there is nothing feminine about these burly-legged gentlemen. Nonetheless, we were never in Fiji long enough for me to follow suit.

The bus brought us to the depot, which was comprised of a widened street area accommodating bus parking, where the bustle of Suva first presented itself. There were excited vendors rushing around! At each bus with people aboard awaiting departure time, vendors were walking about under the windows loudly calling, "BEEEEAN bean bean bean bean bean bean bean!"

For ten cents, a small brown paper bag of very spiced dried peas could be bought. Yes, peas not beans, as we are accustomed to calling them. With care to not break our teeth, we shortly became sufficiently addicted to these "beans" to the point of producing a salvatore response upon hearing the word bean.

The Amex office was found without difficulty. We were graciously received as old friends because many of the employees had become familiar with our name, as evidenced by the stack of mail brought to us. The stake had been growing over quite some time.

I cannot recall when we arrived earlier than planned at any destination. For clocks run more slowly aboard sailing vessels than those mounted in the town squares.

As we had made our way toward the Amex office we passed many small shops selling all manner of things. But one thing seemed common to them all. In each doorway stood an Indian man whose entire aim in life was to urge you with abounding emotion that just inside this very door was the item which he felt assured would be the very thing that our lives needed, and that his price was less than any other in all the earth. Had it not been illegal for him to do so, I suspect that we would have been grabbed by the arm and been drugged inside each succeeding shop, one after the other. Such confidence in one's product is indeed assuring.

It was this bustling of the city of Suva that first spiced our fascination as we were to encounter life in Fiji. For there are two massive cultures rubbing shoulders with each other. The Fijians are the ruling faction. The Indians are the shopkeepers and sugar cane workers. Their stories, in this writing as well, find few instances of communality. We were to learn more.

* * *

We rowed over to *Cat's Paw* to return Jodie and Russ' money that had been advanced to Peggy for those baskets, and as always we enjoyed talking to their sons Garth and Gavin. They were about 5 and 13, each with definite and differing reactions to the constant revelations of the spectacle of life at sea. It was without exception a delight to talk to them.

Chapter 14 — Fiji

Rampatamper also boasted two boys aboard as well. And though they were a couple of years younger, they were no less full of expressive excitements, not the least of which was regarding the bird whose life they had saved. While way out to sea, a gull had landed on the boat. It was unwell and the boys went immediately into rescue mode. They wanted to take it in the cabin for the night to keep it safe but were not permitted.

At first light they had rushed out and to their enormous relief it was still there, having grasped the bow pulpit to which the lifelines are attached. They gave it fresh water and it ate as a royal guest for several days. The entire boat glowed with pride. Harry had been saved.

Two boys can find adventure in a little plot of ground called the backyard. Throw in an ocean full of the spectacle of living creatures and you have the stuff of which dreams are made, and is where the vibrancy of life is truly lived.

Life with children aboard includes home schooling. In most cases, as well as these, when a sailor is reentering formal school classes, the sailors are generally two classes beyond their age group. Well done moms. And well done ye sailors. The world welcomes those who can look beyond a horizon of problems to see a harbor which can be gained. How sweet shall be the taste of your success!

* * *

A few days later Fred arrived, being towed into Suva by a commercial tugboat company. He immediately went to the customs office. He had been instructed to do so by an officer of customs not long after grounding at that island of his arrival. There they had asked the usual questions of him. One of these questions was, "Did anyone other than you travel aboard this vessel?"

Fred, being a jovial fellow answered, "Only a Tongan fly, and he flew off as soon as I hit the reef." The officer was not amused. To him, Fred was confessing to the crime of smuggling a person into Fiji! Fred therefore was a captured criminal.

He tried to explain, but doubt remained in the Office of Custom! And when he came ashore at the yacht club, and saw the prison across the street, he gasped at the mental vision of his being attired in black and white leaning over while cutting grass with a machete for the rest of his life.

He retold his story. I was summoned to the office as witness to the fact that I had towed him off shore at Tonga and that no one else was with him; and that he really was jesting about the Tongan fly. It seems that not all Customs Officials are endowed with Fred's brand of humor. Fred, though still perspiring, walked past the prison a free man.

He also got his rudder back. He had advertised a $200 dollar reward to the person who brought it to him at the island of his mishap. He got his rudder back. Plus the fact that the boat sustained no damage in the grounding seems to show that Fred's membership in the Good Luck Club remains in effect.

** * *

Another day has dawned, and I want to tell you about yellow, and about flowers, and about fire and frenzy, and drums and chanting, and horns that sound like bag pipes, and about men and boys and priests and red paint and spikes, and about prayers and cow urine, about rope and spirits; about what to the first-time viewer seemed like acts of ages past, thrust unchanged into today. Not so, of course, to those who are enlightened.

I found myself at a ceremony, though differing greatly from my personal religious experience; it was indeed of the highest holy endeavor, held sacred by millions of Hindus.

But how, how can I relay to you what I have seen? It seems to have overloaded the circuits of my perception.

I was standing on the shore of a bay. It was not far from Suva. The day was pleasant and sunny. Nothing about the day portrayed how immeasurably removed from my experience this day would reveal itself to be. There were about fifty of us who were on the outside of a U shaped area. We were at the upper half of the area designated by a rope enclosing about forty men and several boys who had been cleansing themselves in the waters of the bay. They were now on the shore, so close that I had to back away to focus the 300 mm lens of my camera. I could have touched the people inside.

Almost everyone inside the ring wore yellow. When I got there, they were in great reverence while dressing one man in red silk of very thin material, almost like a veil. He was covered from head to foot. Others were making mounds of flowers and leaves, which later were to become huge headwear for three men who were to lead the procession. With these three was the man clothed in red who appeared to represent the procession's goddess. Others were having dabs of a red paint-like substance applied to them.

When this was completed, many would stand in prayerful reverence before a picture propped on the sand in the same area where the leader's apparel was being assembled. A small fire was also in that area which was crowded all around by everyone inside the enclosure.

They were kneeling before the priest who put his hands on their heads. All of this was going on simultaneously. The drums, which had been heated by fires outside the enclosure, began the sound of their beating and the several small trumpet-like horns began to blare their one and only note. Everyone began a chanting of what I perceived as being the name of the goddess.

They swayed and bobbed up and down. Some men in attendance were carrying pails full of what I am told is a mixture of water and cow urine, which they sprinkled about with leafed branches. They were making the area purified. And when someone would become too frenzied, they would wet him down with some heavy strokes of the wetted branches to "bring him back again" to the present.

And now, in the midst of the chanting and the drums and the horns and the swaying and the hopping; one at a time they would kneel before a certain man who put spikes through their skin and flesh; through the cheeks first on one side and out the mouth and then another spike through the other cheek and out the mouth, followed by spikes through their eye brows and ears. Three or four more spikes were then pressed through the skin of each man's arms and hands, and other parts of the upper body. Boys of the age of what I would guess to be as young as twelve also presented themselves and were likewise festooned.

The spikes appeared to be about the thickness of the shaft that holds the ink of a ball point pen, silver grey colored, dull pointed at one end and three-pronged at the other; somewhat similar to King Neptune's Trident in appearance The shaft was about eight inches long. A yellow flower was put on the end of each spike after it had passed through the skin. There was no blooding visible. And as each man's festooning was completed, he was led to stand in a rough line of about two or three across.

They stood side by side facing toward the picture and the fire and the headgear and the "goddess." Most stood with palms together at the chest, some still swaying. As soon as each had received the spikes, someone would come with a golden container of some liquid, which was splashed on each wound.

The men wore no shirt. Only the "bride or goddess representor" was covered from head to foot. He wore a high ornate headgear, which was at least two and a half feet wide at the head, and proceeded as a triangle to a pointed high peak. There were silver reflecting discs on the front of it.

Still the chanted repetition continued with swaying and bobbing and dancing to the sound of the instruments and when all was in readiness the procession began. It followed the paved streets from the bay to the temple. For the next two or three miles the sounds and the frenzy was not to lessen. A rope was kept closed around them. The sprinklers lead the way, wetting the area in all directions in their zeal of purification. Most of the time, I managed to stay out of reach of this unknown substance as we proceeded toward the temple.

At the temple was the fire-walking appeasement to the Goddess. You've probably seen it in pictures or movies, so I won't describe it, except to adamantly tell you that this is not a cooled off toasty little affair! This was a red glowing huge mound of coals remaining after the burning of an enormous amount of wood.

The mound had been leveled off with long handled rakes. The pit, which was now ground level with coals, was about twenty-five feet long and approximately eight feet wide. Perhaps twenty feet beyond the end of the fire pit was a shrine. It was composed of flowers and fire and a statue, appearing to have been made of perhaps paper Mache.

Everyone appeared to try to follow the path of those who had gone before him, and then to dance before the shrine of the goddess whose picture was there. The path through the coals became plainly deeper than the rest of the surface, and although not cooler, there appeared to be less sinking above the ankles if one followed the trail of those who had preceded him.

One fellow who got off the track fell forward onto his hands but scrambled on. Mostly everyone strode through the embers with long fast steps. A few ran, and a few walked a slower than normal purposeful stride.

I had arrived at the temple ahead of the procession. I wanted to see their arrival at the location of the fire walking. The fire pit had, of course, been dug in the temple grounds, and the temple was a hundred feet beyond it and in the direction toward which the walkers processed. To the right of the pit and about fifty feet away, was a two-story building of the compound.

The fire pit was parallel to the building. A sidewalk ran the length of the building with a balcony above it serving the second floor where Peggy had saved a place for me to sit with her. A fellow yachtsman also sat on the balcony, but about fifty feet from where we were.

He was closer to the pit. We spoke to him afterwards and saw that his face was bright red from the burning heat of the embers. That's how hot the embers of the fire walk were!

Fortunately, the firewalkers were in such a state upon their arrival that they were getting pails full of "water" thrown over them to subdue their frenzy, which also drenched their skirts. Conceivably, the heat could have otherwise threatened to ignite their clothes.

Thusly, our view of the wide variations which are held holy within the hearts of all who seek to know a guidance in life from a higher plane than one's own, has left us deeply impressed by the devotion of all persons of all faiths whom it has been our great privilege to have even briefly known. I have no experience that can in any way relate to that of those who walked here today. We returned to the boat.

***

Four years ago we had met the folks aboard the boat Jane from the Hamptons in New York. Paul and Jane are lovely people. We had not seen them since then, but after all, it is a big ocean. It was fun to get acquainted again. As we visited back and forth, on one of these occasions Jane told us that she was a graphic artist, whereupon the proverbial light bulb lit in my mind, and I told them about the Tambua.

Fiji at one time was a whaling center. I did not learn the history by which the whale's tooth began being used as part of the tradition of the Fijians, but it came to be deeply imbedded as a huge part of life on these islands.

On major events such as marriages, a Tambua is presented to the patriarch of one family from the patriarch of the other. And if it is accepted, it binds both families to peace forever. The Tambua is also offered at the end of perhaps years of hostility resulting from some ancient event between groups when reconciliation occurs.

A whale's tooth is worn around the neck. A hole is drilled sideways through both ends of the tooth and a woven plant fiber necklace holds the tooth so that it hangs horizontally at about breastbone height. It is a very big deal.

Chapter 14 Fiji

The supply of whale's teeth is unlimited; by virtue of the fact that a good remedy for a shortness of cash is being readily resolved by a walk to an Indian pawn shop where the tooth can be sold. So each tooth seems to move about throughout the community with some rapidity, all to the smiling benevolence of the shopkeepers.

The sight of a whale's tooth immediately kindles nostalgia in the mind of any blue water sailor whose mind conjures up visions of the old square rigged sailing ships whose men created the art form of scrimshaw. Long passages before the effortless tradewinds would have brought boredom to idle hands were it not for the profitable endeavor of this artistic form, which I have always deeply admired.

But alas, as an artist I make a better blacksmith. [An aside: I played the part of a blacksmith in a Paramount movie while in New Zealand.] The light bulb, which lit when I learned that Jane was an artist, was for me to ask if she would be willing to draw something for me that I could trace on a whale's tooth as scrimshaw from our tradition; to be presented as Tambua in the tradition of Emusi and Lanieta when we visit them.

Jane was willing. She asked what I wanted. I told her that I would like to have a stylized fish with long flowing fins and bubbles ascending from its mouth. And wow, she saw exactly what I had in mind. She drew it, and my work began.

I searched for an especially large whale tooth. I found what I wanted, smoothed the tooth to perfection by many hours of vigorous applications of sandpaper and perspiration, traced the pattern onto the tooth with carbon paper, and began my torture.

I say torture because, being a traditionalist, I choose to dig the pattern into the tooth as the old sailors had done. I used a sail needle, grasped between my thumb and next two fingers, and all day long for weeks, I pressed down hard with the needle — endlessly scratching the point into a short part of the line, as the image with torturous slowness began to appear. But appear it did!

My fingers were numb within the first few hours, but I kept on until I felt that permanent damage might be done to my fingers, whereupon I would rest until some feeling and circulation returned.

When finally all of the lines and curves of this wonderful fish had come to life, I bought some black India ink, again as tradition demanded, and scrubbed the ink thoroughly into each crevice. And when I again sanded the surface of the tooth with very fine sandpaper to remove the excess ink from its unmarked surface, there it was!

Thanks to Jane, it is a work of true art! It is Scrimshaw!!

Many weeks passed before normal sensation returned to my fingers. But even as I lightly massaged my fingertips during this time, I must confess to an ever so small smile of satisfaction, which was almost hidden from view. And if truth be known, a detectable quantity of pride remains to this day as I tell the story to you, for as I do so, again I smile.

**

Before venturing to the village of our friends Emusi and Lanieta who are the subsequent recipients of the gift of my scrimshaw as a Tambua, life in the Suva yacht club whirled about in its usual laid back excitement.

There were movies to see, hot showers to take, food was perpetually available, joined with conversations crisp and constant. It was fun to come to the club. It might even be said that we cruisers added to the life of the place. This was also the time that the board members, apparently wanting a jolt of income, offered a lifetime membership to all associate members such as we.

The cost was small and we took the lifetime membership in this, *The Royal Suva Yacht Club*, because it not only sounded snooty, but we were bound from here to New Zealand and Australia, where we had been told by many, that they rule themselves as more British than the British, and permit entry to their club's facilities and anchorage areas only to those who show a yacht

Chapter 14   Fiji

club membership card from elsewhere. This custom exists, whereby reciprocal club amenities are thereby exchanged between clubs for the benefit of each other's membership.

Actually, even though some are a bit formal in dress code requirements, we were to find everyone genuinely welcoming with or without "being in the club." Only once in the future was any deference shown to us, and that was in the US, where surprisingly these folks happened to know that the presence of the word Royal in the name means that the club was chartered by the Queen, making such membership thought to be of added distinction. Well, such are the feathers which are thought to advance the appearance of one's cap!

We were off to find our Fijian friends whom we had met in Tahiti where they were working at the time. We had met them at church, in the English speaking class. It was their choice too, instead of where either French or Tahitian was being spoken.

We had eaten dinners together ashore and on the boat, and they had invited us to visit them when coming to Fiji to which they were planning shortly to return for their retirement.

The plan that had been given us in Tahiti was that we were to ask our way to our biggest church in Suva and make ourselves known to the choir director. He was Lanieta's brother, and he would contact them about our schedule.

So we went to the mission headquarters and asked the mission president where this church was and we told him who we wanted to meet. And with beaming delight, he said, "Oh, I know him well! I'll have him come here to meet you." Etonia, whom we needed to meet, was one of the elders of that church and yes, of course, he knew Emosi and Lanieta, and we were immediately taken over.

However, things are not always as simple as they might seem. Etonia suggested that it would perhaps be best for him to contact a relative of his wife's who lives out in that direction, where we could spend a night. They in turn would contact a relative of our friends, and this person would come to us, escort us to his home for another nights stay, and then arrange for a way to get us to our friend's village which was about six to ten miles "in the bush." There was no transportation to their village.

Well, we don't like to be a burden to people, so I asked about alternatives; we could perhaps just walk, if we could get good directions; or was it possible to arrange for four horses and a guide? (One horse for Peggy and one for the guide, one for me and one for the gifts would also be needed).

Well, all of this would have to be looked into, but no he didn't think that we could arrange for horses in advance, but perhaps we could do so when we arrived. However, he didn't think this would be possible either.

He reminded us that this was the north bush-county and things were, to use his words, "much more primitive up there." But since we weren't ready to go up there yet, due to trying to schedule a "haul out of the boat," he would try to get more information through his relatives.

Actually over a month passed before we finally left Suva making toward the north. The boat hauling schedule, after two months now, is still unresolved; but I'd like to tell you a little about this trip.

* * *

The preparations were not overly extensive but took several weeks in time. I had been investigating the customs involved. One must always visit the chief to request permission to visit his village.

There is a very intricate Yaqona (Kava) ceremony with a gift to the chief. If one Fijian visits and stays with another, custom calls for him to bring enough food with him for his own need. This is presented as a gift to the hostess upon arrival. The hostess may or may not serve this food to the guest, but at least it replaced the quantity of the host's supply. We certainly like the concept and, of course, likewise complied.

Chapter 14 — Fiji

We had now learned that a mission tent-meeting was being held each night at the village of Rabula to which the bus from Suva went, and that the family friends would indeed be there every night. So all of the contact problems dissolved. We were off.

Unlike Tahiti whose buses are trucks with a bench on each side, Fiji has genuine buses, with seats such as we are generally accustomed. On one side, a line equal to the width of two and a half average people, where usually three large persons sat, and on the other side, a line of seats of one and a half persons in width where two people sat, required one to usually push through the over hangings in order to go down the center aisle in order to leave the bus.

There are, however, no windows. At least no glass in the window openings and no frames for glass existed either. I make this correction, due to the fact that there was a large polite sign painted in the front of the bus on the inside which read, "*Please* do not jump out of the windows." The frequency of doing so appears to have caused some injuries.

We were to travel six or seven hours to get to Rubula and the paving ended within the first hour. One quickly learns to take a deep breath just before the dust cloud of an oncoming truck stings the face. But there is no sting that can reach very deeply into excited spirits. It is said that where there is no effort, there is no great reward. We have come with genuine anticipation.

What a beautiful country. It is mountainous and hilly, but not with the straight up and down volcanic walls of Tahiti. This land is mostly usable. We saw oxen teams plowing or hauling sugar cane. The bus would have to swerve on occasions to avoid cattle in the road. People were riding horses, many walking or working or laying in the shade. There's a lot of laying in the shade. But a lot of work is going on too.

I watched the bus driver. It was a tough job keeping the bus on the road due to its being quite crowned, curved, and steeply hilled; and having bridges made mostly of wood having heavy bearing timbers crossing the span, and next, timbers were laid across these, and then two or three planks were laid crossing the span for the tires to roll across. There was nothing much on either side. The driver's aim has to be pretty good.

This is especially true when these bridges seem to suddenly materialize at a hairpin curve at the bottom of a wild full speed down the mountain run. I say good aim, because the bus being long must be lined up with the bridge before entering it. Particularly when the distance between the curve and the bridge seems to be too short to make it possible to achieve. It's amazing how infrequently one can breathe and still sustain life. As I look back on it though, it wasn't really all that bad, maybe.

There was also a conductor on the bus. In addition to collecting the money, he also would unlock the "baggage" areas for people when they got on or off the bus. Everything that one could conceive went in there; from fruits to root, chickens to cases.

After one of these unloading stops, the driver started off again at the usual speed when someone called out to him something in Fijian. He slowed down, looked in his mirror, started out again at full speed. Again, three or four people started talking at once to him. He slowed down, looked out his mirror and started up again. This time six or eight people started talking to him all at once, and excitedly. He slowed down, looked back in his mirror and almost stopped. Looked back again (now everybody was talking at once) and he stopped again, this now about ¼ mile away from where his passengers had gotten off.

He had driven away leaving the conductor. The driver waited for the conductor to arrive. He arrived with a little embarrassed laugh to the passengers and we were off again. The driver never said a word.

We stopped in many places, several towns, and anywhere people were along the road who wanted to take the bus or to leave it. Some places we would be staying for five, ten, or fifteen minutes as announced by the conductor, and I would always be off to explore or to find something to drink for us. The trouble is that I never wear a watch; and although I was always back in time, once I was about to have the conductor's experience — if it hadn't been for Peggy's frantic and loud screams to the great merriment of all.

People were dispersed to look for me, but no one was upset (except Peggy), and I was there in half a minute carrying two plastic cups of cocoa and apologized to all. I had dashed off to ask where I might find something hot to drink, (it had turned cold with all of the wind in the bus).

"Yes, above the restaurant," was the reply as he pointed up the street.

Well, I looked up the street, decided to go in the opposite direction and sure enough I found the "restaurant" upstairs. Above the restaurant meant the restaurant was above. He could also have said on the first floor, which would have meant to us the second floor, since the ground level is not called a floor; the first floor is the first one up. But to have found the place still left some problems.

I explained that I wanted to take drinks with me. Someone else was called. I explained again. "Well how can you do that," was the completely bewildered reply.

So I asked if they had plastic cups and was greatly encouraged to see a sudden half gleam of comprehension of this novel idea cross his face and his lifting of a finger for me to wait a moment told me that he had plastic cups.

Time was passing and although I was shifting my weight from foot to foot, I was still smiling. The cocoa came in glass cups. But with a triumphant expression on his face, two plastic cups came also. I poured in what would fit, gulped part of the remaining boiling brew, and dashed off. I heard my name being called by Peggy. And although I was only half a block away, I would have heard her perhaps half a mile away, due to the "sincerity" of her call.

In Rubula we were to find the tent. We had no idea what was to be involved in that but felt we could ask our way to it without problem. The conductor had told us that there would be no problem about that, and yes he would tell us when we came to Rubula, which he did. The tent was visible from the road and at closest proximity to it the bus stopped for us. So joy reigned supreme.

It was about 3:30, but people were there. Lots of things were going on. Food was being brought and outdoor cooking of it needed firewood. There was water needed for the group of people doing this work, all of which called for quite a number of people in constant attendance, some of whom were related to our friends.

So we were very warmly received, and yes Lanieta would definitely be here this evening, and everybody was happy. Emosi, however, was gone to another area of the island for work and would not be home.

We asked if we might wash our faces of some of the dust and were immediately led off for a much needed bath in the river. The deep pool (three feet deep perhaps), was right at the edge of a side road. This was the village bath. However, a man came with three boys in the middle of our bath who was getting water in big jugs a few yards down stream from where we were. We assured ourselves that he was not getting drinking water.

In any event, they too were very cordial with much waving, welcoming, and smiles. The water was gloriously refreshing and we were soon dressed and back to the tent for conversations before being taken to the home of Lanieta's sister. She lived close by along the main road. We enjoy more conversation, an afternoon sleep, and a change of clothes. A supper was presented before returning to the tent for the evening event, and our meeting with Lanieta.

But she didn't come. We were assured, however, that we would be brought to her village by the village truck that brought everyone to the meeting, and one of Lanieta's brothers, whom we had met earlier at the tent, would bring us to Lanieta's house. I think that word may have gotten to her, and house preparations might have been in progress.

In any event, after the tent meeting, when the lumber truck stopped at her village, Lanieta's 14-year-old brother dashed off and by the time all had climbed down, a lantern was hurrying toward us, showing no light on the face, only on the sulu (a wrap around skirt) and someone shouted, "Here comes Lanieta!" We dropped what we had been permitted to carry (others were carrying everything else) and hurried to meet the lantern. Indeed it was Lanieta, welcoming us with open arms and much joy, and escorted us to the house.

We couldn't see much of the house or the village in the darkness. And since it was late, we were shown to our place to sleep after refreshments and conversation. Peggy did ask if there was a bathroom and no there wasn't. "We use the river," was the response, so she thought it best to learn about that in the daylight. What we learned the next day is another of those language problems we have in the USA, and which it is easy to forget. Namely, of course, that bathroom does not mean toilet. Bathroom means a room in which baths are taken. And joy of joys this village boasted a toilet room, though I never saw anyone else ever going in or out during the time we were at the village. It may have been reserved for us. In the morning, immediately upon dressing, before food or anything else, we were off to see the chief.

The chief's house was higher off the ground than everyone else's. We had taken our shoes off before entering. This is the custom for all homes in Fiji, as it is also in Tonga, Samoa, and even Tahiti. We sat cross-legged on the floor. Lanieta sat to the side as translator. Even though the chief could speak English, he said that he could not speak it well.

I thanked him for the honor of receiving us. Told him of our travels by sail, in the way of the ancient peoples; and how we had met Lanieta and Emosi in Tahiti, and how they had spoken with great affection of the beauty of Fiji, and of their invitation for us to visit them upon our journey here. And that it was for this reason that we had come this morning to ask his permission to visit the village so that we might enjoy the reunion with our friends; and that I hoped that he would forgive us for so small a gift, but that it was none-the-less a token of the very high respect in which we view the chief and his village. All of this being translated as I went on in what was the prescribed manner, but it was felt in the fullest sincerity. The chief accompanied my presentation with solemn grunting, mutterings, and bowings.

The chief's response was of equal length in Fijian, translated as he went along, which I accompanied also by "ahs" and "ohs" with solemn bowings. Yes we could visit the village. We could stay for two weeks if we wished to without paying, etc.

So we were off for breakfast, which was cooked outside. A small fire was lit on the ground beside the door so the smoke wouldn't come inside very much. Three stones were put down to hold the pan.

When it rains, as it did while we were there, the cooking is done inside the house in exactly the same way as done outside. The smoke, after all, does not last very long.

Most of the houses were thatch roofed with woven fiber sides and without windows. Lanieta's house was tin. They had lived for several years outside of Suva, but while they were in Tahiti, her father came to Suva, dismantled the house and took it back to his village and this is where they found it when they returned. But that seemed ok, I think. Lanieta, who is our age, much prefers "the village life" as she referred to it, as compared to Tahiti.

She said that she was worried about us and the village life. We were constantly reassuring her and thankfully, finally succeeded. Our village life had begun.

The traditional Fijian house has a palm tree trunk as a ridgepole for the roof, which extends beyond the walls of the house by a couple of feet. The roof is about a foot thick of closely lain fiber, and the walls of one or two thin weavings of squares of fiber. The house has apparently one reason for being, and that's for practical necessity. There is no embellishment of the type found in Samoa where fiber lashings of framing, etc., are indeed a work of magnificent art.

The bure, as the house is called here, is generally quite small to extreme on occasions but this was not the case with Lanieta house. It was quite large in fact, about 12'x19' with an additional four feet added to the side making about 16'x19'. This four-foot area was without floor at one end and contained a table of boards on boxes beside the propane stove for which, at the time, there was no fuel. This was used when available, during the rainy season, which is not long in this area. The unfloored area is used for the indoor cooking fire and the dining room.

The main house, however, had its floor raised eight or more inches above the ground by rocks on which the planks were laid. Although it made for slightly different levels, it kept all the dampness of a wet earth off the floor. There were no windows, but a door was in each of three walls, which included the cook room, so by opening the doors, the lighting was fine. A rock rolled against the door at night is the most obvious of closure efficiency.

At the end of the house, the end without a door, a plank reached across from wall to wall, which supported pictures and mementos, and also supported one end of the cloth curtain between the sleeping areas and the main room.

The fact that the tin of the outside of the walls does not overlap in all areas has the benefit of letting in the breeze and letting out the smoke.

Our friend's house is close to the chief's. This may have indicated a prestigious honor. The chief's wife is Lanieta's aunt. Emosi comes from the Lau Group of islands, which is the most southeasterly of the country.

The people are very fortunate in Nasayani, the name of this village. There is a river of considerable volume just a couple thousand yards away, and although they have water piped in to outside taps, in drought conditions they don't have far to carry water. And there are fish.

Giant mango trees abound, and in season, since the trees are communal property, one need but to harvest as many mangos as he wishes and by taking them by bus to Suva, the mangos can be sold in the market, whereby money is available for rice, etc. But one's time is not always one's own. Once a week at the village meeting, which everyone attends, a report is given of the work done or not completed during the prior week. And additional jobs are assigned for the coming week.

These people are also fortunate in having many thousands of acres of land, a great portion of which they have contracted to the government for planting of trees at a price at harvest of $6.00 per tree for the timber. Several million trees have been planted.

I did not point out to them, as they were explaining this to me, that since there was no specification to the contrary, the government could wait fifty years before beginning to harvest the biggest and best, but everyone seemed to already be spending the money in their minds, including the chief, or so at least it traveled my mind.

However, they do have a considerable stand of existing timber, which they have already started to harvest. The plan is that it be done by family groups in sequence, for which the village has bought a heavy-duty lumber truck and rented a portable sawmill.

Some of the men were instructed in the operation of this mill before its arrival, and the chief was there this morning to show it to me.

I came not long before lunchtime and they were having a little difficulty with what I think may have been the first tree. There were some cuts out of the upper portion of the log and there appeared to be some small problem. They were just beginning though, and just because the lumber may not have been quite square, does not mean that success would not soon follow.

However, the blade of the saw had a three-foot radius and the lower portion of the log was greater than this. Rolling the log over 180 degrees to join the other cut was a problem without anything but some pry bars with which to turn it.

They also had no carriage to hold a log in a given position, but only pipe-type rollers to push the log into the saw, such as those used by truckers to unload boxes, without any means of controlling a log's speed of travel or even its angle to the blade. It's no wonder there was just a little problem at their beginning. But there was no shortage of men in contact with this log from various angles and each was giving simultaneous advice.

I think the chief sent everyone home early, perhaps because things weren't going too well at the moment. It wasn't the time for demonstrations.

I was careful to show no notice of the difficulty, of course, and gave voice solemnly over the great difficulties of lumbering, but chose my words carefully so that I not be falsely taken to have any knowledge of a saw mill. Despite the fact that I've watched a few in operation, it should not be misconstrued as my having great wisdom and knowledge on the subject. Although, I did know enough about it to see no solution to their problem, with the equipment presently at hand.

This thing was an immense danger to all who might come even remotely close to it! And I needed to not embarrass Lanieta before her chief by telling him that this whole scheme was crazy. He must have been the one who had it brought here.

I found out later that our host had already been asked by the chief if I was going to help them with the saw mill, a fact unrevealed to me before our look at the mill. I did make a drawing of a timber hook used to roll logs, which the blacksmith in the town 30 miles away could make out of bending very heavy rebar, reinforcing the bend and sharply bending the end and sharpening it to take the log. A simple two-part metal collar with bolts through the ears could attach it to a four-foot pole.

The day before we left, it had been arranged that I could go by horseback up into the timber area on the other side of the mountains. But the rains were too much for a pleasant trip. So I enjoyed a book that I had brought along. Although reading may not be the usual pastime, a leisure day at home is a definite part of village life.

***

Fiji boasts a gold mine not far from Nasayani and a day was devoted to a bus trip for a tour below ground to see this fabled metal. But we found that new management had stopped the tours. We could not determine the reason for the change in policy, but security and safety seemed to be the likely reason. An interesting day was enjoyed nonetheless.

Another day that we again traveled with our hostess by bus was to find a tiny Catholic Church way off from any much-populated area, where we had heard of a famous artist having painted some beautiful murals. This we did find, and were appropriately impressed by, as they showed Fijian life and culture interwoven with the life and crucifixion of Christ. The facial colors were dark with the hue of Fiji in the overall mural and did not present Christ as of Jewish ancestry.

But it is often the sidelights of these trips that are of the greater interest to us, such as sharing a table in the nearest town with the Scottish priest of the place that we had just visited. It was a little Indian restaurant with its usual menu of hot curry foods. But the setting and conversation was the thing of interest.

His sharing of some of his activity, his interest in the life and different circumstances of John, the priest whom we had met at the little village of Mole Saint Nicolas in Haiti was an enormous diversion to him.

Strolling through the markets of the various towns and their shops, and mingling with the people, is all part of the fun, as compared to the rigid group control of those in guided tours where only objects are made visible and people fade into the background as props. Spotting reading glasses in a window and finding a pair to enable Lanieta to sew again was a super delight.

At first all the different strength glasses were "just right." But with gentle time I was content that the proper one's passed our tests. She not only smiled her appreciation, she beamed to all near and far.

One day we went fishing. I hope to always be able to remember the scene. The area is very dry even though it rained while we were there. It looks much like some of our country's drier west. Hills, which on this side were almost treeless, are all covered with about two feet of brown grass, which the breeze moved like small waves on a gentle sea. A gigantic cattle ranch, operated by the government, joins the village land and it was across a couple of its grazing areas through which we walked to the fishing area. We scattered a herd of long horned cattle as we went.

Peggy walked ahead in the group of women and boys all single file, because a six-inch wide cow path was being followed. And, as they walked through this scene of waving brown grass on slightly rolling hills with barren mountains beyond, while carrying rolled fishing nets and other necessities, the colors and style of dress of the women just seemed to shout of another place, another continent.

I saw Africa for the first time. And I ran up to get the camera from Peggy and recorded the scene with what turned out to be a malfunctioning Nikon camera. Ah well, I can see it still, with the 20x20 vision by which the mind is forever blessed.

We came upon a lovely little river. It was perhaps an average of less than twenty feet in width and up to about four or five feet deep. The women knew just where to set the net, where the river was narrow enough for the net to reach across, and shallow enough for it to reach from the river bottom to its top. All the women, some ten or so strong, were on one side of the net as the six or eight of us men started from the other side a good distance upstream.

We spread our positions across the river and descended toward the net with much thrashing of our hands on the water surface and filled the air with all manner of manly shouting as commanding instruction in several languages were given to the fish.

And flee they did! But the gill net across their path stopped them for the brief moment before one of the women grabbed it free and bit down on it with her teeth just behind the head. The bloodied fish were strung on a vine, which each woman except Peggy had come with for this most vital of exercise. The fishing gods smiled upon us this day. They seemed to have been of very small benefit, however, to the fish.

***

One of the things we learned is that only the owners of a house use the front door. Therefore, I was not surprised at Lanieta's older brother coming quickly into the house through the cook room door. I was alone in the house, sitting on the cot reading, it did take me a full two seconds to recover from seeing him crawling very fast on hands and knees. But by the time he had gotten to the center of the main room and was in the process of coming to a sitting position, I had very quickly slid myself off the cot and onto the mat in a cross-legged sitting position at the same instant that he positioned himself.

Now, this is what was going on. One does not enter a house with his head above someone of higher rank. He had come regarding something of urgency and rushed into the house not knowing where we would be sitting. It is customary to be sitting on the floor. Therefore, I had two thoughts. One, that he might be embarrassed by having displayed an over-courtesy and two, that I not be aware of the custom, which such a degree of courtesy extends.

So although he never looked at me even though we were within each other's visual scope, and although my act was not noted by any outward sign, I knew that I had scored well. And he went out the way he had come in, but a little less hastily. The good man appeared to not expect my presence in the house, and his miraculously instantaneous drop to the floor, though smoothly done, did show a millisecond of confusion. Our discourse was brief to the extreme, so I never knew for what he had come before he was gone again as he had entered. I again had the house to myself, and the bed for my comfort, and the book for my diversion and pleasure.

Lanieta had a goat with three beautiful frolicking kids who would sometimes bound into the house (usually through the front door) and would be shooed out promptly each time. What delightful pranksters they were, as they romped about outside the house, sometimes two of them would face each other, come up on their hind legs and down they would come with a sounding crash of hornless heads.

There was also a chicken that had taken up residence in the corner of the house by the dining table where she sat noiseless and motionless on her eggs. Once a day she would leave the nest and run at full speed, sometimes flying short distances, but always neck outstretched in full race.

Then, still without eating, she would be back to the eggs. I suppose she needs a little quick exercise to get the blood circulating through the body to maintain the temperature for the eggs. It was a surprise to us to discover the hen occupying her corner. We had been in the house for several days by this time.

* * *

After breakfast and after our things were gathered together for our departure, and while Lanieta was busy in the cook room, I sat on the floor away from the cot. I beckoned to Peggy to sit beside me, and when Lanieta's younger brother happened in, I beckoned to him to sit well to the side and also wait. When Lanieta came in and saw us she knew something was about to happen. I could see the surprise on her face.

She first went quickly into the room where she had been sleeping, perhaps to comb her hair, I don't know. But very quickly came out and sat on the floor in front of us. On the floor in front of me, was a small wooden box without a top. The contents of the box lay on a red cloth. It was concealed by a fold of the red cloth on which it lay. The cord of the Tambua lay out on the floor. Only the whales tooth was concealed, but it was evident that a Tambua was going to be presented. I began to speak.

I told of the time when we had met. Of our kinship in the church; of the warmth of our hearts in our friendship; of the memories to always cherish from the pleasures of her hospitality; of the wholesomeness of village life, of the abundance of the food we had eaten, of our appreciation of the lovely customs of Fiji; each were solemnly enshrined.

The full meaning of the Tambua, as begun by the ancient Fijians was reviewed by me as was the custom of the seamen on the ancient square rigged sailing ships that had also used the whale's tooth to create the art form called scrimshaw.

And as the Tambua was uncovered by lifting the folded cover, lying there on the red cloth in the box was the glistening white ivory on which swam our fabled fish. I said that I wanted to give this Tambua — Scrimshaw to Emosi and I asked that it might represent perpetual peace and love between our families.

Well before the presentation was over (and a speech at such a time should not be too brief by custom) there were many tears in the eyes of Lanieta. I knew that the Tambua was well received. She seemed well pleased indeed with the fish that swims forever on his wave. The Tambua was hung from the plank that holds the pictures of the family.

Lanieta and her father and the minister from the tent, went with us to the next town from which we took a bus toward Suva. Our visit was over.

***

We were to spend the night in Lautoka. While there, we went to see the sugarcane mill. All along the route we saw men with machete-like cane knives harvesting the sugarcane. Oxen teams dragged the cane on to little railroad cars for transport to the mill. The tracks appear to be no more than three feet wide, and the cars maybe eight feet long. The cars are flat-bedded with high ends and the cane protrudes out both sides. Some of those oxen teams are immense.

We enjoyed the tour through the sugar mill. Gigantic roller presses squeeze the sweet juice from the cane. The pulp is resold to the farmers for fertilizer, and the water is boiled away to leave the raw light brown sugar. What huge machinery.

We found a little hotel close to the bus terminal and although a bit stark, it seemed clean except for the tub to which Peggy presented a new concept called a scrubbing.

Chapter 14 *Fiji*

We were awakened before 5:00 the next morning. No, we had not left a wake up call. There was no such service. When I heard the sound, I almost didn't know where we were. It was a beautiful sound, hauntingly beautiful.

We had not realized it before but we were very close to a mosque. And we were hearing the call to prayer. A call, much older than modern time, moved through the air with the sound of mystery. This chanted song is voiced loudly and beautifully from the pinnacles of mosques all over the world, heard by us for the first time. It was a hauntingly exquisite experience.

"Well, now that we're awake anyway, why not take the express bus to Suva?" We had planned a leisure breakfast and an 8 o'clock departure rather than the 6:30 express, but now that we are awake, we might just as well go earlier.

At 5:45 we were packed and at the front door. But to our great amazement, we found it locked. We check the other doors, and found them locked tightly from the inside with pad locks.

Six o'clock came and went. No one came to the front desk. Five after six came without an attendant, as did ten after.

By this time I had opened all doors and drawers behind the little desk and found many interesting things, but I found no keys to the padlocks on the door. Deciding that the attendant must be inside asleep someplace, I stepped to the hallway, whistled shrilly, and very loudly called out as politely as is possible while using both hands forming a trumpet round the mouth, *"Please unlock the front door!"*

Immediately a slender fellow came hurrying out of one of the rooms still trying bleary eyed to fasten the top of his trousers. While he was trying to get the key into the padlock, we were very careful to portray no annoyance by gesture or tone of voice. After all, it's not necessary to beat a man on the head.

A two-block walk brought us to the bus and to the bus driver of whom I spoke at the beginning of this Fiji story. The bus was something very special. There aren't many buses here like this one. It had windows, beautiful high backed seats with armrests. It was a totally modern bus in every possible way!

After an hour or so of travel, I started really to become amazed. Peggy and I were sitting in the seat directly behind the driver so that we could enjoy seeing forward as well as out the side, and absolutely everyone we met in oncoming cars or trucks, or walking along the road, knew the driver.

Virtually without exception there was an excited wave and huge smile, and since the driver's face was fully shown from where I sat, I could see the glorious joy spread instantly across his face. It was pure joy, total and absolute happiness.

I was fascinated. I speculated about whom he might be, to be so well known. I was determined to find out and would have asked him if I had not figured it out myself. For, when a couple hours later, while this recognition was still going on, and always responded to by driver with unbounded pleasure, I saw one fellow standing beside the road turn half way around while shaking his hand from a limp wrist, whistling as he turned, as though the sight was too marvelous to look fully upon. I thought the radiating joy on the face of the driver, might shatter the windshield.

Lanieta had told Peggy that the driver of the village truck had a driving license. That he had studied for it and it was a very, very special achievement. And when Peggy in conversation told her that she had driven a huge truck when she was sixteen, Lanieta's eyes were very big in amazement and she asked if Peggy had a license.

When Peggy said that she did, the eyes were even bigger, and she asked, "Does Dan have a license too?" And being assured that I did, it was almost too much of a marvel.

So now I knew. Now I knew who he was. He was *The Driver*. The licensed driver of a magnificent bus, justifiably proud of the fact, he smiled as homage was presented by all.

Chapter 14   *Fiji*

And a good driver he is. It's a tough road. A big portion of it from Nadi to Suva is dirt. As we were going up one small mountain we met a heavily loaded truck coming down who gave way for us by going to the edge of the road. I saw that he was in trouble as we passed him and I caught the anguish in the bus driver's face as I turned in my seat in my hope for the truck's recovery.

I stole a glance at the bus driver's face in the mirror a couple times, and saw skill and the wet mud of the mountain, contesting each other. Skill won the day, and a contented expression, mingled with the knowledge of dangers over many miles past, lingered on his face.

He was right. We were back in Suva for lunch. It's always good to get back to the boat. There had been some excitement while we were gone. A barge had broken loose from its mooring. It was the one that was a couple hundred yards from the *Osprey*. It had gone right through the yacht anchorage of the Club, with yachts scrambling to get out of the way.

We heard of a wife alone on a boat who saw this thing coming at her. Although not accustomed to handling the boat, she started the engine and ran the boat off at 90 degrees to the end of her anchor chain as the barge went by; and off the other direction when it came back again. Well done!

Not all the yachts were so fortunate, but the damages were surprisingly little as the speed of the barge had been slow enough to just push them aside. The *Osprey* fortunately was not threatened. Even though we had people "keeping an eye on the boat" for us, we always know that hazards cannot be totally avoided.

Another chapter of the voyage rests forever richly in our memories. It is a point in time always to be treasured. We thank you Emosi and Lanieta. You remain, as always, very treasured friends.

In Suva, we had met Jim and Lavina Ahkoy, who graciously invited us to their house several times and Jim visited us aboard the *Osprey*. We had met them at church as with so many of our subsequent friends. Lavina held the prestigious position of Clerk to the National Parliament and she took us on a personally guided tour of these chambers, where varnished mahogany presented an abundance of the patina to the dignity and history from ancient England who stands yet at this writing as protector of the beautiful Isles of Fiji.

Jim is in the import and export business and is endowed with political knowledge and influence. As I have mentioned before, one removes one's shoes upon entering a house. And the aid to their guests for doing so is brought to highest aplomb by the Ahkoys.

When entering their very modern house, one is presented into a foyer ten or twelve feet in width and perhaps twenty-some feet long. It is furnished exclusively by several fine mahogany wooden benches, each with intricate back rests. These benches are placed down each side of the foyer, whereby a number of guests arriving simultaneously may accommodate themselves in the simple process of removing their shoes.

The house is atop a hill overlooking Suva in a very pleasant and commanding area. Jim was amenable to satisfy my interest in the plush oriental carpet, which graced the entire foyer by getting on the floor with me and lifting the corner of this carpet, to improve the limits of my knowledge of this very practical art form. It was indeed a creation of exquisite beauty.

We began taking leave of our friends. Even after only three months of acquaintance, these lovely folks had taken us into their homes and into their lives. We are forever enriched by their kindness.

* * *

It had taken all of these three months to get the boat prepared for our next sail. The brief time that we were able to schedule the boatyard railway by which the *Osprey* was taken out of the water had not been quite long enough to get all of the top sides (the sides of the boat above the water line) entirely painted before we had to get back into the water. The Fijian worker certainly helped immensely more than his eighty cents per hour had cost us. But even

Chapter 14 Fiji

so, Peggy had to hold the dinghy off the side of the boat as I finished spreading white paint after launching. The boat always looks and feels good with fresh paint from her deck to her keel. Changing two of the turnbuckles of the standing rigging which hold the mast up was no problem while in the water. Also, I had seen a very small crack developing in the medal where the wire rigging entered these tightening devises. Another yachtsman had some extra terminals aboard, which he preferred to turn into some cash.

A number of boats had been leaving, though none of us try to sail together. Almost everybody was making toward New Zealand, as are we. Customs seemed just a little short of organized swiftness this time. Actually, it took us two or three days to get cleared. As with all countries, we were required to leave all guns with customs and receive them back upon departure. Well, this time, the key to the locked cabinet couldn't be found. It was determined that the man who had the key was the man who was taking some classes somewhere on the island and that someone would be sent to get it from him. However, that person never came back, although we had waited all day. This problem persisted through the weekend while the office was closed. There is absolutely no reason to think that anyone in the office wanted these guns and hoped that we would leave without them. No office functions without mishap and in the fullness of time the key was found, though not in time for us to get underway for NZ that day either. This was not a problem. We could simply spend a night at anchor at Kandavu Island, which put us in an excellent place for an early departure. However, we didn't leave until five that evening, due to waiting for the wind to shift out of the south.

CHAPTER 15

 A SOUTH PACIFIC STORM

We were poised at Kandavu, on the Great Astrolabe Reef of Fiji, waiting for favorable wind to begin the sail to New Zealand.

At 4 PM of the third day I noticed a change in the wind direction. By 5 o'clock I could feel a breeze in the anchorage from the east. By 5:30 we were underway and for three glorious days the east wind held fresh and we were averaging eight knots for most of the time, which for us is flying.

About midnight of the third day the main and genny had to come down. It looked as though the weather was going to get heavier, so with only four hours till dawn I put up only the working jib and went back for some needed sleep. By morning, instead of having gotten heavier, the wind was very light and although we could have made one or two knots I wanted more speed because it looked as though we could make NZ between storms.

We have amateur radio aboard. And there is a wonderful group of people concerned for the safe passage of yachts from Fiji to NZ who come on the radio each day at 2100 hours Greenwich time, inquiring about the sea conditions, weather, course and speed and position of those at sea. Tony is in NZ, Bruce is in Australia, Joyce is in the Solomon's, and John is on Norfolk Island. Other land-based stations also assist, including Jim, but these were the main four. With changing atmospheric conditions causing interruptions of communications within certain distances, someone is always able to make contact by virtue of this spread of locations.

Chapter 15 — A South Pacific Storm

John, on Norfolk Island, is the weatherman. Weather has been a study of his for over twenty years of note-keeping regarding cloud formations and weather changes, etc., and he daily receives numerous weather forecasts via Morse code and voice radio. He draws detailed weather charts sometimes several times a day, and by inquiring about a specific yacht's position, he is able to tell the skipper that there is a low traveling toward him which is causing his heavy weather; and that it is traveling ESE at ten knots, as an illustration; with winds of forty to fifty knots, 200 miles from its center at present position X and that it is at 995 millibars; and that it's rising or falling; that the winds will be SE and go through E to N; and that the center of the low will have passed him when the winds go NW to W; and that he should get heavy rains with the wind shift of NW; and etc.

What I've described is the normal occurrence of a low passing south of you in the Southern Hemisphere, but to be able to know when to hurry up and when to wait to let a low pass with its winds below you when you're traveling southward is a wonderful thing.

The trouble is that conditions can change very quickly, and good plans oft time "gang a glee" as the ancient expression states.

We had been hearing on the radio about all of our friends getting pounded with heavy weather, with much gear failure, sails shredded, sails in sailbags lost overboard, seas breaking loose things tied on deck, etc.

It seemed to me that the summer to the south was late in coming, and that was easy to learn by general short wave radio broadcast. But the summer had only just arrived in Fiji a week before we left. However, I didn't know how long it may have been hot in the cyclone producing areas, so I was getting uneasy about staying much longer; which is why, when conditions seemed to be eased somewhat around NZ, and the East wind came to Fiji, we were off.

And now, when I heard John say that a huge high was coming off Australia and into the Tasman Sea, and that this was the first appearance of the typical summer high, I was delighted and decided to move along rapidly in the light air with the aid of our Iron Square Sail (our engine), since we had sufficient fuel. I wanted to avoid the development of another low.

On the 18th of November we had rain in the early part of the day, followed by poor visibility of perhaps a mile, with occasional rains. At six PM the storm came. This lovely huge high had taken an opposite partner and we were in for an interruption of our progress toward NZ. We were between a high to the west of us and a low which had been building to the east. Both were throwing wind from the south. Remember, the highs and lows turn in opposite directions in the southern hemisphere than they do in the north.

We knew from John that there were winds in the forty to fifty knot range, dependent upon our area, and when the temperature is down, we knew that a cold southerly wind would be much stronger than the lovely tropical trade wind breezes that we've been enjoying for so long now. A given velocity of cold wind is much heavier than the same velocity of warm wind. There are more molecules in it, strange as that may sound at first hearing.

The storm was fully upon us now. I decided to first lay a hull, and see if we could abide the roll. Our sails are getting weaker all the time. Even though we had our Egyptian cotton jibs re-stitched in Fiji; one of which is our storm jib, the larger one had already torn its batten pockets and 2 or 3 hank fastenings along the wire luff a couple days earlier. So until we were heavily boarded by a sea, I was content to try to keep from losing our southing by just laying a hull. To run before a storm of this strength has the danger of pitch-poling, by which a vessel's speed down the face of a wave is so great that her bow buries in the troth and the oncoming wave throws the stern over you, leaving you upside down. To let the ship make her own way through the seas would be the path of least resistance, and hence the easiest on her. The discomfort wasn't too bad.

Peggy did get airborne on her bunk as the boat snap rolled in the troth and crest of the waves, since her side was to leeward as of course, we primarily lay beam to the wind and seas. This means that the boat met all seas along her side, not with either her bow or stern. Wind gusts were likely well over sixty knots by now, and since the storm had chosen our area as a favorite playground for awhile now, the waves had become mountainous.

During the 19th, while in the cockpit, I managed to be thrown into the compass and broke it off of its pedestal. It used to stand in a binnacle in the center of the cockpit well, and had a frame over it with glass windows in the old style. Everything except the bronze pipe which was its stand hit the deck; the cover with its multiple glass windows, the compass with its light wires severed, the compass housing, and I. Several windows of the binnacle were broken but the compass with its glass globe was not. We have a hand bearing compass bought from the owners of a pirated and then shipwrecked yacht which we could have used although with difficulty due to its small card. So we could read a course with it. We also have a very heavy old bronze gimbaling overhead compass which swings over my pillow and is made to read from underneath, but is not ideal for the helmsman. So although we could have made out all right, it was very nice to see that the main ship's compass itself was not broken.

Earlier in the day, but not associated with the storm, our main cooking stove of pressurized kerosene gave up due to an air leak in the tank. These not being conditions to attempt repairs, I simply brought out our "Sea Swing" stove a little earlier than necessary.

Conditions were shortly to worsen, which would have disabled our regular stove from use anyway. We have a small copper pot with a lid and also a small iron frying pan selected specifically for this stove. Such a stove is specifically designed for use in extreme conditions. It accommodates the boat's roll as well as its violent pitching as under conditions which were developing. This one burner stove swings freely in all directions. So regardless of the unladylike behavior of the boat, the stove stays level. Hunger still rules our lives even though our regular stove is useless. We have the coal stove available for use since we carry 300 pounds of coal, but even with rails around the edge to keep the pans on the stove, we would not have been able to keep the food in the pans due to the wild motion in this seaway. Later on though, we were glad to have the coal stove available to warm up the boat and ourselves.

In the afternoon I noticed the long rope tail of the cleated, port jib sheet over the side. I tried to pull it in but it wouldn't come back aboard. As I looked over the side I couldn't tell if it was in the propeller or possibly had jammed itself between the rudder and the hull. So I attached a long boat hook around the sheet in a way which permitted it to slide on the line and yet remain in contact; shoved the pole down and below the level of the problem, thereby pulling at a different angle. It didn't work, so I went below and told Peggy that I'd have to go over the side to release it. Her sensible imploring, however, and a second look at the seas, postponed that activity. It's amazing in retrospect that as one is busy aboard, one doesn't constantly gaze mesmerized at the seas. The wind was gusting toward perhaps sixty knots or more now, and the seas certainly looked like it as I have now reviewed the photographs of the Beaufort Scale of Sea Conditions as taken from naval vessels. I'd be hard pressed to estimate the wave heights other than by the *Beaufort Scale*, and although not frightening, they were certainly very impressive. As a matter of fact, I remember not wanting to stay above decks unless I was doing something. I seemed to have a suppressed feeling that the spectacle had the capacity to adversely detract my mind from the tasks at hand and from my favorite game of "what if." I always try to be a few steps ahead of the present, so that reactions can be smooth and swift if required. As you can hear in your mind, the sound of the storm as it blasts the sea and the boat and you, the storm shouts with an impolite voice which shrieks in anger, while below by contrast, it was like being in a cathedral—the sounds were so much muffled.

We were boarded by a wave.

According to *"Weather for the Mariner"* by William J. Kotsch, Capt. US Navy, winds of fifty knots for thirty hours produce waves of fifty feet. The sea photos in this book of winds of fifty knots look like our seas, and radio John now gave sustained winds of fifty knots, so although there was gusting, fifty seems to have been the norm and seas of fifty feet the size of the top floor of a six story building could have been the case. And even if the winds were sustained at forty-some knots, with seas of plus forty-something, I could not possibly guess other than by an approximation as compared to what the Navy photo shows.

It didn't seem that we were fiercely boarded, although we took water into the house through the closed main hatch as the *Osprey* was pressed entirely under water, it was by no means a damaging blow. It seemed almost gently that we were curled over by an approaching sea as we disappeared briefly from the earth. As we went under, I had been lying on my bunk and came up instantly to a standing position forward of the companion ladder. Everything moved in what seemed very slow motion as the senses went into automatic fast mode. My first attention went to the ports [windows]. On the lee side I was looking straight down into the very deep dark blue of the South Pacific Ocean. The upper side was covered by what may have only been a few fathoms of lighter blue of the sea.

The *Osprey* refused to linger long in this submerged world, and thrust her mast threateningly at Neptune on the way up, but even with this warning to Neptune that such behavior was not to be tolerated, I decided that it was time to put up the storm jib and start running northward away from the storm.

When I got on deck however, and saw that the wave condition had not in the least changed, and that there was still a good distance between them, and that they were still very full bodied with great areas to the tops of them, and that although the wind was bending some of the tops of them over, there was little real dangerous breaking. In fact most of the wind-born water seemed to be in streaks across the face of the waves, which is understandable when you consider that the surface of the ocean is being hurled up and dropped back down by each wave which seems to suck the airborne water down the face of the wave. I came back below, and we were not hugely boarded again.

On the 20th at 5 AM I put up the reefed main to slow her roll and got ready to go over the side. The waves were down surely to half size, and with appropriate precautions, the job of retrieving the jib sheet could be done in acceptable safety.

I have a wet suit aboard. Without it, a very real danger of shock from temperature loss was an unwanted possibility. At least I had considered the possibility, by putting my hand and arm into a pail of seawater to test for that very thing, confirming why I had decided the need for the wet suit. I could not know how long I may need to be over the side.

A few years had passed since I had worn this wet suit. And it seemed to have gotten considerably smaller during these years. Surely, it was not I who had increased in girth! "Look at this thing Peggy. It's shrunk!" Peggy had told me where it was stowed, and as she held the pants up to me with merriment sparkling in her eyes, I said, "It will stretch!" But what she heard was more the sound of hope than certainty, and we both started to laugh. I suggested corn starch to help my legs to slide into these pants which were somewhat like farmer's overalls in that they extended all the way up to cover the chest and even the back, using shoulder straps to hold the whole thing up. In this case, however, falling off was not remotely part of the equation. My legs were being generously "floured" by white powder, six inches at a time by Peggy as I was trying desperately to breathe between my laughter and my pulling exertion. By this time I was on the floor! We were both laughing our heads off as we both were rolling around, since Peggy had lost her balance and fallen on top of me, cornstarch and all! And for a while laughter was louder than the remnants of the outside storm. And we surrendered our senses to the gay abandon of hilarious literal rolling on the floor; tears in the eyes, howling, belly-aching, exhausting, joyous carefree laughter, that shook us from the soles of our feet to the depth of our being. There is glory in such abandon.

In the end, the cornstarch, what was left of it, didn't work. The rubber wet suit must have shrunk terribly. Eventually, I was very, very glad to find myself inside this thing, after prior rolling the pants inside out and pushing the pants on from ankles up like the reverse of peeling a banana. After the effort, I was warm enough that I almost looked forward to going over board.

We took the mask and snorkel into the cockpit, put on my harness used for heavy weather on deck work; attached a ½ inch diameter nylon line to it, belayed the line to a stout cockpit cleat, and Peggy put some turns on the sheet winch. She was gently instructed to keep the excess on board so that I wouldn't get entangled. A knife and screwdriver were put in easy access for Peggy to hand to me on request. I put on the wet suit hood over my head;

mask, fins and snorkel were next and overboard I went—braced for the first cold water shock.

The wet suit is just that; wet, and your body heat warms this non circulating water which is held within the porous structure of the suit. It is the non-circulating water barrier which keeps you warm. But the first water that hits you is not benefited by any such temperature effect. The body must first warm the water that enters against you and is retained by the sponge-like composition of the wet suit.

Breathing was a little difficult though, because the hood's opening for the face left insufficient space for the mask and snorkel. My full beard may have added some additional difficulty. And if I had the mask over the hood in one area, and on the face elsewhere, the water could not be kept out of the mask due to the edge of the mask having no contact for a short distance between face and hood, and I wouldn't be able to see. So the mask was constantly busy trying to push the snorkel out of my mouth. I was tempted to do without the snorkel but there was so much water motion that I felt that I should try to keep that added elevation for air. It was just another part of the comedy, and I wasn't concerned about it.

So let's take a look at what we've got. By this time the sun was well up, visibility underwater was great and I could see several turns around the prop and then several around the rudder shaft.

The biggest problem was the motion of the boat. I could see that I'd have to dash in while she was down by the stern and work while she was rising; then get out of the way before she crashed down again. It was necessary for me to keep my left arm stiffly against the hull above me. When the boat dropped down, it came very fast and by having the boat stiff-armed away from me when she came down, I would be shot back out of the way rather like a pea from a pod. The mainsail was helping the roll but the bow and stern pitch motion was still violent. At least she wasn't rolling much at all at the propeller level which may have been close to the pivot point and the waves were about fourteen seconds apart, so there was some working time between dodging.

The job was done with reasonable dispatch and without prying with screwdriver or cuttings with the knife. Getting back aboard was done with some small aplomb. I hope that I might be forgiven for voicing a genuine small smile of pleasure in executing this little timing maneuver. Perhaps we should not feel guilty over taking these little pleasures as we find them. The boat was rolling. I was in the water. And as she rolled her starboard deck into the water, I was lucky enough to get the timing just right. I simply rolled onto the submerged deck and the boat brought me up to see Peggy's anxious expression change to a grin which matched my own. Peggy was very quick to have brought that misbehaving jib sheet aboard. And she also seemed flatteringly pleased to have me back. That long sheet [rope] had been securely coiled in the cockpit well, but a wave had reached in there and washed it overboard. Luckily such unusual sea conditions are once in a lifetime experiences for such as we, so although a lesson was learned here, I trust to not find application of it in future, whereas you may.

The compass was the next job that needed consideration. So, after a good breakfast (or perhaps I should modify the word good, since Peggy lets me do the cooking at sea) even so, it seemed especially good to me somehow, as I used the one pot, one burner stove which can swing in 360 degrees. I had it mounted just above shoulder height on the forward end of the centerboard bulkhead where it would do no harm to itself nor to us in passing. I am usually hungry at sea, and this morning was no exception.

After breakfast it was time to go to work again. The work went well. The compass was retrieved out of the top-loading icebox where it had slept well, wrapped in its blanket. The frame, which had held the glass windows, was removed. The housing and standpipe were drilled and bolted together with non-ferrous bolts so as not to affect the compass. The compass was secured in its housing, backwards at first, which only would have meant that the light would have shined on the wrong area when the job was completed. The compass was turned 180 degrees before I went any further.

I decided to not work on the wiring for the compass light, thinking that with the windvane steering the boat, we would not be in the cockpit enough to warrant the work, thinking that a flashlight would suffice when necessary. That turned out to be incorrect.

The windvane was broken. A wave had apparently struck it from the side and forced the servo pendulum gear beyond its designed limit of swing. The teeth of the servo pendulum rudder were no longer engaged to the teeth of the windvane and I could not reengage it. There is an adjustment to permit this, but that hasn't worked since Panama.

So it meant that I had to climb out of the boat, and onto the small platform aft of the transom, which is also aft of the windvane, where the solar panel for charging the batteries lives. There is something foreign about getting out of one's boat at sea. Doing so in less than gentle conditions seems to not detract from that strangeness.

But this time I was suspended over the water instead of in it, except when the boat came down hard by the stern. Then most of the time, only my legs were in the water, and I never went down more deeply than my waist. Entertaining as this may have been, I had work to do out there to reengage the windvane parts.

I had to remove some circlips with a special tool; disassemble one section; engage the teeth of the gears in proper sequence by holding the windvane blade's teeth of the gears in that sequence, while holding the windvane blade in one position with one hand, and pushing the servo pendulum with one foot; while turning part of the disassembled section with one hand, and holding on to the bottom of the two-foot square platform with one leg, while sitting on that slippery wet Plexiglas cover of the solar panel. But I was wearing a safety harness with its line attached to the boat, so there never was any real danger in the exercise.

Years ago, I had tied knots in the harness line to enhance my ability to pull myself back to the boat against her speed through the water. The climb outboard to work on the windvane and the climb back again has been made so many times in the past that I can do it blindfolded. This does not attest to any great skill on my part at all. It's just that the windvane has aged considerably on this trip and requires very regular TLC, so I've been there before. The only reason for mentioning it at all is to share the activities with you in a way which does not give an undo impression of danger.

The ship's wheel, however, was very hard to turn. And had it been necessary for me to have cut the jib sheet off the rudder post instead of having untangled it, I would have suspected the possibility of some piece still being jammed in there. But this not being the case, I spent quite some time with the bolts of the various parts of the super heavy duty Edson worm gear steering. I was trying to assure that forces of the sea motion on the rudder had not perhaps applied such jarring action on the steering gear as to have caused a general misalignment of the worm gears. No success resulted and the steering of the boat was still just as hard. It seemed that the only remaining possibility was the bending of the enormous rudder shaft itself. For, alas, my attempts at solving this problem by adjustments and applications of grease were totally unsuccessful.

When we got underway at 8 AM November 20, the windvane could not handle the job of turning the wheel, and although the very heavy duty drive motor of the Cetrek auto pilot tried valiantly, it too gave up. We were on our own.

Peggy, who until now has been spared this work, was left at the helm on the 21st from 4:30 AM to 11 AM and again from 1 PM to 5 PM and again from 8:30 to 11 PM. During this time I did whatever was necessary for food, radio contacts and glorious sleep. It was tough work for her with the wheel so hard to turn, and I have nothing but praise for her determined performance. All other times, I steered.

She only called me up out of my sleep once, and then with just enough of a sound of stark fear in her voice to send me on deck in one leap.

The boat was over powered. Well actually, we had been getting a gradual wind shift. We had been close hauled on a port tack and the wind was backing. All that was necessary was to ease the sheets of the genny and main, and having done so, Peggy finished her watch without undue apprehensions.

On the 22nd Peggy steered from 4:30-6:45 AM (as you can see by these precise times, Peggy was keeping record), I removed the chain from the auto drive motor that goes to the steering shaft, in the thought that if burned out it could be causing a drag on the steering, but this was not the case either. I again reattached the linkage of the windvane in another attempt at its talents, with no better results than before. During all of these additional problems and labor, spirits were by no means adversely affected. That afternoon, while Peggy was steering, she gave out a loud shriek followed by laughter. I found a foot-long Flying Fish thrashing about in the cockpit seat beside her which she had seen coming at her from the far side of the boat, almost hitting her in flight.

Well, the shriek brought me up like a shot, and I heard the laughter in mid air, so I knew before arrival that all was well. I gently helped the fellow complete his flight plan, and briefly joined Peggy in her merriment. Most of our Flying Fish had been smaller than this one. It is amazing that these fellows have been found as high as thirty feet above the water line on commercial ships, all done by those huge gliding wings called pectoral fins.

We had gotten our latitude from a sun shot the day after the storm, but nothing since. So when Peggy saw a light, she could not wait till the end of her watch to share it with me. She in fact thought it to be a masthead light of friends whom we knew to be in this crossing with us somewhere. The *Cats Paw* also has amateur radio aboard, so we could have called them. But it was better than that. It was a lighthouse on the New Zealand shore. And four hours later, at 3 AM, 23 November 1981, I put the good ship *Osprey* on a few tacks back and forth across the mouth of a bay until dawn enabled our seeing the way in. We had heard by radio that the light characteristics had been changed for the light at the Bay of Islands which was our destination, but since it had a thirty-mile visibility, and north and south of it were lights of only ten and fifteen-mile visibility, and since we could see no other light, I thought that we had arrived. Although we had a chart for this bay with only one hazard in it which we could avoid in the dark, it is not my practice to enter till day light. So I tacked her back and forth, readying her for entry by setting her ensign at the mainsail leech, the New Zealand flag to the starboard spreader, and the

"Q" flag to port. But we weren't half way in before I became suspicious that perhaps we were not at the Bay of Islands at all, and I headed for a twenty-five-foot local fishing boat tending his nets close ashore. By this time it was obvious that we were not at our port of entry and the pleasant fisherman informed us that we were about ten miles north of our destination.

The wind was now coming lighter all the time, and we motored through the Cavalli Islands into the Bay of Islands, finding New Zealand's rocky shore and land mass much like the coast of Maine in the USA, or was it just the joy of remembrances of quiet peaceful rest that made these shores look familiar, the look of home. Perhaps here lies one of the many reasons why yachtsmen like New Zealand so much. If so, it is but one of many other reasons, born of New Zealand's many charms.

There was a thrill on this crossing which I hope always to remember. For if it took this storm and its discomforts to bring that memory which remains thereby always available to our recollection, it is a price gladly paid. Because, just before this storm struck, I had shouted, "Peggy, albatross!"

Huge, gigantic, regal, majestic, magnificent, all bright white with a little contrasting black on the wings, sailed the royal albatross of the great Southern Ocean! Gliding toward us ten feet above the waves; he stayed quite awhile with us, never seeming to move a feather; sailing off to port several hundred yards and back again, passing perhaps twenty feet from us and then on to starboard of the great ship *Osprey*. What a sight!! What a joy!

We were to see ten albatross on the trip and two different species of them, with wing spans of well over ten feet. No other creature on earth can equal his flight; an indescribable thrill can still travel up and down my spine as effortlessly as he made his endless passage just out of the reach of that great ocean who stretches herself southward to feel the cold frozen face of Antarctica itself.

And here, closer to land, we saw the beautiful yellow-headed blue-footed boobies. They dive head first into the water to catch their fish. And they do it with mesmerizing grace.

Once in the bay area, we came across many flocks of hundreds of small black surface diving birds that swim after their fish, and we saw yet another type, one of which wasn't able to get airborne again after the catch which he intends to take home. The fish was bigger than he was. We laughed.

We had not been fishing since leaving Kandavu where we caught our largest Dorado to date. We know the sex of this fish by the different shape of the head.

Perhaps one last impression that still lingers with me about this passage might be shared with you. Upon our securing to the commercial pier at Opua in the Bay of Islands, as required for our entry formalities, an agriculture official left a form for us to fill out, listing certain types of food stuff, and went on to carefully explain that the quantity by size was also necessary to be stated on the form.

Apparently finding us of normal intellect, he went on for sometime talking about how so many people will only say "six tins of beef," which could be of any size whatsoever, and it was a totally amazing and baffling thing to him how people could be so stupid. And yet it happened time and time again.

The list was completed when he returned in an hour or so, and he was incredulous over my having done the very same thing with fish.

He gave it back to me and I only muttered something or other and I corrected it.

I didn't try to explain to him that we were in fact going around in a state of only partial awareness, and that our senses were already beginning to lapse into rest; like some storm-tossed frail bird, staggering to the edge of a fresh water puddle and there to swallow but once; and then as though by some force outside of itself, turn to that mystic, marvelous state, called sleep; for I felt myself akin to such a small creature as this, as though now perched safely on a ledge. My head was drooping downward, my feathers were drenched and bedraggled by the storm; and though awake, part of me already slept.

What a wondrous voyage it was.

***

We were officially entered and welcomed to the storied isles of New Zealand, where white sheep speckle the green grassy hills, and where its south island reaches farther south than Africa's Cape of Good Hope.

The grin that plastered our faces was much more for the anticipation of adventures yet to savor in this new land than the satisfactions of another great voyage completed. All of the days of magic granted to us by the good ship *Osprey* are forever a part of our persons. But grins, joyous as they are, can face a pause. "Our sincerest laughter with some pain is fraught."

Still grinning, we started our engine, took aboard our dock lines as we yelled to friends where we were going to be anchoring, put the gear in reverse to back away, and nothing happened. I tried the forward gear, and nothing happened. So now, with a different kind of grin, I heaved a line back up to the dock where someone was still standing and called out, "Hey, I've just lost my transmission. I need a tow to the anchorage!" And in just about as much time as it takes to tell you about this, we were off again.

Perhaps a quarter of a mile away was the anchorage of the area, adjacent to which is the Deming's Boat Yard, at which I was about to begin a wonderful and prolonged acquaintance.

After the tow, and after getting anchored, I launched the dinghy and rowed ashore to arrange for a rescue of the *Osprey*'s innermost self. I had assumed a linkage had uncoupled. But influenced by the availability of mechanical expertise virtually at the door, plus my discovery learned over the years now, that I really am not a mechanic after all; very happily I headed for the marina.

There was a close and still water beach area to land the dinghy. I brought the bow to the sand, stepped out with the little two-pound Danforth anchor and pressed it into the sand. The anchor line as always was properly secured to the dinghy. I wore short pants and no shoes as I had stepped out of the dink and had gotten wet up to about my knees, which I picture for you because I had looked all about for what I thought would be something like small "sea nettles," because something was stinging my wet feet and legs. Sea nettles are little jellyfish characters who, dependent on size, can cause a stinging sensation to the skin.

The water, however, was absolutely clear as from a drinking fountain, and I saw nothing. Ashore, I washed my legs off from a fresh water faucet. The water was cold. I washed well above my knees and now everything which I had gotten wet was stinging. This was strange, but not unduly painful at all, so I went on to find the marina boss. His name is Les. And we were to become great friends.

I told him the problem; we got the *Osprey* up against the wall of the marina where it could be secured and Les stepped on deck directly from the marina building. Boats can be stood on this grid to be worked on below the water line as the tide goes out, but a railway is also here by which boats can be brought up for longer service.

I liked everything I had seen here and had an instant affinity with Les. The grin was back until I washed my hands with water from the *Osprey*'s tank and instantly had my hands and arms tingling with that stinging sensation which I had felt on my legs. Now this is too strange to not have some meaning.

So out came the medico books and there it was. I had ciguatera poisoning. On the underside of certain coral reef plant leaves, attaches certain biflagellate which are poisonous to fish. Small fish may eat small quantities of these leaves. The problem is that the poison is not eliminated. It stays stored in the tissue. The bigger fish eat the smaller ones and become carriers. I had eaten a really large amount of a really large fish caught in Fiji before leaving. A serious problem arises here, because this is the cause of many islanders having died from this poisoning.

Happily, I was no longer in an area where ciguatera poison flourishes. It only occurs in tropical waters and on certain reef plants. And on a given reef extending past several villages, only one small area may be infected leaving the rest of the reef completely free. The reef inhabitants have very defined territory around their "home" and the poison problem is very localized accordingly.

In the fullness of time, the symptoms declined and I stayed away from fish shipped in to NZ, which were large in size and therefore had the possibility of danger. Even now, I think myself to be poisonous to others who might be inhabiting a lifeboat with me. There seems always to be a silver lining if we search for it.

The coupling problem was readily repaired and life returned to normal, which included visits back and forth with old and new friends afloat and new friends yet unmet ashore. We had been met at the dock by Jim Morgan, one of the amateur radio operators who had faithfully watched over us sailing yachtsmen at sea. And we were delighted to learn that he and his good wife Sylvia lived just up the hill from the boatyard. They welcomed us into their home for fascinating conversations going all the way back to the Second World War when Clair was engaged by England's MI 5.

Les invited us to come to his house which adjoined the boatyard, where we had the delight of meeting Silvia his lovely wife. We guessed the house to predate the boatyard and was wonderfully charming in every way. But we could never have guessed that others occupied the premises as well.

Both Les and Silvia took great enjoyment from our surprise as they revealed the "others" by lifting a previously loosened floor plank. An entire small colony of penguins returns each year to reside there. An occurrence determined by perhaps eons of uninterrupted time which may have predated the house, or even predated anyone's first foot step upon this small island out from a place now called Opua, in the land of New Zealand.

We were enthralled. And Les took my suggestion about cutting some planks away and covering an area a foot or so square with Plexiglas, and hiding the light from them by use of a small carpet if it wouldn't create a hazard of slipperiness to walk over. That way the Fairy Penguins could be shown to friends while also retaining that special aroma to their own area below the house.

Chapter 15 — A South Pacific Storm

* * *

We asked our way to church and were immediately inundated with questions about our sailing. We were fascinated subsequently to learn that it seems that absolutely everyone in the entire country of New Zealand either owns a boat, or is looking to buy a boat, or is in the process of selling one.

We were in our element and one couple of those wanting to see the *Osprey*, let us stumble upon the fact that they would be most pleased to accept a weekend invitation to sail with us from Opua to Whangaroa the following weekend. We were delighted!

The wind was fresh but I felt it not enough to be concerning to our guests, but it was enough to create sufficient lumps upon these waters to have Peggy choose her bunk as we were tacking our way out toward the head of the bay.

I had up a full main and regular genoa as the *Osprey* put her lee deck into the water a few times as we went to windward. A few more hours of this passed when our event occurred. And this one was a doozy.

As I came out of the cockpit and passed the open companionway, I said in no more than a conversationally volumed voice, "Peggy, we've broken the mast."

"What?" I repeated it more loudly since I was farther away, and she was instantly on deck with all ill feelings of seasickness totally gone!

The upper ten feet or so had broken off the mast and was dangling on deck with everything attached; all sails and standing rigging. The rest of the mast remained in place due to the lower shrouds.

In no hurry whatsoever, I brought down the rest of the main, gathered up the sails and rigging, secured all lines, and started the engine. And just that quickly we had become a motorboat, having given our guests an almost dramatic experience aboard a US flagged sailing yacht, apparently "done in" by a little New Zealand breeze.

They were good sports about our change of plans for the weekend and became great friends with whom we were to share other and more completed adventures. The motoring back to Deeming's Boat Yard was uneventful, but the dismasting sent ripples of shock through the foreign yachts visiting New Zealand that year.

The first thing that I did was to write an urgent letter to my authority on all matters regarding yacht design. His good name is Ed Cutts, of Cutts and Case boatyard. And yes, the name Case is in recognition of the great company making Case farm equipment who was an owner of the boatyard with Ed Cutts. Ed in turn is famous for his designs but less known as having been a prodigy of the super famous yacht designer, L. Frances Herreshoff, whom I hold in near reverence.

I told Ed about the most idyllic dismasting in history. I told him why I thought the mast had come down. And I asked him how much longer I could make the mast for more power without making her tender.

I told him that all of the sails were being worn out and that while in Fiji I had found two swaged rigging terminals getting their first small crack in the upper portion of the swage end where the wire enters, and had bought some "Staylock" terminals as replacements. I had become a great fan of the Staylocks and made up a replacement rigging length equal to the longest length aboard to care for an emergency rigging in the event of a failure at sea. Were such a failure to have been in a shorter wire, one of the terminals needed only to be unattached with wrenches and after cutting the wire to the required length the Staylock terminal is simply reattached. The great thing about these terminals is that they are fitted to the wire with simple wrenches, unlike swage terminals, which require special press equipment. I was ready to change all of the rigging, so let's change the mast length as well.

The *Osprey* was designed by Ralph Wiley while he was owner of the boatyard. The person for whom the boat was built happened to be commodore of a prestigious California yacht club, whose financial capacities enabled him to be very exacting about his requirement for the boat. And although this particular requirement resulted in our dismasting, other requirements gave us many years of pleasure, such as the seven-foot length of our bunks; the wonderful and efficient crystal glasses cabinet which never broke even a stemware, the excellent chart locker, stainless steel coal stove and coal bin, etc.

The *Osprey*, her original name, was to be sailed to the Netherlands where his relatives resided, and in order to accommodate ducking under the canal bridges, he wanted to be able to lower the mast without cranes or assistance, wherefore the upper section of the mast was tapered considerably to lessen its weight.

The mast had one set of spreaders. And though I failed to notice what was happening to the mast between the masthead and the spreader in the area where no support is given to a mast, the fact that Peggy was being slightly airborne with each roll of the boat at the trough and crest of each wave's passing, meant that the mast was being snapped back and forth much more wildly due to the fulcrum effect of being so much farther from the point of roll than where we lay.

Therefore, the hollow box construction of the wooden mast was entirely capable of coming down at sea, a great distance from New Zealand, instead of at her door step. Life is good!

Ed Cutts calculated that she should not take more than an additional two and one half feet before the risk of becoming tender, and offered to make up the planks and mast head fitting, etc. and put it all on a ship for New Zealand. But I declined that part of his offer, telling him that I was at a boatyard and that we could proceed with the rebuilding.

I was disappointed in the two and a half feet limit. I wanted six to ten feet! But it's somewhat counter productive to ask for advice only to ignore it, so two and a half feet it shall be!

While I had been waiting for Ed Cutt's response to my letter, I told good Max Deeming, the owner of the boat yard, that I had written to Ed asking his advice, and he immediately told me about a renowned New Zealand yacht designer who was just moving into the neighborhood and suggested that I should go and talk to him as well.

John Spencer turned out to be a great guy and happy to talk boats. He was building a house a quarter mile away from the boatyard and doing most of it himself. I especially liked the sink which he made for his bathroom. It was beautifully made of wood laminations and varnished to that lovely state of glory which when seen graces our faces with the smile of approval that also soothes our souls.

Although the house wasn't completed yet, he was living in it very comfortably, and he permitted my giving him a casual hand in the building process. Before I knew it, a regular routine had established itself. I was helping him with the construction, Peggy was cooking meals for us, and John happily let Peggy use his automatic clothes washing machine. We had no such luxury on the boat.

Peggy has joined many local native women at their river locations for the rituals of scrubbing and rinsing of clothes in various parts of the world. It's all just part of the great romance of sailing to remote and pictorial island paradises, he says with tongue in cheek. She loves automatic clothes washers, although she grew up with a ringer washing machine in the tobacco country of North Carolina. She has quite an affinity with clothes dryers as well.

And if I were able to supply these, I would love for her to enjoy that special part of modern living. Is that what that guy was talking about when he said something about there being no free lunch? I'll have to think about that one.

"John, you know what I think is the most beautiful of all sailing rigs – the schooner."

"I could design a schooner rig for you if you want me to."

And I knew he could, but this boat has yet to sail us the next half way around the world, and as much as I love the look of a schooner rig, a modern narrow-hulled boat like the *Osprey* is more efficient as a sloop. But it's always fun to dream a bit, even though it may not always be about practicality. After all, we are realists aren't we, not romanticists, aren't we? I haven't figured that out yet.

I do, however, know what caused the doors of New Zealand to be opened so widely to welcome us. It is because that's just the way these lovely folks are found to be, with open arms and open hearts. To this day we are honored to list many as friends with whom we still remain in contact, in fact, just moments ago, while writing this page to you, Jim Morgan sent an email to us.

It's a beautiful land. The North Island's rolling hills, green and distinct in the Southern Ocean's bright blue, are alive with the rich wool of hundreds of thousands of sheep! What a sight. Like the mid-ocean sky on a moonless night when countless white specks make the darkness of the sky all but disappear; even so do the sheep almost mask the green of the hills of New Zealand.

It was great fun getting acquainted with the people at church. Someone was good enough to pick us up with their car each week and after diner with one group or other of them, deliver us back again. Our friends Ruth and Neville started taking us around the area. How lovely it is.

We were a bit surprised to find that some roads, though with two way traffic, have only one lane. This was not a particular problem; however, because a pull off section is provided in strategic locations, into which one or the other vehicle can enter, thereby permitting an otherwise unimpeded flow of traffic. Also very commendably, New Zealanders in general take excellent care of their cars, as evidenced by the average age of the national population of vehicles.

Les and Betty were good friends of Ruth and Neville. They were dairy farmers with whom we found ourselves also enjoying time and food and talk and fun. The fun included some effort on the part of the three gentlemen of our group with shovels in our hands as we repaired a dam on Les' property one day. And although I have had limited experience at sea with a shovel, camaraderie is fun in any setting.

***

We made an offer to Ruth and Neville, the acceptance of which brought the entire country before our fascinated eyes and the cherished experience of our memory.

"Have you ever been to the fjords at the end of the South Island?"

"No."

"Well if you would like to take a car trip through the country, we will pay for the car expense and we can all have a leisurely trip to see the sights."

I also needed to find the proper quarter sawn wood planks for the mast rebuilding. This was found outside of Auckland. And the rest of the trip had adventure as its only title.

When you visit New Zealand, if you have even the most remote interest in sheep, do not fail to visit the *NZ Agrodome*. It is located in Rotorua at Riverside Park and although it was very interesting to see how the shepherds command their sheep dogs, inside the building are penned RAMS. I capitalize the word for emphasis, because mere words give small justice to these animals.

Little-boy-type lambsies they are most definitely not. These guys are endowed with the same attitude of dominant possession of all of the earth within their sight as the most pawing of the ground posturing of any bull anywhere, any time, whatsoever. These guys know who they are and what they are and go very much around not only declaring their ability, but performing it with my personal envy. One ram will service an entire flock of hundreds of females in a matter of a few days. His attention to duty is so dedicated that he will lose a huge quantity of weight during his exercise time and will ignore even his customary urge of hunger for food.

The shepherd will have harnessed the ram with a pouch containing a powdered temporary dye, which marks the ewes who have received service. Thereby, the farmer knows when the task of the ram is completed, and the ram is once again removed from temptation for the next year of contemplation to follow.

These rams in appearance have the look of graduates of something like the Arnold Schwarzenegger Body Builder's Club of New Zealand. I doff my cap to such as these. I am impressed!

* * *

We spent a pleasant couple of days at the church's annual "get together" of people around the country and in the local vernacular was *rapt* by the account of a missionary's story of an event which took place on a certain island in Papua New Guinea. Later in this writing, you will join me there.

Fjords have played about in my mind's eye since childhood. The massive stone walled chasms jutting straight upwards from the depth of the sea has always echoed one word within my brain — always the same word, "Wow," and so it was today in Milford Sound. Wow! What a sight.

We stood in the queue for our tickets. It was a sightseeing boat holding about fifty passengers. It took us over the deep cold blue water, along those steep grey walls of smooth rock, and to where jade in its green hues looked back at us. I hope that you enjoy the trip as much as we did when you visit there.

The Kea had done no damage to the car. These are green parrots living all the way down here, just 1030 miles from the South Pole. They are a bit naughty though. If someone is unfortunate enough to have left a car window open, they have been known to tear to shreds the seat covers and anything else they can get their strong beaks into.

Returning northward, we stopped again at Rotoruta for some soaking in their Hot Water Springs and later took an obligatory stop to see the Kiwi Bird, New Zealand's national identifier. But of even greater interest to Peggy and me were the chicks of the royal albatross on a spit of land at Taiaroa

Head, out from Dunedin; the only albatross colony in the world within the boundaries of a city.

It is indeed a very quiet spot, absolutely protected in every smallest detail by the Wildlife Service of NZ. I'm sure the albatross were here first. But it is a high badge of propriety that the great royal albatross who appear to only come ashore to rear their young, find that sufficient accommodation has been maintained by the people over the many years of their presence here, that these giants of the sphere just above the ocean's waves, remain confident in their return.

The museum here gives a very close look at an adult with wings stretched out over ten feet, as we have seen them in their magic motionless gliding over the sea. This one no longer owned that realm where in life he had been king.

But in an area away from the museum, stood a huge full-grown turkey! At least that was a brain cell's first attempt at identification, except that it was covered in thick down, somewhat light brown in color. This large turkey was an albatross chick! It was gigantic. At the end of about 100 days, the chicks down reaches five inches in length and is fed by his parents up to four pounds of food at one sitting.

Late in September, following lesser quantity of feedings over about ten days, the chick, now fully fledged, wanders from its nest to the ridge top, tests its outstretched wings, and eventually takes off with the aid of a strong wind.

His wandering over the oceans has begun, and perhaps, in the fullness of time, he may return to his birthplace, to found yet another generation of the Royals of Taiaroa.

Not far from here, we were delighted to watch the huge yellow-eyed penguins in their regal march of disdain to their surroundings. And the Southern fur seal population is happily beginning to increase its numbers in the last few decades, after the decimating hunts which nearly annihilated them. How wonderfully adaptive with under-water agility, is this air breathing character. Wouldn't it be a hoot to be as acrobatic under water as these seals? But then, I also want to soar as an albatross, but alas I can only sail about on their ocean and watch them. Not bad though, and any of us can do that!

When we returned to the *Osprey*, it was as though seeing a great good friend again after a long absence. And I am actually sure that it is our own smiles which were the cause of our thinking that she was smiling too. What a wondrous woman of the sea, is this creation who has reached up and grabbed a few fistfuls of wind and cast them behind her as she has thrust us across vast reaches of time and of place.

This fine ship, as all vessels, is referred to by the feminine gender. And as is the case with a good wife, she patiently and perpetually has been teaching me her preferences, which are much less complex than Peggy's.

The *Osprey* does not like saltwater filling her cockpit. I had enlarged the size of the cockpit self drainage system, but the heavy weather encountered on the way to New Zealand had certainly shown the ocean's ability to come aboard, to not put too fine a point on it.

In the case of our being entirely submerged by that exceedingly impolite wave, when the *Osprey* pounced back to the surface, she came up side-ways, but the weight of her keel rolled her upright with such speed of indignation that she hurled the water from her cockpit right back at the sea as she shook herself in the appropriate manner of any good sea dog.

On the other hand, had we been running before the wind, and hence the seas, and been boarded from aft, the cockpit would have been filled and perhaps not been relieved of this weight. If this were the case, she would have been pinned down by the stern and held there, resulting in the cockpit not draining at all, due to one ocean looking at another ocean on a horizontal plane.

So if such were a possibility, the best thing to do would be to keep the cockpit protected from the sea. There are seamanly options of handling heavy weather sailing. However, if too much sail is carried, one can be pitch-polled if caught by a rogue wave and thrust forward with too much speed.

Another obvious solution is to reduce the cockpit size. The *Osprey* has a larger than usual cockpit well and long seating which has been a joy of comfortable sleeping while on watch due to being able to stretch out on the seats whose width also afforded the luxury of space.

To be able to set the simple kitchen egg cooking timer to ring in twenty minutes allowed me to awaken, stand and turn 360 degrees to check the horizon for lights of an approaching ship while setting the timer as I turned, and promptly to sleep again. This precaution of perpetual watch was only necessary during the passing through the general area of shipping lanes. Otherwise, the likelihood of a large fishing vessel or research ship hitting this tiny forty-one foot target in a vast ocean had sufficiently unlikely odds for my gambling capacity to accept.

We never saw another vessel, day or night in such areas, and no more than can be counted on the fingers of one hand were seen of ships during all of our sailing. How vast the sea!

But her personality is always present, and always she is able to raise her voice to call up great waves at her beckoning and does so with thunderous sound, sending them crashing around us. A man will love his wife. He may love his boat. But with only few exceptions does a true seaman love the sea. And I don't want it in the cockpit.

Since I don't want to change the cockpit size, and since I can't drain it quickly, a deficiency exists. This danger is remote in my opinion, but none-the-less displeasing. It is unlikely in the extreme to destroy us. And as gambles go, it is one of certainly acceptable odds.

The secondary interest, but of no lesser consideration, was for our personal pleasure of protection from the elements of rain and wind and storm. This venture is for fun! We are not escaping from some terrible homeland!

I decided to build a wheelhouse over the cockpit. It took neither time nor study nor deliberation for the designing. I knew instantly what I wanted to do and how to do it; but first, the mast.

We had a friend at church, who was regularly transporting oranges from Keri Keri in our area and delivered them to Auckland. He offered to take me along so that I could get the lumber for our upper mast rebuilding. Being a very large trailer, the lumber was therefore bedded securely and arrived at Deeming's Boatyard with gentled hands.

We set the planks up where a perpetual breeze blew and would be blowing over and under each plank. A thorough drying was essential, and had begun. But time was not to be hurried in this process, and we could choose to stand and watch it happening, or we could go off on another adventure. It was to be the latter.

***

Our final plane arrived thirty-three hours after the NZ plane tucked its wheels up into itself. We were back to Washington DC, USA and would drive from there to Philadelphia, Pennsylvania, to attend the graduation of our son as Doctor of Optometry, an event which a thirty-three hour plane trip paled to insignificance.

An immense amount of effort had gone into this achievement, for which we applaud him. And he would feel such applauding worthy only as it included the major help and assistance from his good wife Carol.

It was a great celebration and wonderful to see old friends and relatives and feel again the touch of the land where the buffalo still roam.

But there it was again. That horizon thingy. And Peggy knew that the time would come when once again I would answer that call, and wondrous wife that she is, she knew that she would be with me as we cast loose the bonds of home, to stretch our heads upward to get our next glimpse of that horizon always just *beyond here*.

This time I swear the *Osprey* smiled! Well, okay, maybe it was just a reflection on the water, but oh how lovely to be back!

The mast timber was dry and I could begin. The planks needed to be scarfed for joining end to end. Even though solid blocks would be fitted to the inside of the otherwise hollow box mast, to just butt the planks together is not nearly as strong as tapering the plank's thickness over an eighteen-inch distance to zero thickness at the end; and likewise to the plank of the remainder of the mast, and epoxy gluing and screwing this large surface together and to the block in the center.

This long and absolutely perfect planning of these two scarfs can only be achieved by making a "jig" which holds the plank and has tapered edge boards on which to ride a long plane on which the plank will be "shaved" to the required surface.

It was while making this jig that word came about Hollywood's Paramount Motion Picture Company looking for people with whom to make a pirate movie. Well, I really should talk to them, don't you think?

* * *

I went at the appointed time to the appointed place. I heard them talking amongst themselves.

"Yeah, the beard is great. Would you take your shirt off please?"

I did so and upon their finding me to be rather "woolly" I was instantly declared the blacksmith. Doesn't the world realize that I am doing serious business here? I have all manner of urgent matters requiring my attention! Does the world think that I go around just playing at life!

If these objecting questions presented to me at all, they were certainly not given consideration! I was hired to make a movie! And I couldn't have scrubbed the grin off my face if I had tried.

Well, yes. They were making a pirate movie, and yes, I was hired. However, I was hired as an "extra" which is just as a background activity as blacksmith and sundry other crowd activities where the costume required a shirt for disguise.

The movie was nothing of merit, but absolutely fascinating and fun. There were two great square rigged ships in the harbor to which we were brought by super fast big catamaran power vessels where an entire village had been built along the waterfront. The buildings were comprised only of front walls except where indoor activity took place. It was, of course, a world living only within the eye of the camera.

All manner of activity was going on constantly. One very small thing that caught the eye of the camera only in passing, but which delighted me, was a sixteen-foot Whitehall being rowed through the harbor area at one point. If you don't know the Whitehall, but you see beauty in a grandly designed pulling boat, please look it up on the Internet. It is my favorite.

It was being perfectly rowed by a little girl of about ten or so years of age. She was dressed in her finery of the period as though on the way to church. She even had on a little hat which made her even more delightful. And her dog sat attentively on the aft seat as she rowed from the center. It made a perfectly charming sight, especially in contrast to the ruffian cast of pirates. But they had a couple of sailing ships which would call to the heart of any seaman!

So dissolved a month or so of my New Zealand time, our visas were limited, and the boat had already been in the country over a year. But it had been really great fun, and Peggy too had a couple of days spent in buying the day's fish catch in the mock town, so she got into the fun too. Meanwhile, back in the real world, the boatyard had, by arrangement, been rebuilding the mast, which was more than paid for by Paramount Pictures for my presence.

I had the boat out of the water by this time, and after having scrubbed the bottom in the usual way as soon as she had come up so that I could take a close look at her, I noticed a small area of loose bottom paint. And wanting a proper drying, where the paint exposed the wood here, I brought a putty knife with me later in the day, and carefully lifted off the paint.

Not only did I see a couple of square inches of bare wood, but the paint also had brought some wood with it. I was very surprised. I called Les over to see it, since he was standing nearby at that moment. He touched it with a finger tip, pressed it, went entirely through the hull, and dragged his finger along the plank until he came to the next frame. We both gasped! What on earth had we just found?

I took a light hammer, and went over the whole hull below the waterline, listening to the difference in sound as it lightly struck normal hard wood from the sound of softness; rather like the difference of tapping a rock and tapping a potato.

The entire hull was affected. Most of it was less so than others. I took a nail, and proceeded to tap it into the hull every six inches vertically and horizontally. Almost everywhere the nail went at least ¼ inch into softness and vast areas ½ to ¾ of an inch, while large areas didn't resist the nail at all. This was disaster!

She needed to be entirely replanked from the waterline down. Les had the source of good lumber at hand. He estimated the cost for us, and although it was a wonderfully attractive cost, we had two problems, the first of which precluded the second. We did not have the money to pay for the job, and number two, New Zealand was going to demand that if the boat remain in NZ long enough to do the job, the boat would need to be imported into the country. This fee would also have been impossible for us.

So we scraped off all of the bottom paint, replanked the worst areas, left the boat to dry for several months, and covered her bottom with fiberglass before repainting.

Chapter 15 — A South Pacific Storm

Before all of this, I had begun building a wheelhouse on the boat. Just before entering the great Pacific Ocean, while still in the Bay of Panama where Balboa had looked out at this huge bay and thinking that he was seeing the Pacific Ocean, name it "Pacific" for its calm waters. Of course, the ocean beyond the bay is no calmer than another body of water over which the winds can howl uninterrupted by barriers of land and mountain.

While there, I had built a permanent sunshade of PVC pipes the frame which had so admirably held up a canvas between us and the sun. It boasted a fixed extension outboard enough to shade us through more than just the overhead period and was attached by bungee cord to keep it tight while allowing some movement for gusting wind.

During the crossing to NZ, we had rather more than just gusting condition, and I had to cut the canvas down with a knife to ease the boat of her unwanted windage. The pressure of the wind was too great to enable me to free its ties. But we have been spoiled by the pleasure of that otherwise perpetual enjoyment of shade which had not, however, done anything for us during rain or flying spray. (The boat is named *Osprey* and I had named the dinghy, *Ah, Spray*. But spray is not a delight.) And the hazard of being boarded by a sea from which all agility of the boat's maneuverability would be lost, needed resolution.

I had designed a wheelhouse just high enough to sit under, while a huge sliding hatch when open permitted one to enter and leave the cockpit as though there were no wheelhouse, because the entire cockpit well was uncovered by the hatch. And when shoved forward, I could still stand atop the steering box, hold the boom gallows with both hands for balance, and steer with my feet, having gained eye elevation to see where to steer through coral areas of approaching islands for anchoring selections, etc.

The side windows were to be of Plexiglas, hinged at the top and were over six feet long, but alas we had to settle for rolled up canvas with isinglass to help the budget. The aft window and the windows at the forward end of the cockpit seats were fixed. The one forward of the cockpit well was able to

A South Pacific Storm   Chapter 15

be rolled up with the canvas to which the isinglass was sewn, and it was secured closed by a series of snaps.

When the church folks and a few others waved us on our way to sea as we left New Zealand, there had been only enough time to have gotten a lead based priming coat of paint on the wheelhouse, leaving us looking rather odd with a reddish "sore thumb" following an otherwise white sailing yacht. But her flags waved just as gaily as though we were without blemish, and our send-off mixed our anticipations of new adventures beyond the horizon with that familiar hollow feeling in that special place in the pit of our stomachs, that here were friends never to be seen again. Our wavings were never permitted to divulge this, but in the eye of our friends we also saw a moistening.

It was cold. We had checked out of the country with the NZ Customs Service, declaring our destination to be Australia. Two problems presented. Number one, the boat was not ready for sea. There is a place for everything. And everything must be in its place. However, it was necessary to take formal departure with Customs because our extended visa time had expired. When one is cleared for departure, no further commerce may be engaged, etc., but waiting at anchor for acceptable weather is permitted so long as no contact of persons ashore occurs. So we anchored in another bay and prepared for sea.

The second problem was more minor. Australia is to the west of New Zealand, and so was the wind. The old saying is, "Gentlemen do not sail to windward." And slogging to weather is neither pleasant nor productive with our reduced sail inventory. However, wind direction changes perpetually when not in the trade wind belts, so we started out when ready, as required.

We zoomed up the east coast and reduced sail somewhat as we left New Zealand behind taking the eastward running seas abeam. Miles followed miles and days followed days, and still the west wind blew. And after a few more days of our northing, a destination change began forming unbidden in my mind. And a few days later, with Fiji's familiar Suva harbor directly over the horizon before us, Australia faded from our minds as the remembered delights of Fiji called us from afar.

CHAPTER 16

Fiji Again

Here we were on the same track as when we sailed from Fiji to NZ, except, obviously in the opposite direction. And sure enough, there it was, just where we had left it almost two years ago.

We sailed right to Suva Harbor's quarantine buoy, and in the fullness of time we were again processed by officialdom to very familiar surroundings. I had no concern about our having left NZ officially bound for Australia being challenged, and had it been, sea conditions would have been easily confirmed as cause for altering our destination.

Of course, we became instantly reconnected with many church members and clergy, many whom we had not met the first time here due to our early search for Emosi and Lanieta, our friends whom we met in Tahiti. It would have surprised us, had we known at this time that events would conspire to exclude the opportunity to see them this second time in Fiji.

We did, however, meet a gentleman who was employed in the main church office. He had come from a distant, rather isolated village here on the island of Viti Levu where we now were. And when we learned that no roads go there, dirt or otherwise; and that the entire village were members of the church of our attendance we were interested to visit there, and asked if it were possible for us to do so.

The village was contacted, how he did this I don't know, but a plan was made which I fear entailed huge effort on our behalf. He also arranged for the horses and a guide. We had asked for four horses.

When we learned that we would be crossing a river numerous times on the way to the village and would be holding onto the tail of our horse as he swam across where the water would be too deep, our anticipation heightened even more. First time experiences always are a heady drink. Our appointed adventure was to begin in two weeks. We were to later learn that the village was also preparing.

What great fun! We told our friends in the anchorage that we would be gone for a week, so that an eye could be kept on the boat. And at the prearranged bus stop, closest to the path toward the village, we found our guide with the necessary four horses. We unloaded our gear from the bus with many helping hands of fellow passengers, and with delightfully enthusiastic wavings by us and by the passengers and driver, the bus was gone and our guide and his charge of horses rematerialized out of the cloud of dust swirling about by the only known bus speed. It requires the "pedal to the metal," aided by a hardy cry of Fiji's equivalent of "Hi Ho Silver."

We offered some food and drink to the guide who expressed his pleasure to be showing us the way. The horses appeared most able. We were to learn that the horses spoke Fijian. We loaded the pack horse with our things securely aboard and off we went. Well, that's almost correct.

When Peggy got her foot into the stirrup and gave the requisite little jump with the other leg while simultaneously pulling on the saddle horn and pressing vigorously with the stirrup-footed leg, the saddle slid around the poor horse to be dangling from its belly which the guide and I both lunged forward to resolve. The saddle on the horse was properly cinched by our guide, and I tried to tighten Peggy's lost dignity.

With Peggy now properly enthroned, and with the guide and me aboard our horses, he led the way down the trail which instantly became very narrow.

Peggy was the third in line. And an hour or so later, instead of following the pack horse and guide, she turned to the right and started up a different trail.

"Where are you going?" I called.

It seems that she was just so totally dazed by the saddle event, that she had entirely forgotten *how to steer the thing*, as she said. Well yes, she had grown up on a farm, but they didn't have horses. Well, what do you expect, when you have immersed a girl into the strange water world of the oceans? But now, even Peggy can laugh (a little) about her first experience of a trance, and her failed communication with a horse who spoke only Fijian.

* * *

We arrived, not with camels across the desert, but with horses across the mountains. The river water had been low enough that we were able to retain the saddle as the horses walked the crossings rather than having to swim them. It was a beautiful experience; long, but beautiful.

The mountains were a renewed marvel to us seafarers. The mosses and the undergrowth were vibrantly lush, while the forest canopy lent ever-changing patches of shadows which were moved about by what seemed to be the breathing of this enchanted forest. As did the forest, we too listened to the sounds which kept to the soft beat of the horses' steps. They were made by birds that seemed to settle to a melody after the first tuning of their orchestra. None were so impolite as to sing a new song of comedic horsemanship.

The Naraiyawa Village was a wonderful contrast to so many others which we had visited elsewhere. Usually bare dirt occupied "the town square" in the midst of a dozen houses. Here, flowers bloomed all about amidst grasses. Everything was spotless!

Our hosts, Apete Qali and Ositina, rushed up. We were introduced by our guide as we "gracefully" descending from our five hours of polishing the saddles of our horses. Hugs and hand shakes merged into tears of laughter as various episodes of horsemanship were related. The pack horse was unburdened of his load of treasured foods and gifts to be formally presented at the appropriate time. The food was brought to the house of our hostess where we were to be guests. And with more pride than we understood reason for at the moment, we were shown to the necessary facility.

It turned out to be a newly dug outhouse for our exclusive use. Leaves were still on the branches that formed the walls, and a door which had elsewhere performed its duty over many years had been installed for its important function on our behalf. The vines which served as hinges voiced their youth by a soft but high pitched squeaking when employed. There was a hole in the ground in the center of this chamber.

The purpose of this object was indisputable. But there was a certain difficulty in envisioning exactly how its "thronelessness" was to be mounted, when I saw a rope hanging from above and swung to the side. With the rope firmly grasped, one is able to assume a suspended sitting position. High adventures await.

The house of our host was built with woven plant fiber as were all ten of the other houses of the village. And amazingly, all had tin roofs. Remembering the foot paths used by our horses, a very major effort brought these roofs up here! The half of the house which Peggy and I occupied was slightly elevated above the other half and had a double bed with mattress which too was carried up here. The cooking area was in the other half which was kitchen and dining area combined. The house was indeed a perfection of efficiency in every way. And there was no waste of space.

A festive meal was lavishly presented and immensely enjoyed. It was mixed with stories and conversations and with our abundant expressions of gratitude for permitting our visit to their lovely village of happy people. I praised their well being, and applauded their prosperity.

We slept soundly after a long discussion during our privacy, as to how to function our lovely new necessary room. "Just don't let go with both hands," seemed to be the concluding instruction that I offered to Peggy. No trance was to be experienced without a certainty of unspecified but guaranteed unfortunate result. The next few days would hold the answer.

Many people came smiling past as the morning progressed. One man brought a rifle. It was a .22 caliber with a telescopic sight. He said that there was something wrong with the gun and asked if I would be willing to fix it. There seemed to be an intrinsic assumption here. The question was not: can you fix it?

The manner in which I took the question to be asked was inquiring as to my willingness to take the time and interest to do so. It may also simply have been a manipulation strategy useful in the culture, I'll never know. But though certainly no gunsmith, of course, I was willing to look at it and asked questions as to the problem; which was that he couldn't hit anything, though being certain that the object was directly centered in the scope.

This sounded like an easy one. I asked the distance that his object usually was from him, set up a target at that distance, fired the gun, noted the off center direction and quantity, adjusted the scope accordingly and after a few more adjustments hit the center of the target. I gave the gun back to him and a few hours later he returned, trophy in hand, showing the accuracy of his rifle and his skill. He was happy.

By the next day, the word was out. Someone brought a radio that wouldn't work even with new batteries. I had taken classes to qualify for my amateur radio license but had never lived in what I considered the rarefied ether in which this hobby dwells. So I can only claim luck and persistence as the victor in this battle of blind man's bluff. My closed fist was used as a magnifying glass, by permitting just that tiny beam of light through it, as my eye was pressed against the joining of my thumb and forefinger at one end and the radio circuitry at the other. After some effort, the radio worked. Another challenge successfully met!

Our hostess had long possessed a non functioning hand-cranked sewing machine, to which Peggy was introduced. Peggy in turn introduced me to this

Chapter 16 — Fiji Again

interesting relic. My only contributing effort was to oil it in its many and varied mysterious parts. It was Peggy whose patient fortitude at very long last resulted in unscrambling the stitching tension of this device from ages past. We were batting a thousand.

It was Sunday, and Peggy told our hostess that she had brought popping corn and wanted to make some for the children, so an epic six hours began.

The children loved it. They had never heard of popcorn much less actually eaten any. Excitedly they told their parents who came to see what it was. And, of course, it smelled like nothing ever experienced for as long as these mountains had been here! Could it taste as good as it smells?

One adult tasted it, followed by an equivalent for "Yum!"

And six hours later, Peggy had used up all of the popping corn, and the crowd around our hostess' cooking shed slowly made their way to their houses in the village circle, after most fondly expressed gratitude and delight for her wonderful gift to them all. It was a marathon for Peggy, and a bridge to friendship perhaps unexpected by some.

The few small things which opportunity permitted our doing, was our feeble and certainly inadequate attempt to present substance to the expressed voice of our hearts which were so abundantly overflowed by their kindness to us; for suddenly, a week had passed and our departure was at hand, as was our guide and his small herd of horses.

Fond indeed was the taking of leave from each other. And with wavings from the adults and ourselves, and the excited following of the children for a ways — wanting a last wave and callings of "Bulavanaka" to the popcorn lady — we were off.

No poorly cinched saddle surprised Peggy with its disappearance, and the returning horsemanship was indeed a thing of justifiable pride as all trails were properly followed. And Peggy, not having seen it before, marveled over the magnificent grandeur of Fiji as garbed in such glorious garments of green as this the same forest through which we had passed on our journey to that lovely village of friends.

* * *

We were back to the boat with nothing untoward having interrupted our return. We thanked our fellow cruisers for having watched over the *Osprey* in our absence and exchanged stories of the events which transpired during our absence. They were delighted to hear about living a week in a remote village.

I was back with my head full of the departure preparations. This time, however, there were a few more problems to solve than just the usual random requirements of food, water, and fuel. The varying wind conditions of the sail from New Zealand had caused yet more havoc to our dwindling sail inventory of headsails. The drifter was gone, and now the genoa had given up as well.

What we did have, was a very nice selection of small jibs. So the obvious solution is to use two of them at the same time. Using one would always be too small, be it a light weather sail or heavy. Our mast had grown two and a half feet taller, and the bow stay had been moved from two feet inboard from the bow to two feet outboard of the bow on a short bowsprit. I rig a stay (cable) from the new upper mast spreader and tack it (secure it) where the bow stay previously lived, I could work the boat as a double headed sloop.

I had wire and terminals aboard. I needed to fabricate a mast fitting to secure the stay and did so very simply by employing the spreader attachments. The halyard block attachment was made by an angled stainless steel sheet mettle passing under the mainsail track thereby pulling pressure on the entire mast rather than a fitting just screwed to the timber.

This put me up and down the mast very frequently, and what a joy to have the electric anchor windlass. Now, in place of the seven fall block and tackle system by which I could bring myself up the mast, Peggy could just stand comfortably on the cockpit bridge deck and let electricity do all the work.

Chapter 16 — Fiji Again

The first time up, I saw it. It was a hairline crack in the new section of the mast. I knew that craftsmanship had built it, so that left the answer to be that the epoxy glue had let go. The mast, of course, was secured by screw fasteners. The problem was that rain water was now able to penetrate the timber and thereby wood rot would soon follow. The wood had to be re-glued to seal it, and then I needed to re-paint the mast.

To do this, I had to cut the crack open to allow drying and then fit a wood insert to take the place of what I had cut out, and re-glue and paint the mast. Had I just filled the long crack with glue and painted it, this glue would have expanded and contracted at a different rate than the painted wood, thereby tearing loose from the wood, leaving another crack for rot to start, on an unending sequence toward destruction.

This mast work took much time in both labor and drying time, and was not part of my planned schedule. But drying time had its pleasures too. We had the pleasure of friends afloat and ashore to visit. The Akhoys of Fiji's government fame had come one evening with other friends to see the Festival of Lights. They had dinner with us aboard the *Osprey* and we also had great fun joining them for a progressive party. We dashed about Suva with them to a host of houses of their friends. It was great fun.

We toured. We were so graciously cared for while we were there. I was desperately trying to leave due to the expiring of our visa which by now I had extended by an additional month. Happily I had gotten a coat of white paint on the wheelhouse so the boat was now looking her best again. I like her look with the wheelhouse, and I'm absolutely in every way ecstatic over the enhancement of its function.

The work was not completed yet. I had to rig running back stays to counter the forward pull on the mast of the inner jib that the back stay must oppose to keep the mast straight.

As with all things, in the fullness of time if effort is expended, everything comes together, even though the metal work for the new sail rig had to be done twice, we were ready to be sailing over the horizon as a double headed sloop toward yet another adventure of the sea.

Farewells were exchanged afloat and ashore and we were westward bound again. Leaving Fiji the second time seemed accompanied with twice the abundance of friendship being left ashore. Again, we are reminded of the truth in the immortal words, "Our sincerest laughter with some pain is fraught."

How pleasant are our memories of your isles. How warmed by an eternal glow shall be our remembrances of your grace and kindness to us.

Bulavanaka, Fiji.

APPENDIX A

⚙ A Detailed Look ⚙
at the Boat Handling Arrangement

This might be a good time for you to look around the boat to see how we are arranged for ocean passages. Let's look below first. There is a crowned bridge deck between the cockpit and the companion way into the cabin. This is a good arrangement in that were the cockpit well to be filled by a wave coming aboard, this water cannot find its way into the cabin. This is more important than the inconvenience of getting our stuff wet. If the cabin is filled with the weight of the sea, the boat will sink. But even with this barrier protecting the cabin, the cockpit should drain with some dispatch so that the stern not be held down below her water line too long so that she is not refilled by subsequent waves and thereby sunk.

Before starting this venture, I had plugged the drain pipes, filled the cockpit with water from a hose, and timed how long it took to empty. The cockpit is large, and although the motion of the boat in a sea way would throw some water out, I was not satisfied with the time factor. I had the drains enlarged.

A further protection of the cabin is that water on the bridge deck does not have free access to the cabin. One steps over a portion of the structure of the aft of the cabin to place a foot on the top step of the companion way ladder. This step is level with the bridge deck, so ease of entry is maintained.

When entering the cabin, Peggy's bunk is to starboard. Mine is to port. They serve as couches and otherwise and as seats for the dining table during meals. The centerboard trunk which divides the cabin fore and aft has a hinged table leaf which can accommodate two people on each side of the trunk. There is a simple hook which secures the leaves to the trunk when they are not in use for the table, so that they not swing up due to motion in a sea way, which thereby would impede our passing.

Forward, beyond Peggy's bunk, is a lovely cabinet and bulkhead, beyond which rests our stainless steel coal stove not used in the tropics. Now, our regularly used stove is mounted atop the coal stove on its gimbals. It is a two burner kerosene cooking stove. The centerboard trunk continues forward through this area, and a bulkhead built atop it divides the galley from the other side, making a great place to mount Peggy's copper cook pans. The pans simply hang of brass hooks by their handles and are all available as needed. When at sea, the pans are held securely and noiselessly in place, by elastic bungee cords, which are attached to the bulkhead at each side of the lower portion of each pan. To ready the galley for sea, the bungee is lifted over each pan, and all else is stowed in its usual place. Even the sharp knives have a home in the same area as the pans.

On the port side, just forward of the bridge deck and cockpit, where I rest my head in sleep, a gamboling compass is mounted well above my pillow. Mounted on the bulkhead below the compass is a pull switch to light the compass card at night. It has a red lens on it to ease my reading of this compass which is made specifically to be read from the under side. So when in open waters, with no one on watch, I can check our course to see if a wind shift has appreciably put us on another heading. A windvane steering system will, of course, continue following the wind setting which has been chosen. I have used the old system of pulling a hitch in a sheet line brought to a tiller opposed by surgical tubing to maintain a reasonable course, but a good windvane is essential for short handed ocean passages. We also had an autopilot, but while sailing, it is wonderful to have a windvane system to be shipmates with you. As with everything else aboard, this device requires some occasional ingenuity to keep it functional.

There is a space forward of my bunk for currently used books and navigation tools, above which is a mirror fronted cabinet storing the glass crystal wear, none of which was ever broken underway. Beyond the foot of my bed and forward, is a door which encloses the necessary room comprised of the head (toilet) and shower and sink, closed by a door forward of it as well. Forward of this area is a hanging closet and next a built-in chest of drawers. The upper part of this opened by a drop down door in which our charts were stored. The drawers required lifting over a small barrier to be opened, thereby keeping the drawers closed during sailing in protected waters with little heeling, but for our intended voyage I drilled a hole through the framing of the cabinet and through the drawer's side at an angle downward so that a metal pin could be inserted, whereby the drawers were kept closed in severe conditions as well. The inward extension of the forward edge of the dresser enabled my choice of this solution. I formed the pins out of bronze rod with a diameter of about 3/16 of an inch and bent an eye in one end to comfortably fit my finger. The pin hangs comfortably from that finger while extracting the item needed from inside the drawer and the pin thereby was at hand to relock the drawer.

A very important matter for being underway during even modest durations of time is a comfortable sleeping arrangement.

Mine supplies a level sleeping surface regardless of the extent of the *Osprey*'s heeling degree whether on a port or starboard tack. Translated into English, this means that, to whichever side the boat is leaning and regardless of the amount of the lean, I sleep level to the horizon.

<u>*Please* skip this paragraph if you don't want the details of the arrangement regarding this bed</u>, because I shall go into detail describing it. I found this arrangement wonderful in the extreme. And for those who appreciate this comfort, and as I who cannot sleep on airplanes for lack of comfort, I recommend this to you with unbounded enthusiasm! *Please* picture a book, at which you look end on, with the binding to your left. If you place this book in your mind onto the surface of a desk, and now picture the desk toward your left leaning downward from the horizontal, if you had a hinge at the

bottom edge of the book cover as it extends along the opening edge of the book as you open it, you can readily see that by lifting the binding edge of the book, you can bring the book to the level of where the desk had been before its left surface dropped down from the horizontal. And if you have a line from the corners of the book's binding cover, and a third one from the center of the binding edge, and had a place to affix the lines, the book would stay at the level you chose.

Now picture the above desk leaning downward on the right side. If you lift the book, having a hinge at the binding position, you can see how the top cover of the book can be brought level to the horizon. Beds on most boats do not have springs. They boast a comfortable mattress on plywood. Now, for the application of the above, to that of my bunk, I shall finish the picture. On the plywood designed to receive the mattress, I have placed two additional sheets of plywood of the same size and shape. Following the description sequence used above, I placed a hinge the length of the bed at the point where the lower of my two additions meet along its inboard edge of the original plywood, which is along the right side as looking forward. This allows for the mattress to be raised from the left side when the boat heels to the left, resulting in a horizontal mattress. Now, by placing a full length hinge between the two plywoods which I added, along the left length of the plywood, upon the boat heeling to starboard the mattress can be brought to horizontal in like manner.

So let's say that we are on a starboard tack, wherefore the wind is coming over our starboard deck and the boat is heeled to port, (our left side as we face forward). Since my berth is on the port side, I could lie against the hull and sleep quite well. If on the other tack, I would be rolled out of bed unless somehow retained in it. But rather than lying against the hull, I can bring the mattress up to just below horizontal, whereby I am slightly retained in place as the boat rolls as she makes her way through the sea, and my comfort, and hence my rest, is greatly enhanced. The greatest hazard at sea is fatigue. You can readily see that the position of the bed and its mattress is likewise cared for on a port tack. Magic is not used in this accommodation. On the outboard edge of the top plywood a line is attached to each non hinged corner and one midway between them, as likewise the lower of my added plywood received such lines at its non hinged corners and mid point. I tied a knot in each line at strategic points so the knot in the lines could be placed over a retaining hook which carried the weight of the bed. With a certain private jest of my own, I enjoyed thinking of a port heel as being a three knotter or a four knot heel, etc. Mixing word usage can be fun. You can see that on a starboard tack, there are no lines obstructing my entry or leaving from my bed, whereas on a port tack, the center lift-line obstructs my way. This is an inconvenience which is not a hindrance to me in any way. But it is the reason why Peggy refused the arrangement, preferring the more traditional lee board comprised of a canvas slung to leeward when on a starboard tack. On a port tack, she sleeps against the hull. Her bunk is on the starboard side of the boat, opposite from mine.

I wish to emphasize what I said above. *Fatigue is the greatest hazard to which you can be exposed at sea.*

A reader who does not need the minutiae of the boat's seamanship could choose to omit this paragraph. For those who remain, I would like to "show you the ropes" above decks. Let's see what the boat looks like and how she is handled in straight-forward sailing as well as in heavy weather.

She has a short anchor sprit forward which carries two forty-five pound CQR anchors, one on all chain and the other with three fathoms of chain (eighteen feet), and the remainder with half-inch three-lay nylon line. These anchors are lashed in place for passages. A hand-cranking anchor windlass has an open drum to starboard and for the chain rode, there is the usual chain accepting drum to its port. The deck is teak to the topsides. The topsides continue upward beyond deck level by six inches, forming a very generous toe rail on which feet may walk safely when the lee rail is under water. The toe rail is topped by a cap which extends ¾ inch beyond the toe rail both inboard and out. The outer is for aesthetics, while the inboard extension keeps the foot from slipping overboard. The forward end of the cabin terminates about eight feet from the stem. On the deck, at the forward end of the cabin, the life raft canister is chained to the deck. The eye bolts to which the chain is attached are poured in one poring rather than welded parts or the eye being bent to form itself. The bolts are passed through the deck and through large backing plates under it to spread the force of a heavy sea's effort to wash the life raft overboard. Tension of the chains which kept the canister in place between its chocks was done by a lashing. Life rafts are generally patterned after the commercial shipping kind, which wants to try to stay where a ship has sunk in order to be located by another ship plying the same route. In my view, this does not properly serve the yachtsman who seeks to remain outside of shipping lanes when at all possible and who sails from or toward non commercial areas. But I found one made to form a rectangle with two parallel below water pontoons giving direction ability to make way with the square sail and mast which is part of the package. I added fishing gear and more solar stills which make water by condensation. I added some other sundries which you might choose differently, such as hats, some clothing, and medications including sun block and hand bailers, etc.

The *Osprey* is sloop-rigged, having one mast, therefore one mainsail and one jib. Our voyage started with twelve bags of sails. I will only mention two specifically because of my affinity for them. They were made of Egyptian cotton which was of uniquely long fibers grown only in the Aswan valley which has been forever taken away by the building of the Aswan Dam. It caused the valley to disappear below enormous waters. The storm jib would noiselessly set to perfection. It was roped all around for strength and endurance. I always dried the sail carefully before stowing it away, but as they say, nothing is forever, and she and her partner, a storm trysail, were respectfully taken ashore after they had lost their battle with age, the grim reaper. And as time passed, first the drifter disintegrated as did the genoa thereafter, leaving the boat without enough sail power forward. So I rigged a temporary inner stay whereby I could sail her as a cutter instead of as a sloop. I could not logically move the mast farther aft, so she was less efficient than before, but perfectly able nonetheless. There was no self furling system aboard, so I did a reasonable amount of sail changing underway.

The reefing of the mainsail was a one man job as well, which certainly was the requirement. Three rows of reef points crossed the main. Each reefing was set up as the others, so I will describe only one. In the usual manner, there is a clue (ring) at the luff (the edge of the mainsail at the mast) and at the leach (the trailing edge) of the mainsail. Between them are placed a row of reefing points or ties. A few feet from the mast I have placed a winch on the boom, and I made and attached a row of varnished, wooden cleats to the boom as well. I like the base of a cleat to be about 20% wider than the top width and I like this to taper in a straight line as viewed from the end, forming the horns in the same plain. The cleat should be made to fit the size of line to be worked on it and be relieved where the line takes its first full turn around the throat before it turns and lock on the horns. Before we finish our tour, let's look at the mainsail reefing procedure for a one-man operation. I sail with the three luff and three leach reef lines in place, as of course all the reef points have permanent ties on each side of the sail. To reef the mainsail, I ease the main halyard and belay it to the fife rail at the mast. I pull down the luff cringle and belay it so that it aligns with the rest of the reef so that it cannot be pulled aft. The leach line which also is half inch nylon, terminates on the port side of the boom several inches aft of where the leach cringle will be brought when tightly in position. The line from the port side of the boom passes through the leach cringle to the starboard side, and then down to a cheek block attached to the starboard side of the boom opposite the location of the point of its termination which therefore is also a few inches aft of where the leach cringle must be brought, and lead to the winch on the boom where I can bring great force to bear. The position of the cheek block and the lines point of origin, keep the cringle snug to the boom and forms a perfect sail set. If the "bag" formed along the boom by the excess sail is not threatened to be filled with sea or rain, the row of reef points need not be used. However, if wished or needed, these points can easily be tied. To do so, I step on the cabin roof top to the center point of the boom, reach down until my hand stops at the deepest point of the sail pocket, grab the sail at this point and pull it up. The wind will often slam the pocket closed bringing the rest of the loose sail pocket along the windward side of the boom. This sail fabric can now be readily rolled in a tight, neat, even roll along the length of the boom. Tying the reef point ties keeps the reefed sail efficiently and neatly in place. As weather worsens, the second and third reefs can all be taken without disturbing any of the prior ones.

The headsails, of course, are taken down and replaced by smaller sails as required. This too is a one man job, and provision is made at the bow to keep me aboard. The bow pulpit narrows as it passes around the point of the bow. It is wide enough for my hips to pass through. Wherefore, I made a seat out of strips of nylon webbing which hold my posterior about six inches below the pulpit keeping me snuggly in place. I was also able to keep one foot below a projection that kept me from being launched out of my perch. Having eased the jib halyard with the bitter end always secured, I needed only to claw down the jib being replaced, having first brought the next bagged jib and attached its tack as the first part of this action. With the old jib down but still hanked, I could hank the new one, get it up, resettle the sail balance and then get the old jib below to the forecastle Thusly, the *Osprey* lent herself very readily to single-handing, which in this case for several years was in fact single handing with company. And wonderful company it was. This paragraph would have been easier to read perhaps, had I used the normal rules for same, but you may recall that I gave those less interested in these details to identify the paragraphs which they could choose to pass over.

So you now, have had the opportunity to look about before we get underway making toward New Zealand, and after perhaps rereading the above paragraph a time or two, you are now ready to come aboard for a sail in the fabled southern South Pacific Ocean.

APPENDIX B

Peggy's Log I: The Galapagos

2/2 Motored till 7:30 AM and raised main and drifter 7:30 AM and took drifter down at 7:40 AM raising the genny. It rained all night. Still drizzling this morning. Cloudy all day. Dan changed sails so often I lost count.

2/3 Motored 5:30 AM till 7 AM. Still cloudy, seas confused and choppy, some rain. Dan slept some. Moon out. We talked to Bob of *Brown Palace*. He has 125 miles yet to go to get to the Galapagos. Dave and Annie aboard *Pursuit of Nantucket* are somewhere ahead of them. Good to hear from them.

2/4 Lovely day. 96'W 4'.10 S. Sailing well. Slept some.

2/5 Lovely day. Lots of Petrels and flying fish. We attempted an amateur radio patch to our son Dave. We heard the phone ring but he was out. The ham radioman will give him a message for us.

2/6 3 pm to 7 am, rolling is awful / We talked to Bob / Drifter up. I finished sewing it yesterday / I'm feeling better / Now at 3N & 88W / Patrick left yesterday, going to see the blond beauty at Tower Island / Dan is keeping me out of the galley which is helping. / Drifter up till sunset, then switched to genny / Dan called me on deck — Porpoises.

[Dan] It was a dark night, and here came porpoises garbed in the silver light of phosphorescence darting around in wild acrobatics all around us. What a circus! What a LOL (laugh out loud) kind of show!

2/7   I feel great! We changed the clocks an hour due for local time.

2/8   Cloudy – Lots of flying fish – saw frigate bird / talked to Bob and Dave they're about 50 miles out from Galapagos. Getting rough here.

2/9   Cloudy till 2, rough night. School of fish 2 or 3 pounders. Petrel took a couple of bait fish – shearwaters fishing too. Some porpoise after dark. Rough night.

2/10 About 1/3 of the way. Running rig up for first time. Wind east / changed to south east / Feeling pretty good. 2 pm lots of birds / also tropic bird [beautiful thing], porpoises. Tang bottle top came off. Dan helped clean up the mess. We've enjoyed the Tang.

2/11 Lovely day. Light winds. Talked to Bob and Dave / played music. Feel great. Port side jib chaffing. We taped it.

2/12 Dan improved my lee board by rigging block and tackle for me to gain power. It took him 3 hours to carve a cleat for it. Dan got a running sun shot fix. Should be half way tomorrow

2/13 Got radio phone patch to Arnold. He will call my mother that all is well. [Dan speaking – I will tell you about Arnold shortly.]

2/14 Reading. Dan navigating. 6 flying fish about 8 inches long on deck this morning. I backed a chocolate cake in the pressure cooker today. It took 2 hours. Saw loom of ship lights. Need to stand watches. Our lights are on.

2/15 My watch mid night till 2. Dan 2 till 4 but up at 5 and stayed up till 11. He wanted to talk to Bob and Dave and Patrick. Bob has challenged his customs clearing fee. Dave has cleared. Patrick still awaiting outboard motor parts [his main engine]. He is planning then to go see the blond beauty on Tower Island. Beautiful day. Few clouds. Lots of fish including flying fish. One landed on top of the dinghy – Dan got it and tossed it quickly back into the sea.

2/16	I saw phosphorescent covered porpoises again. [Wondrously starry night.] Dan saw looms of 4 ships over the horizon.
2/17	Have slight head ache. Day lovely
2/18	Really rough. Slow speed. Stars beautiful Lots of birds. Made only 85 miles in last 24 hours.
2/20	Slow. / ¾ way. Few birds. Out of shipping lane.
2/21	Slow
2/22	Slow. / Down wind running rig up again / Cloudy till noon / different time zone again. We each had a bath
2/23	Sailing well. / About 560 to Marquises Sighted ship. / Came close. / Would have loved to ask for some chocolate ice cream.
2/24	I read.
2/25	Dan took ages cleaning the hundred feet of taffrail log line, and its fish, and Ruth's rudder.
2/26	Slow. Made 60 miles last 24 hours.
2/27	Slow. / Lots of birds. / 240 miles to go.
2/28	Sailing faster. / Saw frigate bird. / 180 miles to go. / Motored 9:45 pm to 10 am. Calm.
2/29	Heard by radio no customs fees in Marquises – great. / Very close now. Should be there tomorrow.
3/1	At 7 AM saw land!!

APPENDIX C

 Peggy's Log II: Tahiti

6/3 Up early; straighten up boat part way, hung out sheets and other wet things off my bunk. About 10:00 showered, went to immigration, customs, AMX, (40 letters and 4 packages) cashed check, went to bank exchanged into francs, (exchange 69 francs = one US dollar, Bad). To grocery store got hamburger meat. Wow! What a feast. Read letters for 3 or more hours, did a little more work, supper and to bed.

6/4 Little work rest, wrote letters. We had a notice from main P O to pick up package from them. We walk to get packages took 1 ½ hours. They had sent one package back. We got a ride back to boat. To bed early.

6/5 Up early at 600 am after breakfast walked to SDA headquarters, a long walk. Met Pastor Doom and lady named Gloria and couple others I've forgotten names nice folks, Gloria brought us back to boat. Marcel Millaud a head elder of 3 church here on island came and took us around island in his car also took us out for a nice steak lunch. Nice quick drive lovely views.

6/6 Washed by hand, I found out price of Laundromat (260 francs each load one place and second place 320 francs per load. I had 6 loads, so back to boat to get started) I finished in 4 ½ hours. Laundry drying all of boat.

6/7 Dan wired David and gave him our Tahiti address. Walk to church invited Maureen to go with us. The preaching in Tahitian, but a young man interpreter for us. We got a ride back with an America that has lived here 5 years. Met

Appendix C   *Peggy's Log II*

a couple from Fiji he had a skirt on. Rested after dinner. 7:00 pm was picked up to go to movie at church by, Walter (He used to be a Mormon); He had the Fijian couple in his VW Van and his own son with him also. We met another nice Tahitian lady.

6/8   Wrote letters and cards all day. 23

6/9   Wrote letters and cards all day. 28

6/10   Wrote letters and cards all day. 22

6/11   Called Tearu Mercier to get letter from Louise in Marquises. He came with wife and friend Vaea. They stay 1 hour or more. We deliver the honey and bananas from Louise Bremond.

6/12   Had Valise and Tearu and Vaea for supper. Chicken southern fried, Dan made pumpkin soup. They stayed 3 hours, brought us pamplemousse and coconuts. They have 4 children. We are to spend next Sabbath with them. We had a good time talking. They are cousins of Louise.

6/14   June Work putting afghan together. Dan reading. We were picked up by Martin Walker and son Martin in VW camper he also picked up Lanieta and Emose Yalani (the Fiji couple) and taken to church at Paea. This is Gloria's church. Interpreter was Michel Brotherson also SS teacher. A French man John Reynaud spoke in French and was translated in Tahitian for the church and (Michel translated it in to English for us). It was about rebuilding of Jerusalem of old. We were invited to eat by Laniete, but Gloria & her sister in law were feeding preacher so we were all invited and Lanieta added her food (3 meats). It was Gloria brother's house (lovely place), their names are Claude and Dolores Allouche. Gloria's husband is Dominique Pothier; he is treasurer of the SDA Mission. Michel's wife's name is Fanny. We all talked and stayed to 4:00. We all went to Martin home and after sunset he showed picture of his 1964 trip to Pipette. We got home after 9:00. Note on dinghy from Annie Cook. Who was that??? Turned out to be Annie of Josh Taylor's boat.

6/15 Monett and Andrew Leverd (of the big church) came to pick us. We went with them to the mountains and largest river in Tahiti, "Papenod." It means "where water stays long time" big rocks a millions of stones. We went to 2 waterfalls ands swam in 2nd one. Had a lovely time. Andrew cut bamboo in afternoon an hour or so. The mountains were beautiful. We went to end of road but still in valley. Monett's children Silas, Brenda & Joseph had three lunches, Monett gathered ferns to sell. Monett works at hospital as Secretary in X-ray department. Oh! Yes we had a glass of REAL fresh milk and it was COLD. Got home had note that son David had called. About dark, Pastor Doom and son stop to tell of these calls again and while we were talking, John Reynaud and wife and daughter stop by. We talked on beach and finally got to boat.

6/16 Dan called David collect this morning. He is fine just wanted to hear us. Wrote both our mothers again. 76 in boat at 6:00 pm; and 72 outside. (It is middle of winter here.)

6/17 68 degrees at 6:00 am 10:00 am 80 high 82. Dan read, I cleaned and walk for yarn and worked some more on afghan after supper. Valise and Tearu brought us more drinking coconuts and large box of bananas Wow! We went over to *Yacht Jane* and found out they were same yacht we had met in Norfolk, Va., first week of our voyage when our engine had broken down in 1977. Jan and Paul spent time in Costa Rica and so that's how we caught up with them. Small World.

6/18 Finished afghan. Dan reading, *Brigadoon* came in today. Dan helped with lines to shore. Wind blowing hard at that time. About 5 to 6 am evening I notice traffic being stopped and heard a band playing so we quickly went ashore and walk to De Gaul Monument and they had a speaker. Afterward there was a little band and a drill team, and a few officials laid reefs at the monument. Many sailors and soldiers were there with 4 or 5 drill teams and then they march back up the street. We walked on up to quay and saw the boat *Zion* with John the missionary whom we had met last June in Panama. He had a tale to tell and is now going to Samoa to set up a mission there.

6/19	Met a man yesterday in Chinese store from NJ invited him to see boat. He and his daughter came and stayed all morning and about 2:00 or we went with them for hamburgers. Their names are Nate Goldberg and daughter Maxine. They had just been to Fiji and had loads of stories to tell.
6/20	Wrote 3 cards and our mothers. Dan read. I walked to mail letters and to check on our mail. Dan walked to get boat paper signed and we sent to Arnold. Dan walked to get flowers for Valise and Tearu. He picked out orchids lovely little ones but a large bouquet. They came about 5:00 and we went out to their home which is on same road as Faoruumai Waterfalls, where there are 3 of the falls. They live at Tiurli, in a nice house where she can sleep 12 people in beds. Floor pallets are the frequent accommodation in many places. Tearu is building house still, but they live in it. We had a good supper cold fish with lemon, carrots, tomatoes, coconuts, cucumbers, rice, lentils beet root, bread, butter, jelly, crackers, pamplemousse and coconut drink, and hot drinks if you want. After that we went to choir practice with them. The ladies were in the ladies choir. It was great. After that home and cake and lemonade and to bed about 10:30. But we couldn't sleep till after 12:00. 1st time to sleep off boat since Florida. There was a creek behind house and frogs, crickets and other insects. We giggled and tried to be quiet.
6/21	Breakfast was leftovers and great plus cereal if you wanted. To church at Tiarei where Louise used to live across the road from church. It was Velise's mother & father who used to give Bible studies to Louise. Dan talked in youth and at missionary service. We had interrupters each time. Lunch was good, potato salad with beets and carrots in it (no eggs), garlic no onion, 3 vegetarian dishes, lentils, rice bread, baked beans with corn beef, salad with oil and vinegar dressing, coconut water, orange juice, punch, cake and beautiful fruit salad for dessert bananas, papayas, mango in coconut milk and fresh vanilla bean cut into it, and all chilled. GREAT! Rested a few minutes and then to church at Papenoo, were we arrived before 3:00 pm MV meeting. Dan told story of trip from Marquesas – Lots of singing and soon it was sunset and we had a prayer and song outside for this. We talked on and after dark Velise and Tearu brought us back, but on way home we stopped at Chinese restaurant for supper. It was fair and I was hungry. But they wanted to so badly. Dan finally gave in to us

sharing one together. Home around 8:00 pm and to bed. Headache, too much food. Nice to be home.

6/22 Dan reading, me cleaning a little. Had John & Doug over for supper, talked to 10:00 pm. They will be off tomorrow.

6/23 Velise brought Dan his glasses. Dan read, I washed clothes and floor. We walked down to see boats. Uringo was in & we talked with them for a long while.

6/24 We received a nice funny letter from Buddy.

6/25 Wrote letters to sons and our Mothers. *Brigadoon* came over at dark.

6/26 Caught Le Truck to Venus Point where Capt Cook first landed, lovely view of mountains from there. Went into museum had a couple scenes from the past & quite a few maps and pictures. Went shopping later for Dan's glasses (didn't buy any). Had a Big Hamburger out. We went to the trucks (food vendors) for supper. 350 Francs nice steak and plate all filled with fries. Cooked on charcoal right before our eyes. *Brigadoon* was with us. We had lots of fun talking.

6/27 As I was going to shore, I met Paulette and Marilyn and we walked over to town together. They had come to ask us to a light supper. We did go to supper which was fancy bread and fresh fruit, honey, nuts and jam. Very lovely with cold coco or oval teen. Enjoyed talking and opening of Sabbath with them.

6/28 Up at 3:45 am Tangarora next to us had dragged anchor and wasn't at home. His boat was against our port line to land. Dan worked and worked and got it off by using one of our anchors. Dan couldn't find Fred's winch handlers. Any way, he finally had to ask neighbor *Born Free* to easy his port line so we would get him and in that process he lost line and went into *Gunfleet* and finally had to move till day light. It was a full moon. *Myonie* had lost her stern anchor and gone into *Brigadoon*. Current was very, very strong. 8:00 Martin came to pick us up for Gloria. We went to Paea to church and home with Dolores and Claude because they had convinced Gloria to bring us over (35) people. Lovely food several meats, beans, fish stew, chicken, etc. one prune cake with coconut icing was out of this world made by Gloria and Claude's mother. Nice afternoon talking and by 4:00 back at church for MV meeting which lasted till sundown. We were home by 7:00 pm and in bed soon after. Good Sabbath.

6/29 This month has flown by – Went to a Tahitian feast were Tahitian food is cooked in under ground oven "Tamaaraa" (at Velise and Tearu home). They cooked the following: Fafa (greens wrapped around chicken), Tarua (white root), Poe (banana cake), Mitihue (coconut milk), Umara (Tahitian potato), Uru (breadfruit), Ufi (white root), Taro (grey root), and sheep. They also had Fei (red bananas), Salade De Fruits (fruit salad), fried fish, Poisson Cru (Fish with lemonm& onion and coconut milk), and Fafaru (rotten fish in seawater soaking at least 3 days. <u>Everything devious</u>, but the FAFARU it was the worse taste Dan ever had and the worst smell I ever smelled. In old times, they used to cook this way once a week, but now only once a year. After the biggest dinner we ever had eaten we went to Velise's mother's and saw more of her family. Also walked to bottom of the water falls on the same street were Velise lives. We came home with drinking nuts, bananas, and pamplemousse, also some Fafa and Poisson Cru.

6/30 Fred on Tangarora left today. We had neighbors on *Born Free* over to share the Fafa and Poisson Cru with us. Nice folks been gone September, 1977. They have been as far as Australia and now were on their way back to states. Dan wrote some letters.

Welcome ashore after this sail of ours!
It has been fun having you aboard.

If you feel a little adventurous to discover some truly wonderful sailing to some of the most unique places on the planet, come along in our next half of the experiences of a life time; even to where you will find that centuries have stood still and await your presence to walk on their pathway in the remote highlands of Papua New Guinea and to the outback of Australia where the aborigine and kangaroo roam about in:

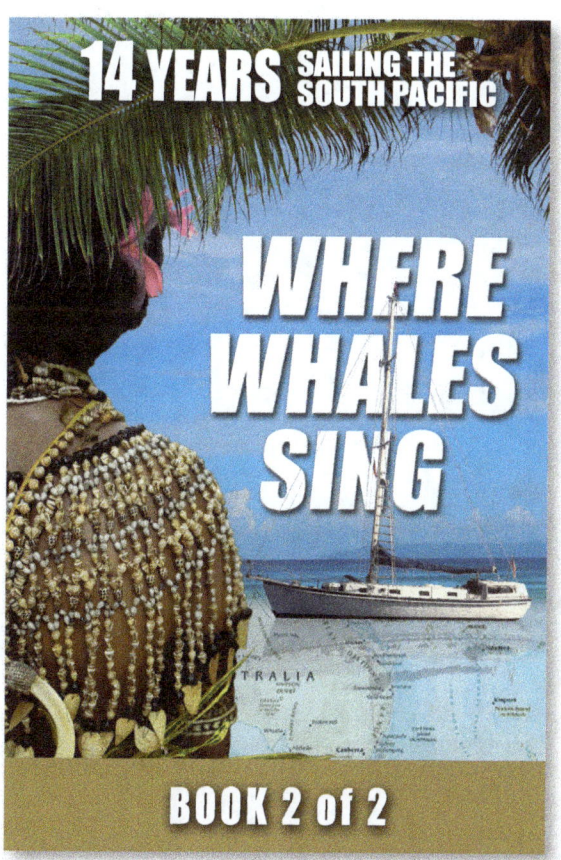

Now available at most eBook retail stores!

www.ingramcontent.com/pod-product-compliance
Lightning Source LLC
Chambersburg PA
CBHW050529300426
44113CB00012B/2019